A History of Flower Arranging

A
History of
Flower
Arranging

Edited by

Dorothy Cooke
and
Pamela McNicol

Published in association with the
National Association of Flower Arrangement Societies
Heinemann Professional Publishing

Heinemann Professional Publishing Ltd
Halley Court, Jordan Hill, Oxford OX2 8EJ

OXFORD LONDON MELBOURNE AUCKLAND SINGAPORE
IBADAN NAIROBI GABORONE KINGSTON

First published 1989

British Library Cataloguing in Publication Data
A history of flower arranging.
  1. Flower arrangement, to 1988
  I. Cooke, Dorothy II. McNicol, Pamela
  III. National Association of Flower Arrangement Societies.
  745.92'09

ISBN 0 434 90252 7

Phototypeset by The Alden Press Ltd, Oxford
and London and printed in Spain by Mateu Cromó

Contents

Contributors

MARIAN AARONSON became interested in flowers 30 years ago when she was inspired by ikebana, and she has since become interested in all aspects of creative design. She has travelled extensively as a national demonstrator, teacher and lecturer, and as such has visited Bermuda, New Zealand, Australia, Canada, the USA, South Africa, Kenya, Zimbabwe, Malta, France, Spain, Belgium, Italy and Monaco. She has judged at many international shows, and she represented Great Britain as a judge for the first WAFA competition in Bath. She has also undertaken several national demonstrations in this country. She is the author of three books: *The Art of Flower Arranging, Design with Plant Material* and *Flowers in the Modern Manner* (Grower Books, 1981). Over the years she has written many articles for gardening and flower arranging publications in this country and abroad. She served on the editorial board of *The Flower Arranger* magazine for nine years, seven of these as its international correspondent. She was made a Special Associate of Honour of NAFAS in 1984.

UMA BASU is Principal of the Kusumika School of Floral Art and a well-known floral artist in India. Her experiments with flower arrangements led to an interest in the history of Indian floral art, and she is now involved in research on ikebana and its Indian connections. Her lectures for the Asiatic Society in Calcutta and articles in leading newspapers and magazines have been well received in India. She has organized many exhibitions in Calcutta, Delhi and Madras since 1964 to demonstrate and promote the art of Indian flower arrangement. She is a founder member of Pushpa Bitan Friendship Society, and is a member of Ikebana International and NAFAS. Her creative activity extends also to oil and watercolour painting, alpana, needlework and photography.

JULIA S. BERRALL, a Vassar graduate, has combined a career of museum work, research, writing, travel and lecturing with home making and gardening. She has lectured extensively throughout the United States and Canada and has planned and escorted European and fine arts tours for small, specialized groups. Her writings have included contributions to horticulture magazines, the *Bulletin* of the Brooklyn Botanic Garden, and the *Encyclopedia Britannica*. She is the author of *The Garden* (Viking, 1966), *A History of Flower Arrangement* (Viking, 1968), *Flowers in Glass* (Studio, 1954) and *Flowers and Table Settings*

(Studio, 1951). She has been named a Chevalier of the Order of the Clou d'Or des Jardins, an international organization of garden authors specializing in history. She has been presented with a Certificate with Gold Seal by the US National Council of State Garden Clubs in recognition of 'distinguished service in garden-oriented authorship and activities'. In November 1970 she was given a citation from the American Horticultural Society for her 'contributions to the literature of horticulture and art'. She is an accredited judge with a life certificate for the US National Council of State Garden Clubs and is a Member-at-Large of the Garden Club of America.

PAOLA BURGER is a sculptress, potter and flower arranger. She has won prizes in many flower arrangement competitions world wide. She has demonstrated in Belgium, Italy, Monte Carlo, South Africa and New Zealand, and is co-author with Loli Marsano of *Scultura Floreale* (Idea Books, Milan, 1986).

BEULAH CANDLISH trained as a painter at Leicester College of Art, where she attained the National Diploma of Design. After a postgraduate year spent partly in Italy, she has continued to paint and lecture in art history, latterly for the Adult Education Department of Leicester University. She is better known by her maiden name of Beulah Wright, under which she continues to exhibit her work.

JULIA CLEMENTS OBE VMH is the author of 20 books on flower arranging. She is a teacher and demonstrator and has judged in the USA, France, Belgium, South Africa, Monte Carlo, Australia, New Zealand, Canada, Italy and Central America. She has travelled widely, lecturing in the USA and other countries of the world, including Japan, and has made two recent visits to India. She writes regularly for *Garden News* and other gardening and women's magazines. She is President of the London and Overseas area of NAFAS, and is a Life Vice-President of NAFAS. She was awarded the Victoria Medal of Honour by the Royal Horicultural Society for her pioneer work in forming flower clubs, and has three roses named after her (Julia Clements, Lady Seton and Julia's Rose). She holds the RNRS medal for 25 years continued service. She was awarded the Order of the British Empire in the Queen's New Year Honours List of 1989.

STELLA COE began studying ikebana when she was living in Japan in the 1920s, with Sofu Teshigahara, the founder of the Sogetsu School, and with Seiko Ogawa. She holds the highest rank of *riji* (master), one of the few non-Japanese to do so. She received the Veitch Memorial Medal from the Royal Horicultural Society in 1979 and the Order of the Precious Crown, Apricot, from the Japanese Government in 1986.

DOROTHY COOKE won her first prize for flower arrangement in 1930, and took the Premier Prix and Medaille d'Or in Paris in 1959. She qualified as a professional gardener and was the first woman to be employed by Manchester Parks Department, 1932–5. She is a Founder Associate of Honour and Life Vice-President of NAFAS, was chairman of the Founding of NAFAS subcommittee, and was a member of the RHS Floral Decoration subcommittee. She has lectured in the USA, Canada, Italy, France and Germany, and was an active chairman of the NAFAS Travel Club. She has been a judge, demonstrator, lecturer and teacher for 35 years.

VALERIE FORD graduated in modern languages from the University of Bristol and then gained the Certificate of Education. She speaks French and German fluently. She is a past National Demonstrator of NAFAS and has travelled widely in the UK and Europe. She was chairman of The Surrey Area of NAFAS 1984–6. She has designed many flower festivals in churches and stately homes, and was codesigner of the festival of flowers in Westminster Abbey in 1981.

JOSEPHINE HUTCHINSON is a professional horticulturist who trained at Pershore College in Worcestershire. Her varied career has seen her employed in the garden seed trade in the Midlands, on a specialist heather nursery in Surrey, a wholesale tree and shrub nursery in Kent, and latterly on a plantsman's nursery in Leicestershire. Over this period she has developed a keen interest in hardy plants, particularly their origins and uses.

PAMELA McNICOL shares her delight in flowers with her love of painting and drawing. She became chairman of the Wessex and Jersey area of NAFAS in 1976, during which time she designed a festival 'Flowers in Pageantry' in Winchester Cathedral. She was a codesigner of the Westminster Abbey Festival in 1981. She became chairman of NAFAS in 1985, and was responsible for the flowers in Westminster Abbey for the wedding of the Duke and Duchess of York in 1986. She was made an Associate of Honour of NAFAS in 1979.

SHEILA MACQUEEN VMH had an early interest in flowers and gardens and was greatly influenced by her mother and grandmother (whose garden was visited by European royalty, including Queen Mary, and many plant collectors). With such a background it was inevitable that she should want to make flowers her career, and she joined the Constance Spry organization in 1931, eventually becoming chief demonstrator and decorator. She assisted with the flowers for the wedding and coronation of the Queen, and has done flowers for many other members of the Royal Family. She travels all over the British Isles lecturing and judging and, following a successful tour of Australia in 1959, has had four further visits to all the capital cities and spoken at the International Rose Convention in Melbourne. She has also lectured in Canada, South and East Africa, Ceylon and countless times in the United States from east to west in 42 states, including the Academy of Art and the Garden Club of Honolulu. She has also talked and judged in France, Belgium and Germany. She has had invitations to judge at both the famous Ghent Floralis and the Concours International de Bouquets in Monaco. The Garden Club of America awarded her the Catherine Thomas Carey Medal for her help in the education of flower arrangement in the United States. She has often broadcast in sound and television, most recently on 'Gardeners' World' and was a regular contributor to *Amateur Gardening.* She is an Associate of Honour of NAFAS, and in 1980 received the Royal Horticultural Society's highest award, the Victoria Medal of Honour. Out of eight books published, the following are in print: *Your Book of Flower Arranging* (Faber and Faber), *Complete Book of Flower Arranging* (Ward Lock: paperback MacMillan) and *New Flower Arranging from your Garden* (MacMillan, 1988).

PAULINE MANN was an experienced writer, judge and teacher and had a special interest in period flower arranging. She had been on the editorial board of *The Flower Arranger* magazine for many years, and had recently been appointed assistant editor. She had been delighted to have been invited to contribute a chapter to this book, and it is sad that she died before its publication.

LOLI MARSANO is a sculptress and flower arranger. She has won prizes in many flower arrangement competitions world wide, and has demonstrated in Belgium, Italy, Monte Carlo and New Zealand. She is a co-author with Paola Burger of *Scultura Floreale* (Idea Books, Milan, 1986).

VIVIAN RICH attended the University of Victoria, Canada, for a BA in art history, and the University of London School of Oriental and African Studies for her PhD in Indian art, which she received in 1981. Her thesis was on the subject of Mogul floral painting. Since graduation she has been lecturing on garden history, the art and folklore of flowers, and the art of the British Raj for the University of Victoria Community Relations Division and she is a regular contributor to local magazines on flower history. Recently she completed research and is awaiting the publication of a book on British Indian garden design.

MARY SMITH lives at Ulverscroft in the heart of the Charnwood Forest area of Leicestershire, where she and her husband enjoy looking after their country garden, specializing in rhododendrons. Gardening and a love of plants led Mary to study City and Guilds flower arrangement and teaching courses. Since then she has taught flower arranging, and has particular interests in working with dried and pressed flowers and in the study of history. Other interests include antiques, travel, walking, theatre, music and photography. She is an active member of the South Leicester Flower Guild and a founder officer of the recently formed Bradgate Flower Club.

PAMELA SOUTH was born in Colombo, Sri Lanka, and has always admired oriental art and loved tropical flowers and exotic foliages. She is a NAFAS judge and speaker, and a teacher and demonstrator in ikebana. She has exhibited at both NAFAS and WAFA competitions and has won prizes in both. She has written on period and abstract flower arrangements, and has contributed to the *Complete Guide to Flower and Foliage Arrangement* edited by Iris Webb and to *More than Meets the Eye* by Sue Phillips. She has presented five programmes on flower arranging on TV. She is the chairman of the Judges, Demonstrators, Speakers and Teachers Committee for the area of Devon and Cornwall, and is on the editorial board of *The Flower Arranger* magazine.

MARY L. STEWART, an American residing in London, has studied ikebana, Sogetsu School, with Margaret East and Stella Coe since 1973. She holds the Sogetsu School rank of Teacher, Second Class, Sanyo. She is also a painter, lecturer, writer and oriental art historian with a PhD in Indian Buddhist archaeology. She has travelled extensively in the Far East and South and Southeast Asia. Author of several books, she is co-author with Stella Coe of *Ikebana: A Practical and Philosophical Guide to Japanese Flower Arrangement*, published in the UK and the USA in 1984.

DAPHNE VAGG was for eight years the editor of *The Flower Arranger* magazine, and has travelled to judge, teach and demonstrate the art of flower arranging in Italy, Germany, Bermuda, South Africa and New Zealand. She has written four books on flower arrangement and compiled and edited the *Guide to Period Arranging* published by NAFAS. Her interest ranges from the styles of ancient times to the abstract of today. Her books are *Flower Arranging* (Ward Lock, 1980), *Flowers for the Table* (Batsford, 1983), *Flower Arranging throughout the Year* (Batsford, 1983) and *Flowers in Every Room* (Batsford, 1985).

Foreword

THE INTEREST OF THE ROYAL HORTICULTURAL SOCIETY IN flower arranging goes back more than thirty-five years. The facilities for flower arrangements to be displayed at the Chelsea Flower Show date from this era and the Royal Horticultural Society regards itself as having been a godparent at the ensuing birth of NAFAS thirty years ago. The interest in flower arranging subsequently, and the success of NAFAS in raising over four million pounds for charity, has exceeded the most extravagant aspirations of its founders and earned world wide admiration for its efforts.

In this book the editors have brought together the collective expertise drawn from all over the world to demonstrate the long and notable history of an art that has brought pleasure and enjoyment to millions. Readers will be able to appreciate the way in which the techniques of flower arranging have evolved over the centuries and will realize that it is a dynamic art with a future that will surely be as distinguished as its past.

Robin Herbert, VHM
President of the Royal Horticultural Society

Preface

FOR MANY YEARS THERE HAS BEEN A GROWING NEED FOR an updated history of flower arranging. With enthusiasm for this subject now stretching to all corners of the globe, it is necessary to embrace new art forms and to accept modern trends whilst appreciating and learning about the old.

This book has involved many enthusiastic contributors, of whom some are members of NAFAS and others are not. Their expertise and that of the editors, Dorothy Cooke and Pamela McNicol, have combined to make this volume one which will be of inestimable value to students of flower arranging in this country and world wide.

I have known Dorothy Cooke for nearly 40 years. She was the instigator of flower arranging in Leicester when she was a lecturer in horticulture at Southfields College, and she formed the very early Leicester and Country Flower Lovers Guild. I have great affection for her and for Pamela McNicol who, as chairman of NAFAS in 1986, designed and directed the flowers in Westminster Abbey for the wedding of the Duke and Duchess of York.

It gives me great pleasure to write this preface, and I send my best wishes for the success of the book.

Mary Pope

OBE, VMH
Founder President of NAFAS

Acknowledgements

Every effort has been made to trace owners of copyright material, but in some cases this has not proved possible. The publisher would be glad to hear from any further copyright owners of material produced in this book whose copyright has unwittingly been infringed.

The editors, contributors and publisher are grateful to the following for their permission to reproduce illustrations:

Accademia Gallery
The Albertina
T. and R. Annan & Sons Ltd
Ashmolean Museum
Bath Museums Service
The British Library
Trustees of The British Museum
British Museum Publications
The Brooklyn Museum
John Calmann and King
Castle Howard Collection
Cheltenham Art Gallery and Museums
The Chester Beatty Library
Ching Chung Koon
The Colonial Williamsburg Foundation, Virginia
David and Charles
Curia Vescovada, Verona
Derby City Museum
East Sussex County Library
Fine Arts Museum of San Francisco
Syndics of the Fitzwilliam Museum, Cambridge
The Flower Arranger
Garden News
Tim Graham
The Griffith Institute, Ashmolean Museum
Trustees of the Holburne Museum, Bath
Hunterian Art Gallery, University of Glasgow, Mackintosh Collection
Idea Books, Italy
Manchester City Art Gallery
Lise Manniche
John Marr
Mead Art Museum, Amherst College
The Metropolitan Museum of Art
Ministry of Culture, Athens
William Morris Gallery, London

Munich State Museum
Museum of Childhood
Museum of Fine Arts, Vienna
NAFAS Ltd
Trustees of The National Gallery, London
National Gallery of Art, Washington
National Museum of Bargello
National Museum, Naples
Newark Public Library
The Pilgrim Society, Plymouth, Massachusetts
Press Association
The Royal Academy of Arts
Trustees of the Royal Collection, London
Royal Crown Derby Museum
Russell-Cotes Art Gallery and Museum, Bournemouth
Scala Institute
State Tretyakov Gallery
Trustees of The Science Museum
Scott Lauder Gallery
Trustees of The Tate Gallery
Board of Trustees of the Victoria and Albert Museum
Uffizi Gallery
University of London, Percival David Foundation
Trustees of the Wallace Collection, London
Ward Lock
Josiah Wedgwood & Sons Ltd

Introduction

LOOKING BACK THROUGH THE CENTURIES AND STUDYING the emergence of plants and their uses, it soon becomes apparent that there are three main factors all of which overlap and intermingle in the history of flower arranging. There is the continuing chronicle of plant representation in formal art found first in the early Egyptian frescoes and continuing through the flower paintings, architecture, embroidery and carving of all periods of history. There is the record of gardens and gardening through the ages, and there are the common customs and uses of plants for medicinal, culinary and decorative purposes.

The transition of plants from being used originally for these purposes to being grown for their beauty and decorative values is seen clearly through the chapters of this book, and one becomes aware that plant material has been used to enhance buildings and people and events from the earliest days, and will indeed continue to do so as far as one looks into the future. At the same time, through the centuries artists have committed the beauty of flowers and foliage to canvas, sculptors have carved them in stone and wood, embroiderers have woven them into tapestries, capturing their transience, immortalizing them for all time, and allowing us everlasting study and enjoyment.

This history of flower arranging, updated through the twentieth century, shows very clearly how throughout the centuries the links between the cultures and civilizations of the world are in many ways dependent on each other and quite certainly have influenced each other. Customs, beliefs and architecture stemming from the Egyptians, the Greeks and the Romans have stood the course of time and many are reflected in our lives today. In the first chapter this ancient Mediterranean world is well described, and one learns how the Romans carried their own and Greek cultures far beyond their homeland and established themselves as powerful global influences.

At the same time the Far East evolved the two entirely independent and highly sophisticated civilizations of China and Japan (Chapter 2) whose art astonished Europe in the merchant trading and colonial periods and still closely affects flower arrangement today.

In many parts of the world gardens have always been places of rest from battle and labour, and of shelter from sun, wind and desert. This is true especially of the ancient Near Eastern civilizations of Sumeria, Assyria, Babylon and Persia, and of the succeeding medieval Islamic cultures that spread from Spain to India and beyond (Chapter 3).

The Middle Ages in Europe were dark times for gardening and flowers, for the freedom of spirit that finds expression in floral art was suffocated by a millenium of war, migration and the heavy hand of religion which frowned upon such frivolous pastimes, and the legacy of antiquity in art and gardens was destroyed.

But owing to the increasing voyages across oceans, the world was soon to shrink and a new chapter for the formal arts and the design of gardens was to open. The Renaissance in arts and science coupled with Dutch Baroque and Rococo is richly described in Chapter 4. These new garden designs which originated in Italy and spread to France were formal and architectural, and in a sense that emphasis on design is echoed four centuries later in the distinctive arrangements of the Modern Italian school described in the final section of this chapter.

The art and architectures of these early ages was normally commissioned by the rulers, merchants or religious leaders, and it has survived because of the quality of the materials chosen by their patrons. The designs were dependent on their requests and the depiction of plants was highly symbolic.

Meanwhile the new found freedoms of the Renaissance coincided with new technologies in printing and the arts, and there developed a much wider recording of the uses of plants in the customs and habitat of ordinary people. An example of this process is described in Chapter 4 associated with Colonial America; and is continued in Chapter 5 which is concerned primarily with the popular uses of plants in Britain through the ages.

It is interesting to remember that the household garden in Europe emerged from the shadows of the Medieval period before the formal gardens of the Renaissance and that the development of post-Renaissance gardening went hand in hand with the introduction to Europe of thousands of species of plants from all around the world.

By the eighteenth century these formal Continental gardens were gradually changing to the more flexible plans of the large landscaped and smaller cottage gardens of the Georgian English styles. These changes are chronicled in Chapter 5. During the Victorian era Britain enjoyed the fruits of a worldwide Empire and the Industrial Revolution. Plants were collected and classified to a greater extent than ever before, and it was said that 'At no other time in history have flowers and foliage been used in such abundance'. To some extent and for those able to afford it, quality became synonymous with quantity in the Victorian and Edwardian periods, and the Art Noveau movement of the 1890s and 1900s was one reaction to this.

The 1930s marks the beginning of modern flower arranging, and at this point the contributions to the book move from historical study to personal experience and recollection (Chapter 6). The reader will enjoy the vivid descriptions of the emergence of floral art as we know it today, the massed cut flowers, the use of foliage and the carefully chosen colour schemes – complementing the interior decoration. The expansion of this popular art form, so welcome after the Second World War, culminated in the formation of a National Association of Flower Arranging and it is interesting to watch its progress and study the contrasts of flowers in the home, flowers for competition, and for public and private occasions.

The final contribution looks to the future and to all the many facets of modern day flower arranging.

If the countries of the world have contributed to this history, certainly the future is in their hands, for this art of flower arranging stretches to every corner of the earth – east, west, north and south. The shared knowledge and inspirations forms a giant patchwork of common interest breaking barriers of languages, creeds and politics, and giving unending excitement in the uses of plant material. From the vibrant carnivals of the Caribbean to the everyday devotion to household gardens around the world, flowers and their arrangement are universal delights.

No book on the history of flower arranging can ever be complete, because it would take at least 10 volumes to attempt that task. Indeed, as one's research begins, it is knowing how to stop that becomes important. By being selective, which was necessary in compiling this book, we know that many parts of the world who have contributed valuable plant species have been omitted from the text.

Let us not forget that the past cultures of Ethiopia and Zimbabwe in Africa, of Cambodia and Burma in South East Asia, of the Polynesians and other Pacific peoples, and of the Aztec and Inca empires in the Americas, all have histories of flowers in art, garden and customs.

In *The Conquest of New Spain*, Bernal Diaz records of Montezuma's Mexico in the early 1500s: 'We must not forget the gardens, with their many varieties of flowers and sweet-scented trees planted in order . . . a wonderful sight.'

This is not a book about *how* to arrange the flowers of past centuries; but is one which we hope will show how they were used in previous civilizations, and throughout history. As we approach the twenty-first century we have new ideas, new inspirations and yet at the same time some methods which are as old as time itself are maintained.

Two great books on the subject of the history of flower arranging have been written, one by Margaret Fairbanks Marcus (1952), the other by Julia Berrall (1953) and both were published in America. We are very grateful to all who have contributed to this book, not least Julia Berrall herself who has provided the chapter on American colonial flowers. Some are authors in their own right, all are experts in their field of knowledge. Their willingness to join with us in this project will, we hope, provide a book, which published in Great Britain will prove a valuable reference book, and will lead to a deeper appreciation of all aspects of flower arranging.

Dorothy Cooke
Pamela McNicol

1

The Ancient World

The plants and flowers of ancient Egypt

JOSEPHINE HUTCHINSON

EGYPT IS A LAND OF EXTREMES. THE RICH FERTILE VALLEY OF the Nile contrasts with the dry rocky cliffs and wind-blown plains that fringe it. The line of demarcation is very pronounced; in a matter of metres one is transported from arid terrain to the lush green of the flood plains. Herodotus described Egypt as the gift of the Nile, and it is the valley created by this great river which forms the home of the ancient civilization.

The land and its people

Around 95 per cent of the land of Egypt has been desert for many thousands of years. Desolate plains, barren mountains, and rocks shattered by extremes of heat and cold form a parched landscape. The river cuts down through this desert from south to north to create the Nile valley, some 625 miles in length from the ancient southern border to the start of the deltaic region near modern Cairo. The sediments carried down by the river have formed the delta where the river enters the Mediterranean. The huge fan-shaped plain of black silt, upwards of 100 miles long and nearly 200 miles wide, slopes gently down to the sea. The high areas of desert cliffs that fringe the Nile valley the Egyptians called *Deshret* or the red land; their homeland, where the Nile runs, they refer to as *Kemet* or the black land.

The lives of all who lived along the river banks were governed by the movements of the waters. Each summer the water would rise and flood the whole valley; in autumn, when the floods had drained away, a thin layer of fine black silt was left behind. It was this regular addition to the land that made it so exceptionally fertile. The rising of the river was unpredictable, so ways of storing water were invented. This water could then be fed from these reservoirs by means of a series of ditches to irrigate the crops during the growing season. However, all these efforts would be to no avail if the Nile failed to rise fully. The annual inundation of the Nile is caused by the rains which fall in central Africa and the rain and snow running off the Ethiopian highlands. Vast quantities of water then flow into the Nile from the various tributaries along its length. The flood is at its highest around the end of August. A flood of 7–8 metres was considered ideal for every purpose; one of 6 metres was perilously low, while one of 9 metres was so high as to cause damage.

The Nile was the principal highway of the land. It offered the obvious means of travel from an early date, as no point in the valley was more than a few miles from the river. During the period of the annual inundation, when most of the cultivated land was under water, the usefulness of the river could be further exploited. Flat-bottomed boats would carry cargoes such as stones directly from the quarries in the cliffs bordering the valley to the sites of temples, tombs and palaces, which were built just beyond the limits of the flood waters. It is in these buildings that we find much of the available information about the lifestyle of the ancient Egyptian people.

Most of the objects and wall paintings characteristic of the ancient civilization have come from temples and tombs. This leads us to suppose that they were a particularly religious people, obsessed by death and burial. They were also probably the first major civilization to leave behind evidence of the use of flowers; bas-relief and wall decorations can provide many clues to this. Their occupation with death appears to spring from the Egyptians' devotion to life and the good things available to them in the fruitful and productive land in which they lived. It was generally thought that the best existence one could have in the afterlife was one that contained all that was available and best on earth. It was this belief which prompted them to inter the personal possessions with the body, together with food and transport for the journey into the next world.

The Egyptians worshipped everything in nature; animals, birds and fish were all considered sacred. The forces of nature – sun, wind and storm – and the flowers, trees and crops were symbols of power and stood for fertility, strength and the continuance of life after death.

Columns with plant form capitals

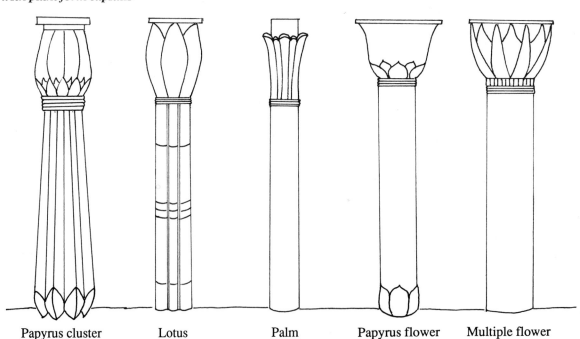

Papyrus cluster   Lotus   Palm   Papyrus flower   Multiple flower

Art and architecture

The nature of the land dictated not only the character of its inhabitants but also the art of the country. The essential conditions prevalent in Egypt are sunshine, little or no rainfall, and the contrast between the vast harshness of the desert region and the prolific vegetation of the narrow valley. The architecture is very symmetrical, following the horizontal lines of the rocks strata and the vertical lines of the cliffs rising from the valley. The tombs, paintings and bas-reliefs follow a very stylized pattern, again echoing the contrasts in the landscape.

It is in the decoration of the stone of buildings that we see inspiration from plant forms. Columns had capitals representing palm fronds, papyrus flowers and the much revered lotus. The tied heads of papyri were repeated in formation to decorate the tops of walls, and the curving tips of the palm gave rise to the corvetto cornice, which stands free above the level of the roof. The wall pictures depict scenes of everyday life: hunting in the swamps, the sowing and harvesting of crops, woodworkers and stonemasons at their crafts, and domestic and recreational scenes, as well as burial and religious rituals. Sculpture featured plants and flowers in addition to animals, birds and the human form. Often works of art are supported on stands representing buds or open flowers; heads are seen rising from an open lotus flower. Jugs, bowls and pitchers are lavishly adorned with flower decoration or made in the shape of a bud, leaf or flower.

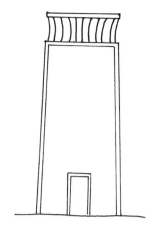

Corvetto cornice

Child Tut'ankhamun rising from a lotus flower
The Griffith Institute, Ashmolean Museum, Oxford

Photo: Lise Manniche

Bouquet of Amùn
From *City of the Dead: Thebes in Egypt*, Lise Manniche, British Museum Publications

The use and inspiration of flowers

Wall paintings, papyrus and bas-relief show us most evidence of how flowers were used by the ancient Egyptians. As well as figuring in many ritual and funerary uses, flowers were given as gifts to friends and used for both personal and domestic decoration. The bouquet of Amun, which was presented in the ceremony of the Feast of the Valley, contained flowers of papyrus, poppy, lotus and mandrake, which was symbolic of death and rebirth. Large ritual arrangements like this bouquet were symmetrical and often of a tall staff shape about the height of a man. The largest flowers were placed at the top, and pairs of fruit and flowers were arranged below; little or no foliage was included. In these ceremonial arrangements there is no evidence of the cut stems being placed in water to extend their life, rather like the bridal bouquets of today.

In some ritual offerings it appears water was used to prolong the life of flowers. The offering to the goddess Hat-Hor shows the use of a bronze bowl containing cut lotus blossoms; at the centre stands the figure of the Hat-Hor cow. The bowl is partly filled with water and the animal appears to be standing in a marshy thicket, reminiscent of the papyrus thickets of Chemmis, where Hat-Hor is reputed to have nursed the infant Horus. The ancient wall paintings also show large vases with narrow necks, often three in number, supporting a large flower head of the lotus in each; again, no foliage is evident.

Both men and women are seen wearing floral collars; these also decorate the mummified bodies of the dead. Representations of collars can be seen in the decoration on the outer coffins and lids, and collars of natural plant material were placed round the face of the inner coffins or the mummified body. These collars could be elaborate or simple in appearance. They were made by sewing or stringing flower petals,

Bronze flower bowl
The Metropolitan Museum of Art. The Theodore M. Davis Collection, bequest of Theodore M. Davis, 1915

Face of the second coffin showing collar of natural flowers
The Griffith Institute, Ashmolean Museum, Oxford

leaves, fruit and blue faience beads on to strips of palm leaf, then securing the whole to a backing of papyrus to form a collar almost circular in shape. The composition of a collar would include the leaves of the olive, the petals of cornflowers, larkspur, acacia and other blooms, and the berries of woody nightshade and other fruits, all interspersed with the blue faience beads.

On all formal occasions great use seems to have been made of garlands. These would be composed of mixed flowers and leaves; the leaves were used with alternate surfaces uppermost to show the effect of silver on green to advantage. Headbands and chaplets were a popular personal adornment. Often a solitary flower was worn low on the forehead or tucked into an armband, and a single flower might be carried in the hand just for the sheer appreciation of its beauty of colour, form or perfume. Banqueting tables were lavishly decorated with baskets and bowls arranged with fruit, flowers and other foods. Vine leaves and flowers were twined around jugs and pitchers containing wines and beers to keep them cool.

Flowers were also the inspiration for love poems. In the Songs of Delight, from Papyrus Harris 500 IIc, the third collection, each poem begins with the name of a flower, followed by a verb of similar sound. In the first the flower has been guessed as portulaca:

> Portulaca: apportioned to you is my heart,
> I do for you what it desires,
> When I am in your arms.
> My longing for you is my eye-paint,
> When I see you my eyes shine;
> I press close to you to look at you,
> Beloved of men, who rules my heart!
> O happiness of this hour,
> Let the hour go on forever!
> Since I have lain with you,
> You raised up my heart;
> Be it sad or gay,
> Do not leave me!
>
> *Saam*-plants here summon us,
> I am your sister, your best one;
> I belong to you like this plot of ground
> That I planted with flowers
> And sweet-smelling herbs.
> Sweet is its stream,
> Dug by your hand,
> Refreshing in the north wind.
> A lovely place to wander in,
> Your hand in my hand.
> My body thrives, my heart exults
> At our walking together;
> Hearing your voice is pomegranate wine,
> I live by hearing it.
> Each look with which you look at me
> Sustains me more than food and drink.

Egyptian style floral collar made by CGLI students at Brooksby College, Leicestershire

Photo: Dorothy Cooke

Photo: Tom Scott

A shadoof being used to water a garden

Horticulture

Egypt has a long tradition of gardening and is the source of the world's oldest pictures of garden designs. Domestic gardens were usually sited close to the house on land raised above or beyond the reach of the flood waters, and were enclosed by high walls. Because the land was raised, cultivation was able to continue throughout the year. Trees were planted around the perimeter and throughout the garden to give shade. Gardens, however small, contained at least one pool which was sited in the shade of trees to produce a cooling effect on the garden. These pools not only were ornamental but also acted as reservoirs for the watering of the garden plots. In large gardens, ditches were also used to carry water to where it was needed. Water was moved from the canals and ditches (which captured it when the Nile's inundation subsided) to different levels by means of a shadoof, a well sweep with a counterpoise. This primitive water lifting device is still in use in upper Egypt today.

In their gardens the Egyptians grew fruit, vegetables, medicinal plants, flowers and trees; all plants had a use or purpose, as water was such a precious commodity. In all gardens there was a place for the much revered lotus and papyrus, their uses being numerous. Papyrus yielded fuel from the roots and a sweetening agent from the lower

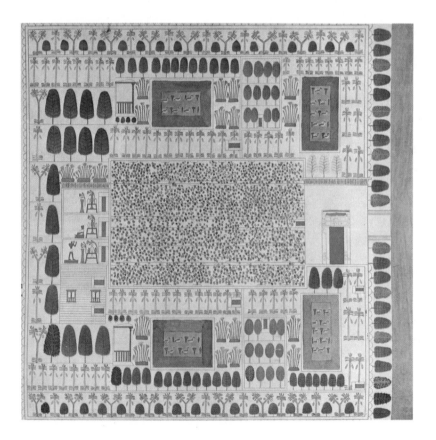

The garden of Amenhotep III about 1400 BC
From *An Illustrated History of Gardening*
Anthony Huxley, Paddington Press

stem. Mats, sandals, candles and torch wicks were made from the bark, and baskets, boats and primitive buildings from the tall stalks. From the lotus we get Egyptian beans, the seeds of *Nymphaea caerulea*, the white/blue lily of the Nile. This species also has edible buds and stems; the seeds have an almond flavour, and the flowers have a perfume reminiscent of anise and are frequently seen carried or held to the nose.

The design of gardens followed the pattern of most Egyptian art, being formal in both style and layout. Groves of trees, straight walkways, matching pools and pavilions gave a feeling of balance, harmony, rhythm and proportion which is still the basis of good design today. Crops commonly grown in gardens included beans, lentils, lettuce, onions, leeks, melons and other gourds; dates, figs and pomegranates; and many kinds of flowers. A subsidiary product of Egyptian horticulture was honey, which was much prized as a sweetening agent.

Agriculture

Ancient Egyptian economy was primarily based on agriculture. Scenes of field cultivation and harvesting are common in tomb paintings, and there is much evidence that the Egyptian farmer worked hard and reaped good rewards. This happy state of affairs was due first to the behaviour of the Nile and secondly to the climate of the country. The agricultural year began when the flood subsided, leaving the earth soaked and overlain with silt. The land was tilled and the crops sown before the soil had dried out and become hard. Canals and ditches would be cleaned out and landmarks re-established. The field crops grown in Egypt in ancient times were annual by nature; sowing and harvesting were completed before the inundation began again the following year.

The principal crops grown were cereals and flax. Of the cereals, emmer was the chief crop followed by barley. Wheat was grown in small quantities until the Ptolemaic period, when it became the principal crop. Barley was grown not only for its primary use in bread making but also for the manufacture of beer, the chief drink of the Egyptians. Flax was the other crop of great importance; this was used mainly in the manufacture of linen, which was almost the only fabric available for clothing. Two other important products were oil and wine. Oil was used for cooking, lighting, cosmetics, ointments and embalming. The main indigenous source of oil was the moringa tree; other plants which produced suitable oils were lettuce, castor, flax (linseed), radish, saffron and sesame. Olive oil was imported until the Ptolemaic period, when successful growing of the olive was achieved. Wine was produced from grapes and dates; grape wine was held in higher regard.

The economy of the country being so dependent on agriculture, the ancient Egyptians fully understood the extent to which their life and prosperity hinged on the unfailing regularity of the inundation. They never regarded the river and its gifts with complacency. Hapy, the god of the inundation, was the constant object of the prayers of the Egyptians. Hapy is represented in image as a bearded plump figure with clusters of water plants about his head. He is shown with pendulous female breasts, indicative of his fertility and the life he brought to the valley.

Egypt was created by the Nile. The river shaped the land and gave it life; without it there would have been no temples and pyramids and no splendid civilization.

Bibliography

Clark, R. T. Rundle. *Myth and Symbol in Ancient Egypt*. Thames and Hudson, 1960.

Hayes, N. C. *Sceptre of Egypt*. Metropolitan Museum of Art, 1960.

Huxley, Anthony. *An Illustrated History of Gardening*. Paddington Press, 1978.

James, T. G. H. *An Introduction to Ancient Egypt*. British Museum Publications, 1979.

Jellico, Goode, and Lancaster. *The Oxford Companion to Gardens*. OUP, 1986.

Johnson, Paul. *The Civilization of Ancient Egypt*. Weidenfeld and Nicolson, 1978.

Lichtheim, Miriam. *Ancient Egyptian Literature*. UCP, 1973.

Manniche, Lise. *City of the Dead: Thebes in Egypt*. British Museum Publications, 1978.

Noblecourt, Desroches. *Tutankhamen*. New York: Graphic Society, 1963.

Petrie, N. M. Flinders. *Arts and Crafts of Ancient Egypt*. New York: Attic Books, 1972.

Posener, Georges. *A Dictionary of Egyptian Civilization*. Methuen, 1962.

Places to visit

British Museum, London.
Fitzwilliam Museum, Cambridge.
Ashmolean Museum, Oxford.
Gulbenkian Museum, Durham.

Many local museums have small Egyptian collections, and from time to time have special exhibitions.

Garlands and wreaths in ancient Greece and Rome

DOROTHY COOKE

IN EVERY SPHERE OF LIFE THE PAST INFLUENCES OUR ACTIONS, and discovering the different ways in which plants have been used by man through the centuries can be of absorbing interest. The world's oldest flowers are considered to be the 80 million-year-old fossils found in Norway; they are thought to be related to the hydrangea, and measure only 1 mm across. Some of the earliest indications of human use of flowers have been found in tombs. In 1950 an important discovery was made when a Neanderthal grave was found in a cave near the village of Shanidor in north-east Iraq. It contained the body of a man who had been laid to rest 60 000 years ago with bunches of carefully placed flowers around him. Analysis of the pollen grains, which are now all that remain of the flowers, shows that they were cornflowers, hollyhocks, ragwort, grape hyacinths, yarrow and a species of centaurea known as St Barnaby's thistle.

The Neanderthal remains greatly predate the civilization with which we are concerned in this section – those of ancient Greece and Rome. These are among the first peoples of which a large body of written material remains today. The literature of Greece expanded rapidly from the fifth century BC onwards, and the earliest Roman works date from the third century BC. Floral decoration has been described as being as old as civilization itself, and indeed the documents of these and other ancient Mediterranean countries show the similarity of their plant material and its cultivation for medicinal purposes, culinary uses and decoration.

But the ancient Greek and Roman writers, whilst proclaiming that flowers played a significant role in the daily life of the people, indicated that their use was almost solely in the form of wreaths and garlands; there was little evidence that flowers were ever actually placed in water. Indeed it is often assumed that the many beautiful painted vases seen in most Western museums were used for flower arranging. Nothing is further from the truth; depending on their shape, they were used for wine, grain, dried fruits and other essentials, and never for flowers.

Most existing Greek paintings are on pottery. The techniques reached their peak with the Athenian red-figured vases of the sixth and fifth century BC; these frequently illustrate chaplets, garlands and bouquets of plant material. In the late part of the fifth century BC a

Attic red-figured skyphos, 490–480 BC
The British Museum

bridal scene was depicted on a thigh guard; the plant material in the vases was almost certainly olive branches, since the olive is associated with weddings. Myrtle was a symbol of love and marriage and was sacred to Aphrodite; it is still used in bridal bouquets today. Garlands were exchanged by lovers, worn at weddings and hung on doors to celebrate the birth of sons. Chaplets – wreaths of flowers and leaves worn round the head – were also popular, and chaplet and garland makers were highly skilled in the choice of suitable plants. Such people were often versed in other uses of plants, such as which would soothe a headache, which would give comfort or joy, and which would inflame the passions.

Many Greek scholars contributed to the very beginnings of the study of plants. Aristotle, scientist and philosopher, began collecting data as a basis for scientific study – and one of the spheres was botany. Whilst Socrates and Plato discussed the nature of beauty, Hippocrates began the practice of medicine at the School of Physicians on the island of Cos. (This is the origin of the Hippocratic oath sworn by medical practitioners today.) Medicinal and herbal plants were cultivated and classified by the early Greeks, and many plants travelled with the soldiers for their use during the wars they fought.

The greatest gift of the Greeks to succeeding Western cultures is their architecture. Plant motifs are found on capitals, bases and pediments, and internally on walls and floors. Foliage was largely used to make the garlands which decorated Greek and Roman temples and houses, and the wreaths which crowned victorious soldiers, civic leaders, athletes and philosophers. Laurel, the sacred plant of the God Apollo, was normally chosen, and laurel wreaths were (and are to this day) given to those who are victorious. In the mosaic floor of a house in Delos (second century BC), the amphora, wreath and palm signify victory in a chariot race at the pan-Athenaic festival. Oak leaves,

Photo: Dorothy Cooke

Modern garland, Greek style.
Arranged by Linda Hyde

Photo: Dorothy Cooke

Modern wreath, Greek style.
Arranged by Janet Everett

Mosaic floor of a house in Delos.
The amphora, wreath and palm
branch refer to the owner's
victory in a chariot race at the
Panathenaic festival
Ministry of Culture, Athens

Maeniad dancing holding thyrus
The Metropolitan Museum of Art, Fletcher
Fund, 1935

acorns, ivy, box and yew were also used for wreaths, and rosemary was added for its aromatic perfume.

The Romans, too, expanded architectural practice. Moreover, their wide conquests were followed by powerful structures and durable building techniques, and the Roman legacy in architecture is clearly visible throughout Western Europe. However, in the other arts the Romans tended to follow Greek styles. Frequently our knowledge of Greek sculpture is derived from Roman copies. The dancing maenad shown is a Roman copy of a Greek sculpture of the fifth century BC; it illustrates garlands and the thyrsus, which was originally carried by Dionysus (the God of wine and fertility) and his votaries. The thyrsus was a tall, slim staff decorated with ivy and vines, often topped with a pine cone and beribboned. Many ancient monuments and buildings throughout the world have been embellished with traditional leaves and garlands carved in stone, emanating from the popularity of this kind of decoration in Greek and Roman times.

The discovery of the ruins at Pompeii – 'the ghost ship' of the Flavian period, buried under Vesuvius's volcanic ash in AD 79 – has given a remarkable insight into Roman daily life, domestic architecture and town planning. The wall paintings in the stricken town provide pictorial information on garland makers. One cartouche in particular shows emblematic Putti with a goat carrying an assortment of flowers, which are placed on a table. The garland makers are constructing the garlands, and then they are seen to be hung on a stand; a woman is shown making her choice.

At its peak, the Roman Empire stretched from the Black Sea in the east to the Pillars of Heracles in the west, and from Britain in the north to Egypt in the south. Behind the armies came administrators and settlers, bringing with them Roman customs. A wonderfully preserved wreath of dried flowers has been found at Hawara in Egypt in the tomb of a Roman matron. The flowers are believed to be anaphalis or immortelles.

The custom of the wearing of garlands and wreaths by the Romans gave rise to the necessity for a great number of people able to make them, and garland makers were doubtless the flower arrangers of the day. Some of the more notable families numbered many garland makers in their household; Darius is said to have had 46 in his! It also became necessary for Roman gardeners to grow special flowers. So clever did they become that with the aid of heated areas they were able to provide vast quantities of roses all the year found.

And acres of roses were grown for many purposes – perfumes, oils and jams. Throughout the history of Imperial Rome, roses were used as a decoration at feasts, and festivals of roses were common events. *Dies rosationis* were commemorative services for the dead, when bereaved families would meet at a rose-bedecked grave. 'Life is no bed of roses' we still say today – and are thus reminded that Anthony and Cleopatra floated down the Nile in a barge decked with flowers, reclining on a bed of rose petals that were refreshed constantly by slaves. Rose petals were thrown in the path of Roman brides, as of course they and confetti still are today. Garlands of roses were worn to ward off the effect of too much wine. A bunch of white roses was hung from a

A wall painting at Pompeii
National Museum, Naples

ceiling, and all spoken beneath them was to be kept secret; *sub rosa* is a legal term to this day. Christianity gradually diffused throughout the Roman empire, eventually becoming the established religion of the Byzantine or Eastern empire in AD 479. The rose was adopted as a Christian emblem, and was attributed to the Virgin Mary; from this comes the Roman Catholic rosary, whose beads correspond to petals.

Another floral tradition was the dancing of maidens in procession through the streets of Rome carrying scarves filled with sweet-smelling flowers and fruit. This ancient Roman Festival was the Floralia or Ludi Florales. It was first celebrated in 238 BC becoming an annual event in 173 BC and always held between 28 April and 3 May. It was designed to honour the Goddess Flora, the Latin deity of fertility and flowers, the protectress of blossom. She had a temple near the Circus Maximus, and a special flamen or priest performed sacrifices by burning on her behalf. It was a time of merriment; men decked themselves with flowers, and women wore bright dresses.

As the Roman conquest of Europe was consolidated, many new plants and herbs were introduced from the homeland. These were needed for culinary purposes and also for garland making; parsley in particular was used for both purposes. When the Roman Empire fell, the cultivation of these plants was continued in monastery gardens. Dioscurides had a great knowledge of healing, and when he came to Britain with the invading Roman army his herbalistic cures became a major influence. Such cures and treatments included the use of poppy seeds as an opiate, pain killer and sleep inducer. The root of Solomon's seal was used to close up wounds (it had 'the power to seal'), and garlic was prescribed for curing worms! Socrates died from a draught of hemlock mixed with other herbs – but he is said to have had a 'serene death'.

Quite the most noteworthy link with flower arranging through the centuries is the remarkable Roman mosaic of a basket of flowers, now

Roman wreath made of immortelles
The British Museum

in the Vatican Museum. It was found in the eighteenth century near Tivoli at Hadrian's Villa, and is thought to date from the beginning of the second century AD. Its grouping of colourful mixed flowers in a basket is a foretaste of the arrangements of flowers in later periods and cultures.

Bibliography

Bandinelli, and Torelli. *L'Arte dell' antichità classica*. Torino: UTET 1976.
Coats, Peter. *Roses*. Putnam 1962.
Grant, Michael. *Cities of Vesuvius*. Hamlyn 1974.
Livingstone, R. W. *The Pageant of Greece*. OUP 1961.
Morris, William. *Life and Death of Jason* (novel). (1867.)
Ragghianti, Licia. *The Magnificent Heritage of Ancient Greece*.
Renault, Mary. *The Last of the Wine* (novel). Sceptre 1986.
Shipway, George. *Imperial Governor* (novel). P. Davies 1968.
Stobart, J. C. *The Grandeur that was Rome*. Maguinness and Scullard 1961.
Wilkins, Eithne. *The Rose Garden Game*.

Places to visit

British Museum, Greek and Roman galleries.
Ashmolean Museum, Oxford.
Chester Museum.
Hadrian's Wall.

The Byzantine age

PAMELA SOUTH

THE BYZANTINE EMPIRE OCCUPIES A CURIOUS POSITION IN history. It was based on Greek civilization and language, the Christian faith, and a Roman style of government. It was a major instrument in the preservation of the culture of ancient Greece and Rome, and in the conversion of the Slavic peoples (especially Russia) to Christianity. At the same time it acted as a buffer between Western Europe and the shock of Islam from the eighth century AD; it suffered attack from the remnants of the Christian Western Empire, notably its Norman successors; and it was rent by internal religious disputes. These factors all affected the development of the arts and therefore of the depiction of plants within them; in particular, classic symbolism was preserved.

After the decline and eventual collapse of the Western Roman Empire, the Eastern Byzantine Empire became the defender of civilization and the Christian religion. Ancient Byzantium was renamed Constantinople in AD 330 when it became the new Roman capital. The city, situated on the great trade routes leading north and south, east and west, flourished as the world's largest mercantile centre until finally it was sacked by the Turks in 1453. The Byzantine Emperor claimed both secular and religious authority as God's representative on earth.

Within its religious confines, Byzantine art was rich and abundant. The culture affected Western Christian society, especially in the decorative and industrial arts. Artistic motifs such as the vine and acanthus were taken from Roman and Greek sources, but oriental influences were also absorbed. Skilful weavers produced sumptuous silks in rich glowing colours of purple, gold, violet, red and emerald, which were worn and used as hangings. Goldsmiths and silversmiths made luxurious objects, especially for church use, and these were often studded with precious stones. Overall, realism and individualism in art were suppressed in favour of religious dedication. The religious arts showed clarity of representation and strict traditional images, both solemn and mysterious, still to be seen in Russian church icons. It was from the Byzantine Church that the Russian Orthodox Church originally stemmed, and the influence can be seen in churches such as the Cathedral of St Basil in Moscow. Byzantium also had a major impact on its subjugated Balkan states, notably Bulgaria.

The icon Virgin Vladimir
State Tretyakov Gallery, Russia

When the famous Emperor Justinian and his Empress Theodora were crowned in 527 they drove in a state coach in procession through the streets of Constantinople wearing their imperial purple cloaks and diadems. The people had 'crowned the town', hanging from windows and balconies their silks, brocades and bunches of spring flowers, whilst the streets themselves were decked with rosemary, myrtle, box and ivy.

Symmetry of arrangement in plant material in a stiff formal manner is in harmony with both the religious art and the pomp and luxury of the imperial palace. Garlands and wreaths were used, but it has become accepted to depict this period with a tall slim tapering arrange-

The Empress Theodora mosaic
Scala Institute

ment of foliage, dotted at regular stages with fruit or flowers, the flowers sometimes being grouped in starry clusters. On occasion a narrow ribbon is wound in a spiral from the base to the top.

It is known that roses were grown in the gardens and their perfume loved. One of the earliest accounts of how rose water was distilled comes from the doctor to the Greek governor of Constantinople writing in the thirteenth century.

The outstandingly beautiful mosaics in the Byzantine churches are our most lasting references for this age. Those in Ravenna in northern Italy are exceptional; the city was the centre of Byzantine rule in Italy under Justinian, and contains greater record in architecture of the First

*The apse of Sant' Appollinare in
Class, Ravenna*
Scala Institute

Golden Age of Byzantine art than Constantinople itself. The apse of
Sant' Apollinare in Classe, Ravenna, displays the charming 'gardens of
Heaven', with St Apollinaris standing in the centre of a curve of twelve
lambs; stylized trees, flowers and plants surround the saints. The
Mausoleum of Galla Placida, also in Ravenna, shows in mosaic form
a very tall spire of foliage and fruit in a deep ornate urn or basket. The
remarkable Hagia Sophia in Constantinople is also of the First Golden
Age. In this church the capitals have the classical Greek acanthus
foliage decoration, but now in a much lighter basketwork pattern.

From the ninth century onwards, Byzantine art was severely
affected first by a prohibition on religious images, and subsequently by
the development of formal rules for iconographic representation. This
led to a revival of classical and secular art as religious art became more
monastic. Famous works of the Second Golden Age from the ninth to

the twelfth centuries include the mosaic of Christ the Pantocrator in the church at Daphne in Greece. Venice, too, was under the rule and later the influence of Byzantium, and St Mark's Cathedral (rebuilt in the eleventh century) is well known for its Greek plan; stylized plant motifs are freely used in the sculpture of capitals and balconies and in the beautiful mosaics. The revival of classicism produced much softer semi-secular works such as the illuminations in the *Paris Psalter*, with its Greek wreaths and garlands, more natural images of plant life, and clear oriental influences.

To the end in the fifteenth century, Byzantium remained essentially a reflection of late Greek antiquity rather than of the medieval developments that were taking place in northern and western Europe.

Bibliography

Grabar, Andre. *Byzantine Painting*. Macmillan, 1979.

Hutter, Irmgard. *Early Christian and Byzantine*, 2nd ed. Herbert Press, 1988.

Mango, Cyril A. *Art of the Byzantine Empire*. Prentice Hall, 1972.

Paolucci Antonio. *Ravenna*. Constable, 1978.

Rice, David Talbot. *Appreciation of Byzantine Art*. OUP, 1972.

A capital from Hagia Sophia in Constantinople showing design of acanthus
Scala Institute

2

Far Eastern floral art

Chinese flower arrangement from the Tang to the Qing dynasties

PAMELA SOUTH

A thousand flowers, a thousand dreams

THE DESTINY OF CIVILIZATION ITSELF IS INEXTRICABLY bound up in the carrying forward of knowledge through time. We stand today on the top layer of a series of cultures, ever shifting, ever evolving through the ebb and flow of human history.

The country of China has enjoyed the unique distinction of benefiting from the longest unbroken civilization in human history, reaching back nearly 4000 years. This cultural continuum, coupled with her vastness of territory and enormous population, has meant that China has seldom felt the need to look outside her own boundaries for any purposes. Not surprisingly, there resulted a great reverence for the traditions of her own past, combined with totally distinctive cultural forms including that of flower arrangement.

Seller of flowering plants. Water-colour on paper
Victoria and Albert Museum

27

In pre-revolutionary China, art was the work of heaven, the result of inspiration that could not be learnt. This is a daunting prospect for the modern interpreter, until deeper personal insights into the underlying culture are developed. Traditional Chinese flower arrangement is characterized by a linear rhythmic quality, within an asymmetrical form having a strong main placement. Space is important within the design, with no overcrowding or fussiness. The whole has a certain joyous, flowing line; it expresses a love of irregularity but within an overall control. The key idea is to express a life-giving vitality.

Flowers were often selected for their symbolic or seasonal associations, such careful selection heightening the appreciation of the informed viewer. Many of the Chinese plants that so excited nineteenth-century European plant hunters had not been used by the Chinese themselves in their gardens or floral arrangements. These plants lacked appropriate traditional associations and were, as a result, not highly esteemed. To understand the style of a different culture one cannot count on one's own technique or rules; one needs to understand why.

Until the end of the Qing dynasty in AD 1911, the three greatest influences on Chinese culture, known as the 'three ways of thought', were Confucianism, Taoism and Buddhism. Confucius (K'ung-fu-tzu), China's greatest philosopher and teacher, was born about 551 BC. He taught restraint, propriety of behaviour and a general respect for one's ancestors and the past. This tradition-based way of thinking has had

A collection of bronze vases now used for flower arrangement
Top left: *a 'Ku' goblet, a wine drinking vessel*
Top centre: *heavily ornamented vase, late Qing, 19th century*
Top right: *brass vase on a lacquer stand*
Bottom left: *a 'Chueh', a three-legged vessel for heating wine*
Bottom centre: *a 'Ting', a tripod cauldron food vessel*
Bottom right: *a 'Tsun', a ritual square bodied wine vase*

Photo: Pamela South

Chinese watercolour interior showing furniture dwarfed trees
Victoria and Albert Museum

a lasting effect upon all the arts in China and has led to the maintenance of considerable design continuity in the visual arts.

An example of this continuity is the design of the ritual bronze food and wine vessels of the Zhou dynasty. These continued to be produced first in bronze and then much later in porcelain, thousands of years after their original religious purposes had all but disappeared. The trumpet-mouthed *ku* (wine-drinking vessel) has a particularly elegant form most suited to flower arrangements.

The Confucian code of social conduct led to the establishment of a system of government run by cultured scholar-officials, selected by a competitive examination system. Their intellectual training for the rigours of government included lessons in painting, calligraphy and poetry, with gardening and flower arrangement being seen as essential relaxations associated with the art of refined living. The Confucian 'ideal man' was represented by the bamboo, strong but resilient, bending with but not breaking in a storm, taking the weight of any burden but always springing upright again. The naturally straight growth of the bamboo stem was associated with a good man's moral uprightness.

Respect for one's ancestors required a family to have many sons, in order that the necessary ancestral rites might be regularly performed. Traditional Chinese houses were designed so that upon entering the house and the main room, one was faced with a small altar for the worship of both household gods and ancestors. On the altar were to be found named ancestral tablets, incense burners and paired vessels; fresh flowers and food were placed there daily. The culturally requisite unity of the family group meant that different generations of the same family often lived within the same compound of houses. The connecting passages and inner courtyards within these compounds usually featured potted plants, whilst the big communal reception hall would be decorated with a large flower arrangement.

The founder of the Taoist school of thought, Lao Tzu, was said to have been born under a plum tree around 600 BC. Hence the plum came to represent Taoism because of its beauty and its independence, flowering on leafless branches. The Taoists' purpose was to study the natural order of things and to work with it rather than against it. Oriental man has never felt the underlying Western sense of aggression against nature, or the overriding need to tame and dominate it for his own purposes. This springs from a more deeply held respect for and kinship with other living animals, plants and inanimate facets of nature such as rocks and mountains.

The *Tao* (way) is seen as a seamless web of unbroken movement and change, of which human beings are but a small part. Taoism appeals to the individual in his quest for long life and search for spiritual immortality. This explains the underlying appeal in the use of aged and gnarled branches as the dominant line element in a classical flower arrangement; as we have already seen, age has always been prized and venerated in the Orient.

Rocks with unusual forms and shapes are particularly highly prized for use in landscape gardening and tray gardens (*p'en-ching*). Rocks, particularly those eroded and hollowed by water, show an image of *Tao*, symbolizing the rule of time and change. They were collected and mounted on individual stands and displayed in association with flower arrangements and tray landscapes. Flower arrangements were rarely displayed in isolation; rather they were grouped with other objects.

The most familiar Taoist elements are the mutual opposites, or energies, called yin and yang. These are oscillating polarities which provide movement. The yin element is female and dark, deep and passive. It is found in negative forces, the earth, valleys, vases, the moon, flowers and the autumn and winter seasons. Green is the dominant yin colour, signifying everlasting qualities and perpetual youth. In the plant world evergreens portray these attributes, and the shady undersides of leaves are also yin.

The yang qualities are found in the male element, heaven, the sun, dragons, mountains, positive forces and the spring and summer seasons. The strongest and largest branch in an arrangement is yang and must be supported and balanced by a smaller yin branch or flowers. The upper surface of a leaf, that nearest the sun, is also yang. Red is the dominant yang colour and is particularly used for celebrations, such as weddings and birthdays, where it denotes happiness and a sense of occasion.

It would not be correct to say that yin and yang are direct contrasts, for in China everything is seen to hold within itself its own direct opposite. Within a man there is often some female streak, and the opposite is equally true. For this reason a pair of Chinese vases should never be separated, for the artist who conceived them saw the pair as an immutable whole rather than each vase as a separate entity.

Yin Yang symbol

Similarly, doubled or paired blossoms or seed heads are considered auspicious when used in a flower arrangement or painting.

Both yin and yang working together are as essential to the creation of harmony in a flower arrangement as they are in the workings of the forces that hold the universe together. The addition of mankind creates the unity between yang heaven and yin earth. The trio can be expressed in an asymmetrical triangle with three levels, man being placed between heaven and earth. This asymmetrical triangle was subsequently adopted by the Japanese in their flower arrangements.

As one of those footnotes to history, the symbolic Taoist plum is incorrectly named in much literature, being in fact the *Prunus mume* or Japanese apricot. Although it is of Chinese origin, where it is called the *mei*, it first came to the notice of Western botanists via Japan; hence the misnomer. This flower was held in such high regard in China that a specific form of vase, called the *mei ping*, was designed for it, having a small mouth and short neck to hold but a single branch. Plum branches which are gnarled and twisted, thereby showing their male yang characteristics, are particularly prized and are known as 'sleeping dragons'. The fragrant delicate plum blossoms show the feminine ying qualities, the contrast being charmingly called 'dry limbs clad in jade white blossoms', whilst the passing of winter and coming of spring was called 'the plum blossoms falling on the cracked ice'.

In addition to the colours mentioned, others also convey symbolic meanings to the Chinese. White is the colour of mourning in both flowers and funeral hangings. White flowers would be placed on a table along with a portrait or name card of the deceased. Yellow was the dynastic colour of the Manchu; their dynasty, the Qing, the last in China, ruled from 1644 to 1911. Their imperial robes and palace roofs were of bright yellow, the yin colour for earth. Buddhist priests also wore yellow, it being their colour for temple decorations.

Buddhism, the third great cultural force in the formation of Chinese thought, slowly filtered from India into China from the first century BC onwards, bringing with it a reverence for all forms of life and daily temple offerings of flowers. It was said that 'One should handle even one leaf of green in such a way that it manifests the body of Buddha. This in turn allows Buddha to become manifest through the leaf.' Floral temple offerings were upright and stiffly formal in paired vases. An altar set would include a cauldron, two vases and two candlesticks, usually of bronze, later embellished with *cloisonné* or replaced by porcelain. In time this style was taken on to Japan from the Chinese court of the Tang dynasty.

The Indian or Chinese lotus (*Nelumbo speciosum*) has always been considered the flower of Buddha, who is often depicted sitting on the open petals of the flower. The Goddess of Mercy, Kuan-yin, is worshipped by both Taoists and Buddhists for her many attributes, which include the bestowing and protection of children; she too is often depicted holding a lotus. All parts of the lotus have beautiful form, and so the flower came to be a symbol of purity. It rises majestically on its long stalk out of the muddy waters, the large upturned leaves being held like canopies above the surface.

*Mountain pine (cascade plant)
shows dramatic rock*
Ching Chung Koon

The lotus also became a symbol for the spirit of man ascending from 'the dust of the world' to the purity of the Nirvana. It is one of the 'flowers of the four seasons', standing for summer. In paintings it is often depicted with mandarin ducks, which when paired symbolize marital bliss. Chinese royal pavilions were often surrounded by lotus-filled canals which were spanned by picturesque red-lacquered and ornamented bridges.

It was the Buddhist monks of China who, from the seventh century AD onwards, perfected the unique art called *p'en-tsai* (bonsai) of dwarfing trees for pot culture. The tips of growing shoots are pinched back and the roots are pruned, whilst branches are tied with twine or wire both to limit growth and to produce the effect of a miniature tree twisted and gnarled by great age. Evergreen trees are preferred for their year-round interest, often being planted alongside rocks of rugged character. The evergreen pine, the most revered of trees, is itself a symbol of longevity, endurance and the constancy of friendship so much a part of Buddhism. The traditional winter arrangement composed of plum, pine and bamboo is called 'the three friends of winter' and also represents the three ways of thought, Taoism, Buddhism and Confucianism.

A further development of the art of dwarfing is called *p'en-ching*, consisting of landscaped scenes in long, shallow tray containers. The layout follows the principles of the Chinese form of landscape gardening, enabling idealized miniature natural scenes to be brought indoors. The trays are composed of dwarfed trees, mosses, rocks, water and sometimes miniature pottery figures, temples, bridges and boats.

To understand what was most admired in Chinese flower arranging, it is essential to know what was admired in the most esteemed of Chinese arts – painting and calligraphy. Flower arranging did not have rigid rules of its own; rather it followed artistic principles found in painting and calligraphy, those visual arts that shared brush, paper and ink in their creation of a linearly dominant form.

Hsieh Ho, a noted painter and art critic *c.* AD 500, laid down the *Ku-hua p'in-lu* or Six Canons, which subsequently became the Chinese standard for the aesthetic criticism of painting. Differing translations of these have been made through the centuries. However, the first and most important canon is that the work must possess a 'living spirit' or life force, *ch'i-yun*, a rhythmic vitality that flows through all things. A short poem written at the end of the eleventh century AD by the poet Su Tung-h'o succinctly encapsulates this idea:

> He who judges pictures by the likeness of shapes
> must be thought of as a child.
> He who hammers out verse by rule
> shows that he is not yet a poet.
> Poetry and painting are rooted in the same law,
> the work of heaven and of the first cause.

The second canon is also applicable to flower arrangement, namely that the essential form or structure, the bones, must be correctly established first, otherwise all subsequent work, colouring and

Photo: Pamela South   Photo: Pamela South

addition of detail are useless. To quote Confucius in the *Analects*: 'Applying colour comes after the groundwork.' In flower arranging, as in brush painting, you cannot disguise a bad shape or an incorrect placement.

The fifth of Hsieh Ho's canons states that good painting should be properly planned and composed. There must be 'proper planning in the placing of elements', or unity and cohesion of the parts cannot be achieved. In Chinese flower arrangement it is particularly important to achieve unity at the base, so as to give the effect of lines arising from the same point. This grouped and upward-thrusting movement gives strength and vitality; it should be remembered that the vase, being ying, symbolizes the very earth from which all plants grow.

The Mustard Seed Garden Manual of Painting (Chieh Tzǔ Yüan Hua Ch'uan: 1679–1701) set out further principles of painting, also applicable to flower arrangements. Form and balance are asymmetrical, with beauty of line being emphasized. The composition includes well-defined spaces; the main line to one side of the centre is balanced by subsidiary placements. Odd numbers of components are to be preferred, there being no symmetrical patterns or straight lines. Curving and upward-pointing lines are to be used to suggest rhythmic movement.

Other guidelines to Chinese flower arranging include an acknowledgement that the flowers used in any one vase should be of one colour, or of only two or three harmonious colours, with no strongly contrasting colours. Furthermore, the number of kinds of flower in a vase should be restricted, ideally to one type but certainly to no more than three kinds, all set out at different heights. Whilst the colours of the flowers should be in harmony, the colour of the vase should contrast with the flowers.

In an arrangement, sequence of growth from bud to open flower should be shown both for variety and to express the passage of time. The height of the arrangement should average one to one and a half times that of the vase, be it slender or massive. Branches are to be selected for their interesting shape; curving lines are particularly admired, even if these have been induced by gentle bending or manipulation. Heavy branches may be partially sawn, with wedges of stone or wood being inserted in order to force a curving line. Branches to be used with wide-mouthed vases can be cut and then tied together with bass or string in the desired juxtaposition before they are lowered into the vase, whilst hidden forked sticks can provide mechanical support.

The most important classical Chinese book specifically written about flower arranging was *A Treatise of Vase Flowers* by Chang Ch'ien-tê; it appeared in 1595, during the Ming dynasty. It not only covers principles of design and the selection of vases together with techniques of cutting and preservation but also, most interestingly, grades flowers in ranks of desirability. The most highly prized are moutan peony, spring orchid (*Cymbidium virescens*), Japanese apricot, chrysanthemum, wintersweet, *Daphne odora*, sweetflag (*Acorus gramineus*), *Camellia reticulata* and *Narcissus tazetta*. Some of these flowers, like the moutan or tree peony and the chrysanthemum, are showy and decorative; others have small flowers combined with a powerful scent, such as *Daphne odora*, wintersweet and summer orchid (*Cymbidium ensifolium*). Fragrance was always highly prized in flowers and fruits, with fragrant woods being burnt specifically to scent the air.

The tree peony, with its sumptuous blooms and ornamental form, was considered to be the 'king of flowers' as well as the flower of the spring season. It symbolized high position, wealth and honour and, because of this association, was placed in large vases in reception halls as well as often being grown in specially raised marble flower beds. The peony is the flower most often depicted on all art objects – vases, screens, paintings and embroideries.

The tea plant (*Camellia sinensis*) has been grown as a crop for over 3000 years and has been in common usage to produce tea leaves since 2000 BC. The ornamental camellias, particularly *Camellia reticulata*, have been intensively cultivated, often being used in New Year arrangements; the New Year festival under the old Chinese calendar was in February. Yet it is the *Narcissus tazetta*, the Chinese sacred lily, that particularly symbolizes this festival. Special bulbs were skilfully grown in shallow dishes, needing only pebbles and water to flower. Thus the charming Chinese name for narcissus translates as 'water fairy'.

Chrysanthemums, the flower of the autumn season, are also associated with long life. This flower was known before 5000 BC in a small yellow form. With intensive cultivation many colours and forms have evolved; white and purple blooms had already appeared by the time of the Tang dynasty. The showier fancy forms were always prized for use

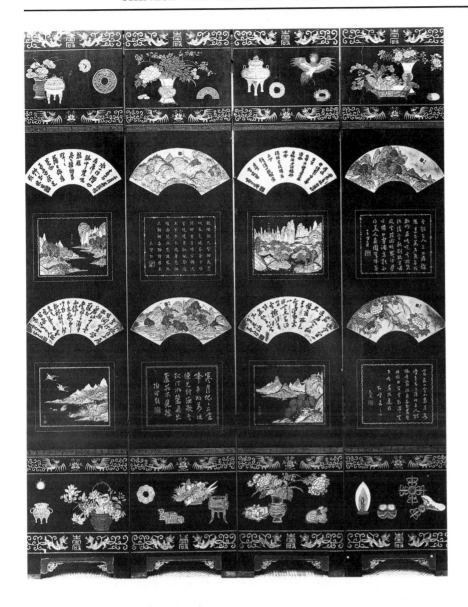

Coromandel screen
Victoria and Albert Museum

in flower arrangements. Popular as house and courtyard plants, they were trained to produce desired shapes, a descending cascade of blooms being very effective. Flowers grown for specifically medicinal purposes had their petals infused in wine to produce a Taoist elixir, whilst a fragrant chrysanthemum tea was often drunk to promote good health.

Chinese orchids are the subtropical terraneous cymbidiums, with small flowers, soft colourings and a delicate sweet scent. Orchids were likened to a superior man or an elegant woman and were all termed *lan*. Confucius said: 'The association with a superior person is like entering a hall of orchids.' He believed their scent was the sweetest of all the flowers. Orchids have long been a favourite motif in Chinese art, and their flowers were frequently used in arrangements, but it is really the graceful form of the whole plant that is most prized in pot cultures.

Roses have also long been enjoyed as garden flowers, coming to prominence first around the time of the Tang dynasty. The introduc-

Coromandel lacquer cabinet
Victoria and Albert Museum

tion of Chinese roses to Europe, some with their recurrent flowering habit and tea scent, was to have a profound effect on the evolution of our modern garden roses. In China roses were not used in bouquets, possibly because of their thorns, but *Rosa rugosa*, *chinensis*, *laevigata* and *banksiae* were used in arrangements.

Because China is a vast country, with such ranges of climate and terrain, the natural flora is very varied and there were many regional differences in what flowers were or could be grown and selected. The following were some of the additional flowers that were used in floral decorations: magnolias, wisteria, lilac, jasmine (*Jasminum officinalis* and *polyanthum*), hostas, quince (*Chaenomelis*), *Viburnum fragrans*, Chinese witch-hazel (*Hamamelis mollis*), hydrangeas, *Iris kaempferi*, hibiscus, *Hemerocallis*, *Lilium regale*, *henryii* and *tigrinum*, herbaceous peony (*Paeonia albiflora*), *Chimonanthus praecox*, *Osmanthus fragrans*, crab apple and kumquat (*Fortunella japonica*).

Bowls of auspicious fruits might also be displayed with flower arrangements. Pomegranates, full of seeds, conveyed the message 'may you have many progeny', whilst given at a wedding they meant 'may you have many sons'. Peaches recalled the mythical Queen Mother of the West, Hsi Wang-mu, who guarded the tree bearing the peaches of immortality; peaches were therefore given or displayed on birthdays or at weddings as symbols of long life. A fungus *ling chih* (*Polyporous lucidus*) when dried is very long lasting and thus came to be a symbol of immortality. Lotus fruits signified wisdom and purity. A fragrant citron, *Citrus sarcodactylus*, was known as 'Buddha's hand' because long finger-like lobes extend from the rind, resembling Buddha's hand bestowing a blessing.

Other objects displayed with arrangements could include branches of coral, an emblem of longevity and official promotion, and peacock feathers in painting or calligraphy brush pots, representing beauty, dignity and rank. Incense burners, carved jade and ivory figurines might also appear.

China's vast and hard-working peasant population, primarily engaged in dawn to dusk agriculture, had no time available for the leisure pursuits of refined scholars and artists. Festivals and celebrations allowed some emotional release for the peasantry, a warm and cheerful people. Festive decorations, like their fireworks, exploded with colours verging on the gaudy. In like vein, the peasants' joyous massed flower baskets and bouquets were very different from the formalized vase arrangements.

China was almost certainly the first country to design baskets

Chinese robe
Victoria and Albert Museum

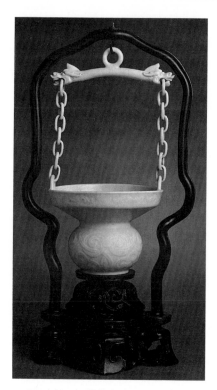

White porcelain flower holder with relief decoration. Qing, 18th century
University of London, Percival David Foundation of Chinese Art

specifically for holding flowers, probably originating along the Chang Jiang (Yangtze) river in the Tang dynasty. In baskets, massed flowers symbolized an abundance of good wishes for birthdays, weddings and happy occasions. Flowers arranged in this unsophisticated manner appealed to everyone, but were the particular favourites of the common folk.

Baskets were made of bamboo, willow, reed and wood, with some being lacquered for both durability and adornment. A particularly elegant form originating in the eighteenth century featured the basket in porcelain suspended from its own mahogany stand. In paintings and ceramics, flower baskets are depicted with *ju-i*, a stylized decorative form of a mystic fungus attached to the handles with flying ribbons, which implied the granting of every good wish and fortunate blessing. One of the Hundred Antiquities, dating from the period of the Qing emperor Kang Xi (1661–1722), is the flower basket.

Lan Ts'ai-ho, one of the Taoist Eight Immortals, is the patron deity of florists and is usually depicted with a flower-filled basket. Another Immortal, Ho Hsien-ku, carries a lotus blossom or seed pod. On the twelfth day of the second month of the old lunar calendar a festival was held in honour of the goddess or spirit of flowers, Hua-Shên, when red papers were tied on flowering trees and shrubs.

Porcelain is undoubtedly one of the most universally admired of Chinese inventions. True porcelain was in use by the time of the Tang dynasty and had been fully refined by the Sung dynasty. It epitomized the spirit of a highly civilized era and, against this highly cultivated background, the arts of gardening and flower arrangement flourished.

Celadon sea-green ware was developed in this period and was greatly prized, for its colour complemented green tea. When used on a vase it is also a beautiful soft colour against which to display flowers. The famous cobalt blue and white patterned vase became the most popular type in Europe from the sixteenth century onwards and was made in vast quantities, being one of China's chief exports at this time. Certainly the beautiful glazes and shapes of the vases produced by Chinese potters were a considerable stimulus to flower arrangement. Seasonal variations in the choice of suitable container were important. Bronze vases were considered best for spring and winter, whilst porcelain was right for summer and autumn.

Bamboo, less expensive and more easily obtainable, was often made into heavily carved and decorated tubular vases. Vases with a flattened side were made for hanging on walls or pillars and looked particularly attractive when holding trailing morning glory, vines or weeping willow.

It is worth noting here that in Chinese flower arrangements the rim of the vase is never covered and that branches should not lean against the sides. This convention ensures added emphasis for the form and importance of the vase.

China has also long been famed for her artificial flowers; those displaying the soft sheen of silk cloth look particularly lifelike. In the Sui dynasty of AD 581–618, which preceded the Tang, Emperor Yang in late autumn and winter had flowers and leaves of coloured silk tied to the bare branches of trees and shrubs in his garden, and aquatic plants made of silk in his ponds.

Silk flowers have been found in excavations of some antiquity near the oasis town of Turpan, in north-west China. Sir Aurel Stein, the noted explorer, discovered some particularly fine paper flowers (which may be seen today in the British Museum) in the Buddhist caves at Dunhuang, also in north-west China. Both groups of flowers date from the Tang dynasty and both locations were places on the famed Silk Route. The flowers were wonderfully preserved, including their delicate colouring, because of the dry desert climate. Did someone long for a fresh flower in that harsh and barren land?

Truly, the Chinese love of flowers comes down to us across the centuries, and although 'flowers cannot tell when people are no more . . . year after year they go right on holding their own beauty contests.' May you too find that, as the lady poet Chu Shu Chen wrote in the twelfth century, 'Man and flowers have in their hearts their own fragrance.'

Ceramic figure of Immortal with flower basket
Victoria and Albert Museum

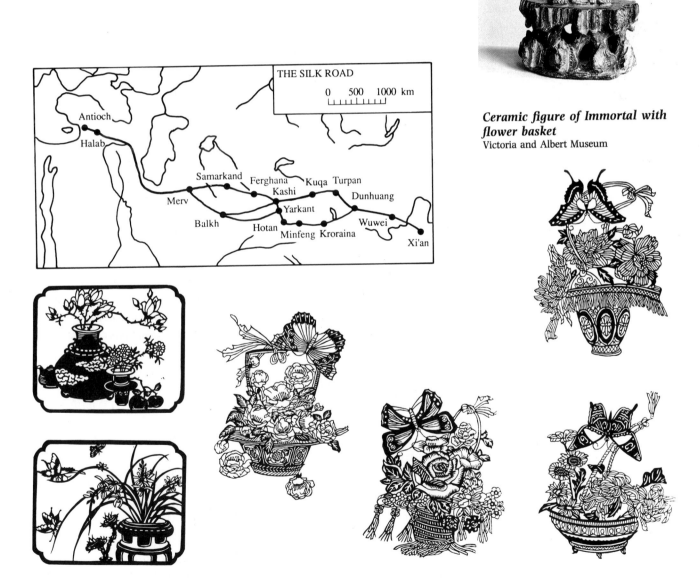

The silk road and examples of paper flowers

Taoism also taught the power of emptiness for it is the hollow of space in a vase that makes it servicable. The chinese have a unique way of handling space as an element of design. In flower arrangement this is shown in the emphasis space gives to the limited selection of line material chosen. Space and the placing of objects in correct balanced relationships to one another is important in the popular groupings of arrangements with other accessories to make a harmonious whole.

Bibliography

Chavannes, Edouard. *The Five Happinesses: Symbolism in Chinese Popular Art*. New York: Weatherhill, 1973.

Cooper, J. *Taoism, the Way of the Mystic*. Wellingborough: Aquarian, 1972.

Cooper, J. *Yin and Yang*. Wellingborough: Aquarian, 1981.

Fourcade, François. *Art Treasures of the Peking Museum*. New York: Abrams, 1966.

Keswick, Maggie. *The Chinese Garden*. London: Academy, 1978.

Lao Tzu. *Tao Te Ching*. London: Wildwood, 1973.

Laufer, H. *Chinese Baskets*. Field Museum of Natural History, Anthropology Design Series no. 3, 1925.

Li, H. L. *The Garden Flowers of China*. New York: Ronald, 1959.

Li, H. L. *Chinese Flower Arrangement*. Princeton, NJ: Van Nostrand, 1959.

Li Zhiyan and Cheng Wen. *Chinese Pottery and Porcelain*. Beijing: Foreign Languages Press, 1986.

Mai-mai-Sze (ed.). *The Mustard Seed Garden Manual of Painting*. Princeton, NJ: Princeton University Press, 1977.

Medley, Margaret. *A Handbook of Chinese Art*. London: Bell and Hyman, 1977.

Sirén, Osvald. *Gardens of China*. New York: Ronald, 1949.

Tsai Hsiang-Ping. *Blossoms of Life*. Taipei: Ho Tsai Hsiang-Ping, 1981.

Vedlich, Joseph (ed.). *The Prints of the Ten Bamboo Studio*. New York: Crescent, 1979.

Watt, James Y. *The Sumptuous Basket*. China House Gallery, China Institute in America.

Williams, C. A. S. *Outlines of Chinese Symbolism and Art Motifs*. New York: Dover, 1976.

Yang Hongxun. *The Classical Gardens of China*. New York: Van Nostrand Reinhold, 1982.

Chinese Treasures and Splendors (catalogue), Palais de la Civilisation, Montreal. Paris: Arthaud, 1986.

The Genius of China Exhibition (catalogue), Royal Academy, London. William Watson, *Times Newspapers*, 1973.

Chinese collections in Great Britain

Bristol, City Art Gallery and Museum: ceramics;

Burnley, Lancashire, Townley Hall Art Gallery and Museum: later ceramics.

Cambridge, Fitzwilliam Museum: ceramics.

Durham, Gulbenkian Museum: bronzes, ceramics.

Edinburgh, Royal Scottish Museum: general collection.

Glasgow, the Burrell Collection: bronzes, porcelain.

Leeds, Temple Newsam: general collection, late ceramics.

Liverpool, Port Sunlight, Lady Lever Art Gallery: Qing porcelains.

London, British Museum: finest collection in UK, especially bronzes, early ceramics.

London, Percival David Foundation of Chinese Art: imperial porcelains, tenth to eighteenth centuries.

London, Victoria and Albert Museum: important general collection, ceramics.

Manchester, Wythenshawe Hall: ceramics.

Oxford, Ashmolean Museum: bronzes, pottery, porcelain.

Ikebana: Japanese flower arranging

STELLA COE and MARY L. STEWART

THE JAPANESE WORD *IKEBANA* IS USUALLY TRANSLATED AS 'flower arrangement'. But a more accurate interpretation would be 'living plant material', for ikebana is the art of arranging more than just flowers. In fact, the flowers are generally the least important part – unless they are used as one or more of the three main lines which form the basic structure of most ikebana arrangements, representing heaven, man and earth.

Our concern is with an Oriental rather than a Western form of flower arranging, a Japanese art form perfected through centuries of tradition and development. Consequently, from the outset we must appreciate a very different way of thinking about flowers and how they are arranged. In Japanese Buddhist terms, ikebana is one of the *do* or ways to enlightenment. So, while an ikebana arrangement can be purely decorative, there remains even in the modern schools a vestige of religious and philosophical symbolism.

Ikebana is not about built-up masses of flowers, even when an arrangement is fairly large. The Japanese thinking is just the opposite:

Photo: Tim Imrie

A basic slanting moribana arrangement using japonica and sonia roses

(*Note*: The arrangements in this section are examples of ikebana of the Sogetsu School. They are from *Ikebana: A Practical and Philosophical Guide to Japanese Flower Arrangement* by Stella Coe and Mary L. Stewart, Century 1984. Copyright of photographs John Calmann and King.)

the fewer flowers the better. What is important is the overall environ-ment in which flowers – if they are used at all – are a natural part. Each piece of material used in an arrangement can also have its own meaning. The Japanese emphasize the significance of the whole of a flower or branch, its life cycle, so that whatever part of it is used can represent the eternal processes of the universe. The full-blown flower, the half-open bud and the tight bud have the meanings of past, present and future and would be used accordingly. Similarly, branches with leaves that are newly budding, fully open or even withered can give a specific meaning to an arrangement.

This detailed interest in meaning is not utterly impractical: quite the contrary. By learning to focus our attention on arranging in a wider and ultimately deeper context, we come to understand and respect the nature of the material we are working with in the same practical and direct manner as a gardener.

By the same token, ikebana attaches great importance to the seasons, as will be demonstrated by some of the arrangements chosen to illustrate this chapter. The range and subtlety of seasonal material is astounding, and again reflects the Japanese understanding of and respect for nature in all its manifold aspects. By using seasonal materials we put ourselves in harmony with nature. While we can certainly buy flowers and materials which are out of season – and there are no hard and fast rules in any of the schools on the matter – by choosing material from the garden or the countryside we become much more aware of what is going on around us and thus more in tune with the spirit of each climate and season. Our ingenuity and imagination are brought into play as well.

As indicated above, ikebana is decorative in the broader sense as a symbolic representation of nature. A bit of the out-of-doors is brought inside. This idea can be carried over into modern, abstract arrange-

Photo: Tim Imrie

On a summer evening: clematis and hosta leaves in an Anthony Stern glass vase. Arrangement by Stella Coe

Photo: Tim Imrie

Photo: Tim Imrie

Above *An autumn breeze: Fuji chrysanthemums, a bleached root and beech branches in a copper bowl*

Right *Winter's wind: hellebore and heather root with driftwood on a slate base*

ments where plastic, metal and glass objects can be combined with or replace branches and flowers as the basic elements. Just as much care in selecting material is then required in order to make a statement which is harmonizing rather than accentuating.

The decorative function of ikebana is so important because a traditional Japanese house is a room without furniture. Cushions and tables are brought out of cupboards when needed and put straight back when not in use. The walls are actually sliding doors, glass for the outer ones and paper for the inner. There is an alcove on the garden side of the room, known as the *tokonoma*. It is usually 2 metres wide and 1 metre deep. An ikebana arrangement is placed in the *tokonoma*. It is offset by a *kakemono*, or hanging scroll picture, which is changed with the seasons. The ikebana arrangement is designed to harmonize with the season, the *kakemono* and the view outside. However, harmony does not mean duplication. If chrysanthemums appear in the *kakemono* or are blooming in the garden, something else would definitely be chosen for the ikebana.

The Japanese are equally fond of evoking moods or memories and expressing them in poetry or ikebana, and their expressions are direct, concrete and visual rather than abstract and theoretical. The communication is intended to be intuitive rather than intellectual, illustrating a characteristically Japanese talent for reconciling seeming opposites. An ikebana arrangement conceived for this purpose can express a specific thought or feeling across an infinitely wide range according to the intuition of the arranger. And it can create a similar response in the viewer at the same level. This added dimension gives such an arrangement its vitality.

Once we have readjusted our thinking about flower arranging to the Japanese mode, it is not difficult to translate ikebana into a Western environment. It is not necessary for us to build a *tokonoma*, or hide all of our furniture in a cupboard, to accommodate ikebana. We simply need to find a place where an arrangement can be seen against a plain background so that its linear structure is clearly emphasized. A Japanese screen made of wood and paper sets the ikebana into relief without competing with the furniture – and possibly the wallpaper – of our homes. Similarly, if we do not have a garden readily at hand, the highways and byways, forests and moors are wonderful sources of material for ikebana arrangements. Here we may find stones, mosses and gnarled bits of wood as well as grasses and lichen-covered branches. Those of us who have gardens have developed a new interest in growing seasonal shrubs, trees and flowers.

Today it is very unusual to meet a Japanese woman who has not studied ikebana, regardless of her social or economic status, as the adornment of her home depends on her skill and ingenuity. Even though Western-style living quarters are increasingly prevalent in Japanese cities, ikebana has been cleverly adapted to suit the surroundings.

Historically, ikebana was not a gentle art of the housewife. Women are comparative newcomers to the art. Most headmasters and senior teachers of the ikebana schools in Japan are men. And it is not in the least surprising that business executives take ikebana lessons. Ikebana arrangements are a common feature in office buildings and factories – where courses may be offered to employees – as well as in hotel lobbies, restaurants and department stores. The major Tokyo depart-

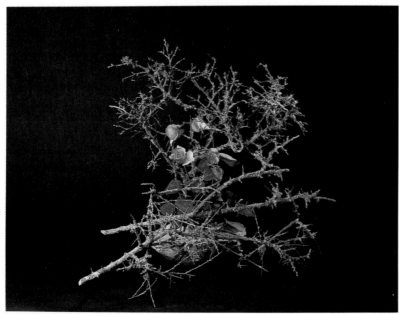

Photo: Tim Imrie

An arrangement on a philosophical theme: the unconditioned state of search. Pink roses and lichen-covered hawthorn in a Phil Sherwood ceramic bowl

Photo: Tim Imrie

An arrangement on a philosophical theme: the timeless communion of the nameless unknown. Agapanthus with driftwood on a stone base

ment stores have facilities for and often sponsor ikebana exhibitions.

The original site of an ikebana arrangement was a Shinto shrine or a Buddhist temple. Shinto, the native Japanese religion, is quite simply reverence for the *kami* or spirits that live in all natural things. While other cultures practised offering flowers to their gods, or personifications of natural forces, the early Shinto priests revered the entire living plant – roots and all – in which the *kami* resided. Offerings are placed before a tree, or a rope is tied ceremonially around a tree. Images are found throughout the countryside in front of rocks as supplication to the *kami* within.

Buddhism was brought to Japan from Korea in the sixth century AD, and with it came the Korean and Chinese custom of placing flowers before an image of Buddha. So in this sense ikebana represents a synthesis of the two types of religious offering: the whole plant and the flower. It was the Japanese genius which reconciled the apparent religious conflict and created an art form.

The early practitioners of ikebana were priests, noblemen and *samurai*, or warriors. The first arrangements were devised by a seventh-century court noble, Ono-no-Imoko, who took the robes of a Buddhist priest when he retired. While he was serving as an envoy to the imperial court of China he was impressed by the way the Chinese designed their gardens. When he returned to Japan he built himself a garden in the Chinese fashion but with much greater refinement and restraint. But Ono-no-Imoko was not as enthusiastic about the haphazard manner in which Chinese Buddhist priests placed their floral offerings before the Buddha image. In the interest of creating a more formal, fitting way of offering flowers to the Buddha, he built himself a small hut beside a pond in his garden, and spent the rest of his life developing the art of ikebana.

The task he set for himself was typically paradoxical. He was trying to find a way to cut the flower (or branch) from its native stem, thereby shortening its life, and then to place it in water in order to prolong its life. He went beyond that endeavour. As a Buddhist priest he felt that an arrangement of such material placed before an image of the Buddha, the symbol of the universe, should itself symbolize the natural world and its process. On this humble spot – *ike-no-bo* – the style known as *rikka*, or 'standing-up plant cuttings', came into being. For hundreds of years the techniques were passed on from master to master, each taking Ikenobo as their name.

Ikenobo art produced many brilliant exponents, but none so illustrious as the fifteenth-century priest Senkei Ikenobo. So many pilgrims came to his temple in Kyoto – at that time the capital of Japan – to admire his arrangements that he decided to start his own school of ikebana, the Ikenobo School. It is still flourishing today.

Early *rikka* arrangements could be 4–7 metres in height and take weeks to construct. The flowers and branch tips were all manipulated in such a way that they pointed to heaven. The style was well suited to the spaciousness of the Buddhist temple. The time and trouble

An arrangement on a philosophical theme: the mind doors burst open. Tree fungus with tiger Lilies and dried fatsia on a black wooden base

An arrangement on a philosophical theme: the cloud of the unknowing. Blackthorn branches, arum lily and dieffenbachia on a stone base

Photo: Tim Imrie

involved in creating an arrangement served the religious function of calming and purifying the mind. Eventually noblemen took up the art, and *rikka* arrangements were made in palaces.

In the eleventh century the *shogun*, or military ruler, replaced the emperor, and Kamakura became the capital of Japan. The *shogun* Yorimoto chose the meditational form of Buddhism known in Japan as Zen for his warrior way of life. Ikebana was adapted to the training needs of the *samurai*. They practised ikebana as a means of composing their minds, to be at one with nature and to experience neither hesitation nor fear in combat.

The *tokonoma* was built as the quiet place in the *samurai*'s home where he could meditate and study. There he could create an arrangement with a single flower or branch in a tall vase. This style, known as *nageire*, or 'thrown-in', dates from the twelfth century. He might also take a brush, ink and rice paper and create a painting or a poem. His painting, mounted on a silk scroll, would be hung in the *tokonoma*, the ikebana arrangement placed on the floor nearby.

The tea ceremony evolved in this period, and also came to be regarded as one of the ways to enlightenment. As tea houses were built in Japanese gardens, the *tokonoma* became an integral part. A form known as the *chabana*, or tea arrangement, was developed. This is a small, natural arrangement, often done with one flower, suited to the starkness and simplicity of the ceremony.

The ikebana and tea master, Ippo, wrote the first book on ikebana, the *Sendenshō*. In it he explains how to arrange flowers in accordance with the seasons for special occasions. The terms *shin*, referring to the main branch, and *soé*, referring to the secondary branch in an arrangement, first appeared in the *Sendenshō*.

Whereas the *rikka* and its modified form the *seika* (a triad symbolic of heaven, man and earth) were designed for Buddhist rituals and court ceremonies, the styles which developed out of the Zen influence represented the unity of nature, and brought composure and tranquillity to the arranger as well as to the viewer. But both styles had their exponents and continued to be practised in the different schools of ikebana that sprang up over the centuries.

As the merchant class emerged from the seventeenth century onwards, and the capital shifted to Edo (Tokyo), ikebana underwent a variety of refinements which took it away from a strictly religious and elite pursuit. It gradually came to be regarded by all Japanese as an essential part of their cultural inheritance.

The refinement of the art had taken place in isolation, however. Foreigners were kept from Japanese shores for two centuries. When the isolation ended in the middle of the nineteenth century, Western influences in the art of flower arranging reaching Japan were quickly met and absorbed. New schools came into being; old schools were modified to accord with the demands of the slowly modernizing population. New styles appeared, such as *moribana* or 'piled-up flowers', usually in a shallow, ceramic container. Western flowers were used, and the *kenzan*, or pinholder, was invented.

All of the schools of ikebana evolved their own adaptations of these styles and techniques. Of the popular schools today, Ikenobo is the oldest. Enshu dates from the sixteenth century, and Koryu from the eighteenth century. The new schools include Ohara, founded in the 1890s, and Sogetsu, founded in the 1920s. The latter was begun by Sofu Teshigahara; his son Hiroshi, who is also a potter and a film maker, is the present Grand Master.

The larger schools of ikebana – and there are about a dozen – have representatives outside Japan who carry on the traditions and who are authorized to teach students and give demonstrations to the public. They return to Japan from time to time to study with a master. The masters themselves maintain a busy schedule of touring the world teaching and giving demonstrations.

Ikebana arrangers have a common meeting ground in an organization known as Ikebana International. This was the brainchild of Ellen Gordon Allen, wife of an American general posted to Japan after the Second World War. After having spent two years in Tokyo, where she studied ikebana, Mrs Allen returned to the United States. She not only missed her associations with ikebana, but also found a number of compatriots who shared her enthusiasm for the art. The masters of the leading ikebana schools encouraged her to establish an international organization which would maintain direct contact with Japan as well as link ikebana practitioners throughout the world. Ikebana International came into being on 17 August 1955 in Tokyo.

The motto of Ikebana International is 'Friendship through flowers'. Its aims are:

1   To stimulate and cultivate the continuous study and spread of ikebana;
2   To develop thereby a better understanding of the Japanese people,

and likewise a better understanding between all nationalities;

3 To strengthen the friendship between masters, teachers and students and, above all;

4 To encourage friendship and goodwill everywhere.

The first British chapter, the London Chapter, was founded by Stella Coe in 1958. Its honorary president is the wife of the Japanese ambassador. There are ten other British chapters, located in Manchester, Birmingham, Leicester, Truro, Huddersfield, Edinburgh, north-west Lancashire, Durham, Belfast and Sheffield. The Ikebana International First European Regional Conference was held at Maidstone on 6–10 June 1983, under the auspices of the British chapters. Its co-chairmen were Stella Coe and Takashi Sawano. The Second Regional Conference took place in Luxemburg in June 1987.

Each of the ikebana schools represented in England – Sogetsu, Enshu, Ikenobo, Ichiyo and Ohara – consists of teachers and students and has its own annual schedule of meetings, workshops and

The new year dawns: white orchids, dried Japanese vine and pine branches. Arrangement by Stella Coe

demonstrations. Ikebana International offers an annual programme as well, and provides a meeting place for anyone interested in learning this ancient and fascinating art.

Bibliography

Carr, Rachel E. *Japanese Floral Art*. Princeton, New Jersey: Van Nostrand, 1961.

Coe, Stella and Stewart, Mary L. *Ikebana: a Practical and Philosophical Guide to Japanese Flower Arrangement*. London: Century, 1984 (paperback: Octopus, 1986).

Conway, J. Gregory. *Conway's Treasury of Flower Arrangements*. London: Routledge and Kegan Paul, 1953.

Donald, Elsie Burch. 'Ikebana', in *Flower Arranging*. London: Royal Horticultural Society, Octopus, 1972, pp. 150–65.

Ikenobo, Senei. *Best of Ikebana III: the Ikenobo School*. Tokyo: Shufunotomo, 1962.

Koehn, Alfred. *The Way of Japanese Flower Arrangement*. Tokyo: Kyo Bun Kwan, 1937.

Komoda, Shusui and Pointner, Hurst. *Ikebana Spirit and Technique*. Poole, Dorset: Blandford, 1980.

March-Penny, John. *The Masters' Book of Ikebana*. Maidenhead: Samson How, 1976.

Ohara, Houn. *Best of Ikebana I: the Ohara School*. Tokyo: Shufunotomo, 1962.

Ohara, Houn. *Creation with Flowers: the Ohara School of Japanese Flower Arrangement*. London: Kodansha, Ward Lock, 1966.

Ohi, Minobu. *Best of Ikebana IV: History of Ikebana*. Tokyo, Shufunotomo, 1962.

Oshikawa, J. and Gorham, Hazel H. *Manual of Japanese Flower Arrangement*. Tokyo: Cosmo, 1947.

Sawano, Takashi. *Ikebana*. London: Ward Lock, 1981.

Sparnon, Norman. *Japanese Flower Arrangement, Classical and Modern*. Rutland, Vermont: Tuttle, 1960.

Teshigahara, Sofu. *Best of Ikebana II: the Sogetsu School*. Tokyo: Shufunotomo, 1962.

Teshigahara, Sofu. *Ikebana*. Tokyo: Sōgetsukai, 1962.

Teshigahara, Sofu. *Sofu: his Boundless World of Flowers and Form*. Tokyo: Kodansha, 1966.

Tsuji, H. K. *The Mastery of Japanese Flower Arranging*. Kyoto: Mitsu-hana, 1962.

Webb, Iris (ed.). 'Ikebana: the Japanese art of flower arrangement', in *The Complete Guide to Flower and Foliage Arrangement*. London: National Association of Flower Arrangement Societies, Ebury, 1979, pp. 224–34.

3

The Islamic influence

Floral art in Iran

UMA BASU

AN APPRECIATION OF ARRANGING FLOWERS ARTISTICALLY has drawn together people with varied cultural backgrounds into a bond of friendship through flowers, and many local and international societies and clubs have been established to develop this art. The history of the floral art of different countries is under investigation, and new avenues open up as research workers explore this aspect of cultural activity.

In India in the medieval period, Mogul rulers had great respect for Persian culture and both Mogul art and architecture bear the testimony of its influence. My interest in the study of Persian floral art began as an endeavour to ascertain the extent of its influence on Indian floral art. Whereas there are innumerable books on Persian art and culture in different languages, there is unfortunately very little information on floral art. Despite clear evidence of its existence, there appears to have been no comprehensive study as yet.

Persia, now known as Iran, is one of the civilized countries of the old world. The great caravan route that passed through Baghdad from North Africa and on through the Mediterranean countries to China and India resulted in an intellectual atmosphere amongst Iran's people and rulers. In the ruins of Pasargadae and Persepolis, built by the Achaemanian kings in the fifth century BC, glimpses of this past glory can be found. With such a brilliant and diverse backdrop, it is no wonder that the cultural progress of Persia is as chequered as its history.

The admiration for plants and flowers in Iran can be traced back to very early days, when roses and gardens played an important role in the lives of the people. Now-Ruz (new rose), the day of celebration for the New Year, is said to have been started by the legendary King Jemshed, and symbolized the day on which the first rose flowered, heralding the approach of spring. Later a fixed date in the third week of March was chosen for this celebration to take place. The word 'paradise' is derived from the Persian word *pairidaeza*, meaning the enclosed area of a garden, a sanctuary from the surroundings of the desert. Persian gardens (or *bagh*) invariably contained shady trees, flowering shrubs and flowing water. It has been recorded that the Achaemanian King Cyrus the Great loved gardens, and in many monuments one can recognize a royal presence by a bunch of pomegranate flowers in the hand.

In most old cities in Iran, ruins of a garden or garden pavilion can be found, and in many gardens were built the mausoleums of poets and intellectuals. It is a part of recreation for Iranian families to visit gardens and relax in the tranquil atmosphere, resting in the shade of tall trees and walking amongst the rose and jasmine bushes.

Shiraz is famous for its garden and is known as the city of the rose, wine and poets. All through history the rose has been of great importance, and even today the extensive rose fields around Shiraz are a joy to see. Attar, rose-water, sweets and cold drinks made from rose petals are popular throughout Iran.

There is no dearth of floral wealth in Iran. Many English flowering plants grow in a wild state, often of a single variety and smaller in size. Near the shores of the Caspian Sea, fruit trees and flowering plants usually found in the Mediterranean area grow in abundance.

From the Sasanian period (AD 224–650) a few vase-like glazed potteries have been found, but it is difficult to state with any certainty that these were used as flower vases. The floral art of India was mentioned as one of 64 varieties of art in the fourth century AD by Vatsayan. Likewise in China, Italy and Greece flower arrangement can be traced to that century. As Persia is situated between these countries it is quite possible that some form of floral art was started there, and there is evidence of this continuous process of development in other art works in the Sasanian period.

From the tenth century onwards there was a great development in cultural life in Persia. The turmoil created by the Islamic conquests subsided, and art and culture flourished with renewed vigour. The Iranians' love of nature can be gleaned from such works of art as carpets, metalwork, ceramic ware, tile painting, textiles and architec-

Sixteenth century wall painting of a flower arrangement in a tall vase standing in a shallow container of water

Photo: Julia Clements

ture. These show elegance of detail combined with jewellers' fineness of decoration. By the time of Seljuqs, beautiful artwork was being eagerly sought by princes, nobles, officials, merchants and also for decoration of mosques.

The elaborate composition of Persian carpets and the detailed work involved reflect a poetic vision of the world. In some Iranian homes the carpets were often the only place on which to sit, and their quality symbolized the status of the owner in high society. There was very little variation in colour and composition in the designs for these carpets, and often they were simulated Persian garden scenes. There were also the vase designs: a tall vase with flowers stood as a central motif, with a cluster of flowers or flowering shrubs strewn all around in arabesque. In the vase design it can be seen that the height of the arranged flowers is not in proportion to the height of the vase, and the flowers are not well spread out. Perhaps this is because in a hot climate flowers, especially roses, stay fresh if they are bunched together with leaves, and it may be that, owing to lack of technical knowledge, flowers were arranged near the mouth of the vase. As with carpets, the vase motif was used to represent a vase of fresh flowers as if on a tile or bas-reliefed wall; Indo-Sasanian architects in India used similar vase patterns in much greater variety.

This evidence of flowers arranged in containers is indicative of the availability of vases. Hand-blown glass objects such as goblets, decanters, candlesticks and vases were also made in Persia in a rich spectrum of blue or green with gold patterns. Beautiful ceramic and glass vases were brought from China and Europe. Inside the archaeological monuments of Delhi and Agra in India, paintings of Chinese and Iranian vase designs may be found. A beautiful vase pattern can be seen in the fourteenth-century polychrome tilework of Masjed-e-Jom'eh in the Iranian town of Yazd. This has a symmetrical arrangement of roses and seasonal flowers in a dark blue vase with a gold ornamental design. In the centre there is an open red rose with two

Photo: Julia Clements

A flower arrangement in a vase

Photos: Uma Basu

Left *Floral decoration in a vase design in tile from 14th century*

Right *Stylized flower and vase design with a peacock pair from Golestan Palace. 19th century*

rosebuds drooping down from the rim in both directions; they look more realistic than the surrounding flowers, which could well be larkspur or buddleia spike and aster. The vase designs in the royal mosque (early seventeenth century) in Isfahan and in the Gulistan Palace (nineteenth century) in Tehran are more stylized. The design in the tilework of the Gulistan Palace has a tall vase at the bottom and a smaller one above. The tall vase is of blue and gold and contains roses and dahlias; it stands against a lighter blue background. The smaller vase is against a yellow background, and is a combination of blue, yellow and white. This vase stands between two peacocks, and above it there is a design with an archer on horseback. A small garland is held by the bird, and another garland with pink roses hangs from the vase. Flowers in arabesque decorate the whole panel.

The formal conventions governing these patterns on carpets and tiles do not constitute the only evidence that fresh flower arrangements were a common feature in medieval Persia. Miniature paintings and books also carry convincing evidence. An early fifteenth-century painting of *Shah Nama* shows the interior of Rustom's chamber in which a pair of vases with flowers is arranged in an oval shape in the foreground beside a low table. In a sixteenth-century miniature from the *Jahangir Album* one can see courtesans, musicians and poets sitting in two groups facing the royal canopy, and in front of them are three vases together with food and drink. The central large vase has long-stemmed flowers spreading out from the top, and the two flanking vases are of a lighter tone with flowers in the usual cluster formation. Iranians normally eat and drink whilst sitting on the floor, and a special sheet called *dasterkhan* is spread over the carpet. In the wealthier houses a low table is used for serving food. In medieval times, flowers and fruit were placed decoratively on the *dasterkhan*; sometimes they were arranged together on the same platter, often using local and imported porcelain vases.

Flowers were often placed on tombs in mausoleums, and on special occasions flowers were knotted together into a colourful mantle or a floral carpet. A miniature painting (sixteenth century) shows a Chinese girl attendant carrying a vase of iris on a salver. These few iris placed informally in a vase are similar to arrangements found inside a modern Iranian house. Does this suggest that a gardener or retainer with a talent for flower arrangement was engaged to render this service? If so, flowers were arranged more often and in greater variety than has been generally believed. In early Indian literature there are ample examples of rich merchants and their consorts vying with each other to engage men or women with deft fingers to make garlands or to decorate the houses for the spring festival. Lady Shell, who in the late nineteenth century was invited to the residence of the Lieutenant of the Emperor in Alupka made this observation: 'I admired the exquisite taste with which the vases were filled with flowers and fruits, and I was told that the Princess's reception rooms and boudoir were decorated with fresh fruit and flowers by an artist.'

From the nineteenth century onwards, the influence of Western civilization progressively infiltrated high society around the Persian court, and the imitation of the decoration of the interior of rooms in

Western style can be traced. Furniture and other decorative Western items were bought by princes, high officials and rich merchants. Similarly, the flower arrangement style also began to follow the Western pattern. Flowers arranged in big Chinese vases near an entrance, table arrangements in porticos, and flowers for the centre table in the dining room became popular. In the early twentieth century Reza Shah Pahlavi, and later his son, tried to introduce modern ideas into the lives of tradition-bound Iranians. The impact of this change may be seen in many ways, not least in the informal flower arrangements in the homes of modern-day Iranians.

Photos: Uma Basu

Floral decoration in Persian home

Beautifully decorated fruit stall in Tehran

Ikebana (see Chapter 2) was introduced into Iran when members of Ikebana International opened a chapter in Tehran in 1967. Several exhibitions using local arts and crafts, including ceramic and glass vases, have been organized by its members.

For a variety of reasons the flower arranging art did not flourish in Iran. The frail art of fresh flower decoration suffered largely because the climatic conditions did not allow flowers to survive long once cut. Further, the lifestyle of Iranian women was one of little freedom even in the management of their household; traditional ideas had to be followed, and little allowance was made for arts such as flower arranging. However the Iranians' great love of nature has been immortalized in forms of art of a more permanent nature – carpets, metalwork and tiles – and in gardens.

Bibliography

Frye, Richard N. *Iran.* Variorum Reprints, 1979.

Hureau, Jean. *Iran Today* (transl. E. Burton). Jeune Afrique, 1976.

Jackson, William. *Persia Past and Present.* Massachusetts: Norwood, 1906.

Lal, B. B. *Studies in Early and Medieval Indian Ceramics.*

Massoudi, Ali (ed.). *The Land of Kings.* Ministry of Information and Tourism, Iran.

Morris, James, Wood, Roger and Wright, Denis. *Persia.* 1969.

Perrot, Georges and Charles. *History of Art in Persia.*

Pope, Arthur Upham. *Masterpieces of Persian Art.* Skilton, 1972.

Pope, Arthur Upham. *Introduction to Persian Art since the Seventh Century.* Greenwood Press, 1972.

Ross, Denison E. *Persian Art.*

Shell, Lady. *Glimpses of Life and Manners in Persia.*

Terry, John. *Charm of Indo-Islamic Architecture.*

Ikebana International Magazine

Persian Miniatures from Ancient Manuscript. Fontana

Indian flower arranging

VIVIAN A. RICH

LOWERS HAVE ALWAYS HELD AN IMPORTANT PLACE IN THE religious and domestic life of India. In a country of such cultural diversity, flowers take on numerous different meanings, and the dividing line is often fine between sacred and decorative usage. The majority of people in India follow the religious faith of Hinduism and they use flowers in the worship of their gods and goddesses. Flowers are presented as offerings. Blossoms are heaped in shallow dishes placed before the deity or flower petals are arranged to create multi-coloured geometric patterns on the ground. Flowers are also strung into garlands which are hung on the image of the deity. The most popular of these devotional flowers are marigold, rose and jasmine.

In Hinduism, and later in Buddhism, certain plants are considered sacred. The lotus is the pre-eminent sacred flower. It is viewed as a symbol of purity since the flower rises unsullied from the mud. The lotus is an integral part of the process of creation in the Hindu cosmos; Lakshmi, goddess of good luck and prosperity, is also known as the lotus goddess. In Buddhism the lotus was used artistically to represent the Buddha. It is also the symbol of Avalokiteshvara, the Bodhisattva or saviour of compassion, who is also named Padmapani or lotus bearing. On a more domestic level, no Hindu household would be complete without its *tulsi* (sweet basil) plant, which is worshipped daily.

The third century BC to the thirteenth century AD was the great period of Hindu and Buddhist art. The emphasis was on religious art, and when secular scenes were portrayed they were placed in the context of religion. As a result flowers were shown for their religious symbolism or association, and the decorative arrangement of flowers in vases was not represented. The courts of the rulers of this period in Indian history were wealthy, and it would be reasonable to assume that flowers were arranged in some form in vases for decoration. However, owing to the religious nature of the art, there are no pictorial images available to us.

It is not until the arrival of the Muslim invaders, and in particular the Moguls, that flower arrangements make their appearance in Indian art. The Mogul empire was founded in the sixteenth century AD by the Babur, a Central Asian prince, and the dynasty ruled in northern India until 1857 when the last emperor was sent into exile by the British. Mogul culture reached its peak under three early emperors: Akbar (reigned 1556–1605), Jahangir (1605–27) and Shah Jahan (1627–58). It spread throughout the region, influencing not only the numerous Hindu kingdoms under Mogul control but also the separate Muslim kingdoms bordering on the vast empire. In this way Mogul culture was distributed across large areas of India to Hindu and Muslim alike. So strong was the influence of this culture that, even when the empire began to break up at the end of the eighteenth century, it was the Mogul artistic style which dominated in the new Muslim and Hindu kingdoms that emerged.

The Moguls took their flowers seriously. Both emperors Babur and Jahangir wrote diaries in which they praised the beauties of flowers seen in their travels. Akbar's reign produced the *Ain-i Akbari*, a fascinating collection of information about life in his empire. One section is devoted to flowers and includes a list of flowers noted for their beauty, such as the lotus, hibiscus, jasmine and oleander. A further list indicates an important concept in the Moguls' attitude towards flowers: scent was equal in importance to beauty. The rose, jasmine and narcissus rated highly among the scented flowers, and the emperor Jahangir tells us in his diary that 'from the excellencies of its sweet-scented flowers one may prefer the fragrances of India to those of the flowers of the whole world.'

Flowers formed an important image in Mogul poetry. In the Islamic religion, paradise is seen as a garden and flowers are therefore associated with paradise and the divine. They were initially used in Sufi poetry as a symbolic expression of man's love and search for God (Sufism is an Islamic mystical movement). As a result of this symbolic usage, certain flowers acquired a religious significance. By the time of the Mogul emperors the floral image had become a general form of literary expression in both religious and secular poetry, although the religious connotations remained.

Of all the flowers used in Mogul poetry, the rose is the most important since it is the symbol of God. The narcissus, because of its large white petals and yellow corona, is the symbol of an eye and in particular the eye of the devotee worshipping before God. The tulip is referred to as the cup of Jemshid. This is a wine cup which belonged to the legendary King Jemshid, and it had the power to reflect within it the whole world and confer all knowledge on to him who drank from it. As an extension of this idea the tulip became a symbol of the wine cup in general. Wine was another poetic symbol, relating to its use in mystical religious practices as a means of communing with God. The violet, lily, jasmine and hyacinth are just a few of the other flowers with mystical symbolic meanings. They refer to parts of the face of the devotee: the violet to the hairs on the lip; the lily to the tongue; the jasmine to the cheeks; and the hyacinth to curly hair.

Mogul art was rich in flowers. By the reign of Shah Jahan flowers had become the single most frequently illustrated decorative motif. Very few objects were not decorated with flowers. They appear inlaid, carved or painted on the walls of buildings, woven or embroidered on to textiles, carved in jade or crystal cups, inlaid into dagger handles, and so on. One could not move within the imperial palace or the home of a Mogul noble without being inundated with floral images.

Flowers were the subjects of paintings. The largest single collection is in the *Dara Shukoh Album* (India Office Library and Records, London) and among these 68 paintings which Prince Dara Shukoh (eldest son of Shah Jahan) gave to his wife are 18 of flowers. These paintings represent an interesting collection of different styles. The majority consist of one or two flowers set against a plain sky. Some contain representations of flowers found in India such as the iris, narcissus and rose, while others illustrate complex flowers created by the artist through the combination of parts of many different flowers. There are even copies from European prints of flowers such as the snowflake (*Leucojum*) which are native to Europe and would never have been grown in India at this time.

Unlike the famous Dutch and Flemish flower painters of the seventeenth and eighteenth centuries, the Mogul artists did not consider accuracy important. Apart from their obvious enjoyment in creating their own flowers, the artists often sacrificed realism for composition. The pattern created by the flowers was of paramount importance. Symmetry in the placement of the blossoms was a standard compositional device, and the pattern effect was further enhanced by strongly curved stems. Exaggeration was common, especially in the illustration of the stamens and in the elaborate twists given to the petals and leaves. Colours were often incorrect. The artists preferred strong, bright colours such as red, pink, orange and yellow, while bright blue was not uncommon for daffodils and other flowers of the narcissus family. The overall artistic impression was a stylized and static representation of exotic, artificially contrived, vibrantly coloured hybrids.

Our knowledge of Mogul flower arranging is derived from written records and visual images. There is a large corpus of material written both by the Moguls and by European visitors to the empire. However, references to flower arrangements are negligible. Perhaps the Moguls considered flower arrangements too common to be worthy of mention. The Europeans may not have found themselves in a position to view flower arrangements inside a Mogul home or, being caught up in the exotic splendour of the courts and the wonderment of a strange land, they may not have considered flower arranging important compared with the other more fascinating aspects of life around them.

Visual images present their own problems. Mogul painting gives the appearance of realism but in that respect it is deceptive. Furthermore the Mogul artists were selective in what they illustrated. The image of the flower arrangement is not common in Mogul interior scenes. This does not mean that the Moguls did not decorate their living quarters with vases of flowers. Instead, the absence of flower arrangements could merely be a case of artistic selection.

The Moguls did not utilize furniture in the European style. Rooms would contain mattresses, cushions or bolsters for the inhabitants to lie and sit upon. However, tables, sideboards and of course the fireplace mantelpiece, the usual sites for flower vases, would not be there. Instead, niches were carved into the walls for the placement of lamps, glasses, bottles and flower vases. This is confirmed by François Bernier, a Frenchman travelling in India in the 1660s, who provides the following description of a room from a 'good' house at Delhi: 'Five or six feet from the floor, the sides of the room are full of niches, cut in a variety of shapes, tasteful and well proportioned, in which are seen porcelain vases and flower-pots.'

Climate and the garden played their parts in the history of the use of flowers. In a hot country the garden is of more practical importance than in a temperate climate where the amount of time spent in the garden is determined by the weather. The Moguls literally lived in their gardens – a logical practice given the climatic conditions of the Indo-Gangetic plain where the empire was centred. A look at Mogul architecture suggests the same idea. Few buildings were entirely enclosed, and most opened on to a garden. A traditional Mogul garden was symmetrical with two main intersecting watercourses. A pavilion was placed at the point of intersection, and fountains ran the length of the watercourses. The garden pavilions were a place for entertainment during the day and for sleep at night.

Gardens were so important to the Moguls that one of the first acts of the Emperor Babur, after his conquest in India, was to lay out a garden. Extensive gardens were constructed in the imperial capitals of Delhi, Agra, Lahore and later in Kashmir, which was popular with the Moguls owing to the ready supply of running water and the greater variety of flowers in bloom. Jahangir, who built a number of gardens in Kashmir, writes that at Achabel outside the capital city of Srinagar: 'As far as one could see, in a beautiful garden, *ja'fari* [marigold] flowers had bloomed, so that one might say it was a piece of Paradise.'

Mogul gardens were planted predominantly with roses, narcissus, jasmine and oleander. Garden flowers were chosen for their beauty and their scent and the gardens often had a theme. In the Red Fort at Delhi, Shah Jahan planted two gardens: the Hayat Baksh Bagh and the Mahtab Bagh (*bagh* meaning garden). The Mahtab Bagh or Moonlight Garden received its name because it was planted with pale-coloured flowers such as jasmine and narcissus. The Hayat Baksh Bagh, the Life-Giving Garden, was planted with brightly coloured flowers chosen for their scent. Considering the amount of time that the Moguls spent in their gardens, the necessity for flowers in vases would be diminished since they would be surrounded by living flowers almost daily.

Flowers in vases were used as a decorative motif in architecture, and Mogul paintings show vases of flowers as they were used in daily living. Architectural decoration is one of the major visual sources for Mogul flower arrangements, and this is due partly to the Islamic religious edict prohibiting the representation of living beings. In private art this restriction was broken, but not in public art and architecture. As a result, the traditional decoration for buildings has been geometric designs, calligraphy, flowers and the arabesque (ornamental conventionalized scrollwork, Greco-Roman in origin). The Moguls consistently used flowers for decoration, and vases of flowers intermixed with images of individual flowers were used in the reigns of Akbar, Jahangir and Shah Jahan. Some well-known buildings with flower vase decoration are the Jahangiri Mahal (*c.* 1570) and the Diwan-i-Khas (*c.* 1635) at the Agra Fort, the tomb of Salim Chishti (*c.*

1571) at Fathepur Sikri, the abandoned capital city outside Agra, the Emperor Akbar's tomb (1613) at Sikandra, also outside Agra, the tomb of Itimad-ud-daula (1628) in Agra, and the Mosque of Wazir Khan (1634) in Lahore in present-day Pakistan.

The Moguls used a variety of different shapes of vases. These ranged from typical Indian pot designs, through Chinese blue and white ceramic ware, to ornate European Sèvres and ormolu vases. This reflects the various cultural influences on Mogul India. The majority of Mogul vases are of the Chinese blue and white ware, which are basically simple shapes. Chinese ceramics became popular in Islamic countries after the Mongol invasions of the thirteenth century, the Mongols having conquered northern China earlier in the same century. The Moguls themselves were descended from Genghis Khan and Timur. Chinese ceramics were highly prized by the Mogul emperors, and it is told that when a retainer broke a ceramic cup the Emperor Jahangir sent him all the way to China to replace it. The Mogul Chinese vases were mainly rounded near the neck and narrow near the foot. Tall narrow-necked bottle jars were also popular. The majority of Mogul vases, no matter what the style, had narrow necks. Ceramic vases, other than blue and white ware, were plain white and followed the same pattern of a rounded body with a long, narrow neck, although some had double handles on the sides.

Brass and silver were also popular materials for vases. Some were quite elaborate in the delineation between the neck, body and foot, while others showed a European influence in design. The majority followed simple Indian shapes; some were rounded like the traditional Indian *lóta* or water pot, and others were bottle shaped with a long, narrow neck.

Europeans had been in contact with the Moguls since the sixteenth century, and European goods were highly prized by the Mogul courtiers. As a result, European vases came into the possession of the nobles. A painting of the *Emperor Shah Alam* in the Victoria and Albert Museum shows painted porcelain vases with ornately gilded necks and feet.

One interesting feature in the representation of flower arrangements is the placement of the vase in a low, wide dish. This occurs consistently on the wall decorations but seldom in paintings and it is possible that the format was used artistically long after it had gone out of common usage. Among the few paintings that show the vase with its dish is one in the Victoria and Albert Museum entitled *Woman with Servant*, which is an Indianized version of a European Annunciation scene. Instead of the Virgin Mary receiving a lily from the Archangel Gabriel, a Mogul woman is receiving a vase of narcissus from a servant. The vase is standing inside a dish. This format appears again in a painting in the Chester Beatty Library, Dublin. This is the only known study of a flower arrangement in Mogul art, and shows the vase placed in a shallow dish. The use of the dish is probably an extension of the Chinese practice of each vase having its own stand, another carryover from the Mongol invasions.

The type of flower vase reflects some important concepts of Mogul flower arranging. The arrangements are limited in both the overall

Photo: Julia Clements

Flowers in vase. Mogul period, 15th century

Vase of flowers
The Chester Beatty Library, Dublin

number of flowers and in the number of different floral species. Mogul flower arrangements, particularly in the early years, were very simple groupings of flowers in bouquets or just a single flower in a vase. The majority of flower arrangements had one or two different kinds of flowers, and rarely were more than four different species of flower seen in a flower arrangement.

The narcissus was the most commonly used flower, and a typical flower arrangement would consist simply of a vase of narcissus, either alone or with a couple of blossoms of another flower. Vases containing just narcissus can be seen at the tombs of Akbar at Sikandra and of Itimad-ud-daula at Agra. In paintings, vases of narcissus can be seen in the *Darab Nama* (British Library), *Akbar Nama* (Victoria and Albert Museum), the *Two Princes Conversing at Night* (Victoria and Albert Museum), and the *Diwan of Anwari* (Fogg Museum, Cambridge, Massachusetts). The previously mentioned painting *Woman with Servant* has a vase with five stems of narcissus and two stems of an unidentifiable flower. The majority of the early paintings and wall decorations of the sixteenth to the mid seventeenth century show vases with only a few narcissus, but in later paintings such as the *Two*

Line drawing of woman with servant
Victoria and Albert Museum

Photo: Vivian Rich

Tomb of Itimad-ud-Daula

Princes Conversing at Night (*c.* 1680) and the *Shah Alam* (*c.* 1800) the narcissus are being massed together in the vases.

Iris, tulip, lily, rose and poppy are the other commonly used flowers in Mogul flower arrangements. Like the narcissus, these flowers often occur alone in vases. In the tomb of Itimad-ud-daula, vases with just roses, poppies or irises can be found. Again these are in vases with very narrow necks suited for a small number of flowers.

When more than one species of flower is used there is often a central, important flower to which the others are added. In the Jahangiri Mahal one can see a vase with five irises and two tulips. At the tomb of Itimad-ud-daula there is a vase with one large central spray of six narcissus blossoms and an iris on either side. In a painting entitled *Shah Jahan Honours the Religious Orthodoxy* (Freer Gallery, Washington DC) there is a vase containing marigolds and white roses around a central red rose.

Occasionally an exotic is the central flower. At the Jahangiri Mahal a crown imperial appears surrounded by lilies. In the Freer Gallery painting of *Shah Jahan* there is another vase with the crown imperial in the centre between lilies, irises, a yellow ranunculus and a rose. The crown imperial was a popular flower with the Mogul emperors and appears often in art. The *Dara Shukoh Album* contains a portrait of a double-tiered crown imperial, and the flower appears regularly in the floral borders around paintings. The Moguls must have viewed the crown imperial with the same sense of wonder that led the flower to be the centre of so many paintings by Dutch and Flemish artists.

In keeping with the Mogul artists' fascination with the pattern qualities of floral representation, the flower arrangements are also shown as symmetrical and two-dimensional, so that the arrangement can be divided down the middle with an equal number of flowers on each side. This artistic formula is used in two of the drawings shown of the paintings in the tomb of Itimad-ud-daula. One drawing shows the narcissus evenly divided into three groups of three blossoms with the leaves again evenly divided and placed between the stems. One side is a mirror image of the other. The other drawing shows two central poppies with an iris and a spray of narcissus on either side. Again the leaves are arranged evenly between the stems. In reality, this symmetrical arrangement would translate into a simple bunching together of a small number of flowers.

There are, however, examples of bouquets which show a more complex, naturalistic arrangement. One such bouquet is found at the Mosque of Wazir Khan in Lahore (drawing in Victoria and Albert Museum). A white ceramic vase is placed within a gold-coloured dish. The bouquet is a massing of roses, irises, poppies and a variety of lily-like flowers. The *Dara Shukoh Album* provides one of the more complex flower arrangements. It is a painting of a *Prince in Persian Costume* by Muhammad Khan, dated 1633–4. The prince is kneeling and pouring wine into a cup. Beside him is a blue and white Chinese vase with an extensive bouquet of flowers. The flowers consist of a grouping of six pink roses, a white anemone, purple irises, orange tulips and small white and burgundy unidentifiable flowers. Greenery is intermixed throughout the bouquet. The flowers are typical of those found in the other arrangements, but there appears to be a deliberate attempt to arrange the blossoms, particularly the roses, as compared with the almost random placement of the blossoms in previous bouquets.

The painting of the flower vase in the Chester Beatty Library does not show a conscious attempt at arrangement. The flowers, of which there is considerable variety including roses, lilies and a daisy, poppy, tulip, narcissus, anemone and peony, are massed together in a wide-necked vase without any real sense of design.

In Mogul society vases of flowers were placed in a different context from European society. One of the earliest paintings showing a flower vase is in the manuscript called the *Darab Nama* mentioned earlier; this recounts the deeds of King Darab, who in Islamic tradition is the grandfather of Alexander the Great. Gifts are being brought from a

Left *Tomb of Itimad-ud-Daula*

Right *Tomb of Itimad-ud-Daula*

Photos: Vivian Rich

Dara Shukoh Album
The British Library

beseiged fort to King Darab. Among the gifts, which include an elephant, cloth and wine jugs, is a bronze vase with three stems of narcissus. This would suggest that flowers were considered an acceptable gift of tribute to a conqueror. This idea is again shown in the *Akbar Nama* which recounts the life of the Emperor Akbar. In one painting Akbar is receiving gifts as the result of a military campaign, and one of these gifts is a white ceramic vase with seven narcissus blossoms.

The primary function of flowers was to decorate rooms. Apart from being placed in niches in the wall, the flowers were also placed on the floor near people. In the *Two Princes Conversing at Night* nine flower vases are placed on a carpet inside a garden pavilion where the princes are seated. Blue and white ceramic vases with narcissus alternate with silver vases. The silver vases contain bouquets of orange poppies, pink roses, yellow ranunculus and pink and white unidentifiable flowers. Dishes heaped with flower blossoms, in the Indian Hindu tradition, are placed before the princes.

The placing of blossoms in dishes is a Hindu custom taken over by the Moguls. The emperors married the daughters of Hindu kings to forge political alliances, which also resulted in the spread of Hindu customs into Mogul culture. The Emperor Akbar used flowers in this form for religious purposes. In the *Ain-i Akbari*, the author Abul Fazl

Two Princes Conversing at Night
Victoria and Albert Museum

states that 'His Majesty is very fond of perfumes, and encourages this department from religious motives ... incense is daily burnt in gold and silver censers of various shapes; whilst sweet-smelling flowers are used in large quantities.'

Flower vases were popular decorations for entertainments. A painting in the *Large Clive Album* (*c.* 1725: Victoria and Albert Museum) shows dancers performing before the Emperor Muhammad Shah who was noted for his pleasure-loving lifestyle. The emperor and a young woman are seated on a raised plinth on an outdoor terrace watching a dancing performance. On the plinth is one vase and on the carpet below are four more vases. These vases are brass and rounded like the traditional *lota*. They are narrow necked and hold bunches of red and yellow unidentifiable flowers. In a painting entitled *Muhammad Shah Entertained by Musicians and Dancers* (*c.* 1720:

Kasturbhai Lalbhai Collection, Ahmedabad, India) Muhammad Shah is seated on a carpet in a garden pavilion. Around the three sides of the carpet are placed small bottle-shaped vases containing narcissus.

The style of Mogul flower arrangement was determined by the available flora. India is a country rich in plant life, but the majority of floral species are found in the Himalayan region, not in the Indo-Gangetic plain where the Mogul capitals of Delhi and Agra were situated. The flora of the Gangetic plain is sparse, and only a few different species of flowers were available to the Moguls. This would account for the limited variety of flowers used in their arrangements. Mogul flower arrangements were also characterized by a lack of obvious planned arrangement to the flowers. The general approach was to bunch the flowers together in a vase. Scent was probably an important factor in determining which flowers were used, as was availability according to season and the location of the imperial court. In spite of the formal effect given to floral arrangements in art and wall decoration, the flower arrangements in reality would have been basically informal groupings of a few favourite flowers.

Bibliography

Abul Fazl. *The Ain-i Akbari* (trans. H. Blochman). Delhi: Oriental Books Reprint, 1977.

Babur. *Babur Nama* (trans. Annette S. Beveridge). Delhi: Oriental Books Reprint, 1970.

Bernier, François. *Travels in the Mogul Empire* (trans. Archibald Constable). Delhi: Chand, 1972.

British Library. *Paintings from the Muslim Courts of India* (British Library exhibition). London: World of Islam Festival, 1976.

Jahangir. *The Tuzuk-i-Jahangiri: or Memoirs of Jahangir* (trans. Alexander Rogers, ed. Henry Beveridge). New Delhi: Munshiram Manoharlal, 1978.

Losty, Jeremiah P. *The Art of the Book in India*. London: British Library, 1982.

Schimmel, Annemarie and Welch, Stuart Cary. *Anvari's Divan: A Pocket Book for Akbar*. New York: Metropolitan Museum of Art, 1983.

Welch, Stuart Cary. *The Art of Mughal India*. New York: Asia Society, 1963.

Welch, Stuart. Cary *Imperial Mughal Painting*. London: Chatto and Windus, 1978.

4

The Renaissance and the modern world

The flowers of the Italian Renaissance

PAULINE MANN

IT IS FORTUNATE THAT THERE IS SO MUCH EVIDENCE OF THE use of flowers in Renaissance paintings. They appear scattered around the Virgin and Child in open air settings; simply arranged in altar vases; woven into wreaths and garlands (the latter frequently adorning altarpieces); and placed in homes in containers in window embrasures, on shelves, benches and writing tables. The flowers are seldom obtrusive and never the main feature, and often they have to be searched for. Plants, as living and marvellous creations of individual beauty, were not stressed in paintings, and they were not drawn with scientific accuracy until the coming of Dürer in Nuremberg (1471–1528) and Leonardo da Vinci in Italy (1452–1519).

During the last years of the thirteenth and throughout the fourteenth centuries the Italians were intensely conscious of their past grandeur and strived to recapture it. Painters, poets, architects and sculptors were stimulated by the works of the ancient Greek philosophers, and there was also a revival of interest in the figurative arts and classical Latin literature. The rebirth of learning was recorded in altarpieces, frescos, sculptures and canvases, beginning with Giotto (1266–1337) and continuing into the cinquecento (sixteenth century), the High Renaissance and most famous period of Italian art. This revival of learning eventually spread across the whole of Europe. It was not then called the Renaissance; it was a Frenchman – Michelet – who gave a name to the vital movement in 1855.

All through this time Italian art was Christian in its roots and meaning, but the new spirit of humanism proclaimed man a free being, in bondage to neither religion nor state. This freedom showed in the enthusiastic study of the natural world in all its aspects. Although the main theme of the paintings was religious, the characters were human rather than spiritual beings and they reflected the real world. The quattrocento (fifteenth-century) pictures had a purpose; they were to instruct the illiterate people in the mystery of the Incarnation and the lives of the saints. The paintings had to tell a story either by the scene actually depicted or by the symbolic attributes of items incorporated. This is where the symbolic flowers had such importance, bringing to mind events not actually happening in the picture. Italy was not alone in using paintings as a means of instruction; the entire Gothic world had been permeated by Christian symbolism. The preoccupation with religious signs was to continue for a long time and was to pervade the works of the great Dutch and Flemish flower painters of the seventeenth century.

Flower symbolism

Although the symbolism of Renaissance Italy was mostly Christian, there were some associations with classical and pagan figures. Pre-Christian Rome had adopted the plants connected with the Greek deities as emblems for their own gods and goddesses: Aphrodite's rose and myrtle became the companions of Venus, the Roman goddess of love. Then with the advent and spread of Christianity the Virgin Mary was endowed with a wealth of flowers, including the rose in all its varieties. One of the names given to the Madonna in the Middle Ages was 'the Mystic Rose', and Dante called the Mother of Christ 'the rose wherein the word divine was made Incarnate'. The rose was featured in numerous religious pictures from the fourteenth century onwards

The Annunciation by Simone Martini
Uffizi Gallery, Florence

by artists from the Netherlands, Germany and Italy. There is a very charming picture *The Virgin the Rose Bower* by Stefan Lochner (died 1451), but in Botticelli's *Primavera* and *The Birth of Venus* the scattered roses have reverted to their classical mistress, Venus.

Although the rose was important in classical symbolism, the *Lilium candidum* ranked first in Christian flower symbols. Once these flowers represented celestial happiness, but the matchless whiteness of their petals naturally suggested purity; from the twelfth century they were invested in sacred art with this meaning, and so became inseparable from the spotless Virgin. They became known as Madonna lilies.

Paintings of the Annunciation were rare before the fourteenth century. One of the earliest known was by Simone Martini (1333); in it Gabriel holds and is wreathed with olive, a symbol of the reconciliation between God and man. The lilies in this picture are in a vase near the Virgin. Later every artist appears to have painted this scene at least once, and they nearly all incorporate the lily. In some pictures the angel Gabriel holds the flower. Lilies were not confined to the Annunciation, but were often shown when the Virgin Mary was present. In the *Madonna of the Pomegranate* by Botticelli (*c*. 1445–1510) the attending angels hold lilies and are girded with roses. A further symbol in this painting is in the hand of the Holy Child; he holds the pomegranate, a symbol of immortality.

The small clumps of growing plants and the scattered flowers have a touching simplicity. They could so easily be overlooked, especially in the groups of the Holy Family in outdoor settings. Only if the viewer understands what he is to look for does he appreciate and comprehend the messages the flowers give.

In the famous *Portinari Altarpiece* (Hugo van der Goes, *c*. 1440–82) the flowers stand out clearly; they are so obviously there for a purpose. Never before had they been so prominent. The blue iris is a royal bloom for the Queen of Heaven, for blue is the colour of heaven and of goodness. The leaves of the iris are reminders of the piercing spear. The orange lily is also a royal flower, this time for the Christ Child. The violets strewn on the ground on which the Babe lies represent humility. The three carnations call to mind the Incarnation and the three persons of the Trinity. The aquilegia is said to refer to the seven sorrows of Mary – or the seven gifts of the Holy Spirit. The Eucharist is portrayed by the wheatsheaf, and by the vase decorated with grapes and vine.

Floral detail by Hugo van der Goes
Uffizi Gallery, Florence

There is a very gentle picture by Botticelli of the *Madonna and Child* where the Child's wrist is encircled by a bracelet of thorns. The Mother has three nails in her hand, and in the background stands a bowl of cherries – the fruit of paradise.

In her book *Period Flower Arrangement* Margaret Marcus suggests that Raphael, in the *Alba Madonna*,

> painted growing plants with particular attention to symbolic meaning – anemones, cyclamen, dandelions, *Epimedium alpinum*, bedstraw, plantain, sorrel and violets. These plants speak in this way: Mary, image of humility (violet), on Her bed of straw (galium), bore Him who led us out of the barren pagan world

Madonna and Child by Sandro Botticelli
The Art Division, Newark Public Library, New Jersey

(*Epimedium alpinum*). All men find their way to Him (plaintain). He suffered death (anemone); bitter was the Virgin's sorrow (cyclamen, dandelion, sorrel).

Flowers in vases

The vases containing cut flowers were magnificent, whether they were placed informally near to the Virgin and Child in simple domestic settings or used in a manner similar to our altar decorations today. The flowers chosen were always symbolic – irises, lilies, roses, aquilegia – and the foliage was frequently juniper and palm. The vases were made in pottery, glass, silvergilt, copper, stone and gold. Shapes varied from wide bowls and baskets, *tazze*, goblets, jugs and jars, to tall pedestals and a version of the epergne or compound vase. In the Flemish paintings of the period the familiar blue and white Delft pottery was used.

Wreaths and garlands

The fifteenth-century Italian world called for wreaths and garlands for celebrations. It was from ancient Greece and its pagan rites – now many centuries away – that Italy inherited the love of this form of decoration (see Chapter 1). Wreaths and garlands were used for the many festivals, masques and pageants that were part of the Italian life. Young men would stretch beribboned flowery garlands across the street for a wedding, and on religious festivals the girls, with wreaths on their heads, carried leafy branches. In the theatre it was the popular thing to attire the actresses as nymphs and place wreaths of leaves and flowers on their brows.

The small angels' wreaths, in Italian paintings, were usually circlets of closely packed flowers with little foliage amongst them, whilst adult figures were often wreathed with a single lissom branch of myrtle or juniper. In Botticelli's allegorical picture *Primavera* the figure of Flora wears, on her head and around her neck, wreaths of mixed small flowers and leaves: cornflowers, daisies, briar roses, strawberry fruit and leaves, and ivy can be identified.

Luca della Robbia (1400–82) was a sculptor famous for his colourful glazed plaques of terracotta. Usually his works were fairly small, with figures in white against a clear blue background, surrounded with borders of leaves, fruit and flowers. The plant material was grouped with almost mathematical precision, and the sections were frequently bound with ribbon. Andrea della Robbia (1435–1525), Luca's nephew and pupil, worked in similar style. Our present-day door decorations for Christmas may well have been inspired by the della Robbias!

Virgin with Child by Luca Della Robbia
National Museum of Bargello, Florence

The Renaissance garlands shown in many paintings are heavy with fruit and dark, overlapping leaves; they are curved in like manner to the Greek encarpa. There is a splendid example in the *St Zeno Altarpiece* by Mantegna (*c.* 1431–1506). The strange holders seem to be forms of the ram's horn or cornucopia, and are a feature of the altarpieces. The whole effect is rich and impressive. Other garlands are lighter in weight and look as though they were made entirely of flowers. There is one ascribed to Lorenzo Monaco (died 1425) which is in the National Gallery; it is made up of light and dark pink roses apparently strung together in fours, with a background of blue sky. This has none of the solid quality that is so characteristic of the altarpieces.

Nero's Domus Aurea (Golden House) took up one-quarter of the area of republican Rome when it was built in AD 65. It was partly destroyed by the Flavian emperors in order to make room for the Colosseum and was left in ruins, half buried. During the late fifteenth century Raphael and other Renaissance artists approached the ruins of this once magnificent palace from above, which made them feel as though they were about to enter caves or grottos. They had to be let down into the chambers by ropes. When they clambered into the buried rooms and saw the frescos of festoons and cupids they called them *pittura grotesca*. From this discovery came the word 'grotesque'. Raphael and his

St Zeno Altarpiece by Mantegna
Curia Vescovada, Verona

companions were reported to have been delighted with the grotesques, and copied them in order to cover and embellish the vast walls of grand buildings.

Raphael's designs for the Vatican loggia were based on the frescos from the Golden House. The rope garland is one of Raphael's designs; there are many of these, all showing foliage of various sorts, fruit, vegetables and a small number of flowers. We can only speculate as to how the various garlands and wreaths were assembled, but probably the plant material was bound or sewn on to hemp rope, fig or vine stems. In the Vatican loggia drawings Raphael makes the rope a part of the design. They have an extraordinary delicacy as they hang against their blue background.

It is apparent that the plant material during the early Renaissance was still a mixture of classical and Christian symbolism. By the end of the sixteenth century, however, plants had assumed an importance in their own right, and although the hierarchy of flowers lingered in the Dutch and Flemish paintings this gradually became less, leaving the canvases for the flowers to be painted for their own beauty.

Bibliography

Baxandall, Michael *Painting and Experience in Fifteenth-century Italy*. OUP, 1988.
Ettlinger, L. D. and H. S. *Botticelli*. Thames and Hudson, 1976.
Levey, Michael *Early Renaissance*. Penguin, 1967.
Lucas-Dubreton, J. *Daily Life in Florence*. Allen and Unwin, 1960.
Marcus, Margaret. *Period Flower Arrangement*. New York: M. Barrows, 1952.
Morton, H. V. *A Traveller in Rome*. Methuen, 1984.

Raphael rope garland
From the Castle Howard Collection

Dutch and Flemish Baroque flower painting

BEULAH CANDLISH

OF THE VARIOUS SECTIONS IN THIS BOOK, IT IS PROBABLY the subject of this one which would first occur to anyone asked to cite an instance of shared interest between the art of the painter and the art of the flower arranger. Even though the name of an individual artist may not be known, the Dutch flower piece of the seventeenth and eighteenth centuries, as a genre, has penetrated the awareness of most people inclined towards the visual arts.

For the flower arranger, of course, the style is often invoked as a model or designated for practical demonstration. In this lies the greatest paradox of all, for the question must be asked: did the great symmetrical bouquets of the earlier paintings, and the sinuous and sensuous arrangements of the later, ever exist in reality? When one looks carefully at the evidence, all the indications are that the answer must be 'no' – at least in the sense of the painter having before him, as a model, the entire arrangement which is seen transcribed in the finished painting.

In the first instance, supposing all the flowers to have been available, the speed at which even the most accomplished flower painter in oils could work, given the great fidelity to nature that was consistently achieved, would mean a faded and wilting model long before the whole had been represented. In any case, as the slightest enquiry will reveal, all the flowers were not available at one time, for it is part of the subtlety and joy of these paintings that they frequently include flowers from a long season: snowdrops and narcissi, lilies of the valley, tulips, irises, anemones and aquilegia, roses, lilies, pinks or carnations, peonies and poppies. In other words, the early Netherlandish flower piece as we know it is an elaborate fantasy, which has been built up blossom by blossom according to the painter's design, and probably from studies of individual flowers kept as a permanent record by the artist and copied many times. This is certainly borne out by the existence of several versions of one painting, such as Jan Bruegel's *Sheaf of Flowers in a Wooden Bucket*, also known as the *Crown Imperial Bouquet*, of which there is a version in Munich and another in Vienna! Finally, the total absence of any flower arrangement as such in all the many paintings of Dutch interiors – which were painted by and for a people determined to display in fine detail their worldly goods – must surely argue against their having ever existed in the terms by which we understand them.

Facing page *Sheaf of flowers in a wooden bucket by Jan Bruegel the Elder*
Museum of Fine Arts, Vienna

82

What then can be the relationship between Dutch and Flemish flower painting of the Baroque and Rococo periods and the present flower arranger? What lessons may be learned or inspiration gained? It would be helpful at this point to differentiate more precisely between the earlier and later phases of Lowland flower painting. 'Early' should be understood as covering the period from the 1580s to around 1630, and is best typified and indeed dominated by the style of the Flemish painter Jan Bruegel the Elder (1568–1625). The 'later' period runs from the 1630s through to the middle of the following century, and is represented by such artists as Nicolas van Verendael (*c.* 1640–91), Simon Verelst (1644–1721), Jan de Heem (1606–84) and by no means least Rachel Ruysch (1664–1750), who was still painting at the time of her death.

Small bouquet in a ceramic vase by Jan Bruegel the Elder
Museum of Fine Arts, Vienna

The early type of flower piece usually presents a densely packed oval-shaped arrangement, well filling the canvas, with little suggestion of depth. It relies for effect on changes of scale between individual blossoms and the excitement of their many colours against a dark background, thus achieving rather an embroidered or tapestry effect. The containers in these paintings are usually simple country vessels (a wooden tub or an earthenware jar) and are discreetly indicated by the painter, often toning with the background in order not to detract from the flowers themselves. A perfect example of this form is Jan Bruegel's *Small Bouquet in a Ceramic Vase* in the Museum of Fine Arts in Vienna. Perhaps the only suggestion element here for the flower arranger is the combination of large, conspicuous blossoms with demure meadow flowers; perhaps flowers are too often classified and segregated by flower arrangers.

It must be remembered that these early paintings were frequently painted for gardeners and plant collectors, the Netherlands already being a horticultural centre for Europe. Thus often they are used to exhibit a newly introduced exotic, as in the *Crown Imperial Bouquet*, or to show a collector's newest acquisition, a choice tulip for instance, which may have cost as much or more than the painting itself. In such instances the 'star turn' often has a special space created around it to isolate its form and colour, and not surprisingly it is usually placed at the apex of the arrangement. Bruegel just succeeds in incorporating these difficult, top-heavy scene stealers, though one might question the peony at the top right-hand side of the *Crown Imperial Bouquet* and even wonder whether it was a later addition. Bruegel's skill is perhaps best appreciated by considering an attempt by a lesser painter. For this I would cite a painting by A. Boschaert (*c.* 1588–1645), in the Fitzwilliam Museum, Cambridge, which has at its apex a large and dreadful sunflower. Yet could this painting, admittedly unintentionally, suggest the idea of 'the joke' in flower arranging?

Early and later paintings have in common the almost universal use by the painter of a dark background to offset the luminous quality of the flowers. The effectiveness of this device may easily be gauged by looking at an arrangement evenly lighted against a pale background, and then placing the same arrangement at night against an uncurtained window, when it will almost certainly acquire an enhanced radiancy. This is a difficult element to interpret in practice, for the actual arrangement in its full, three-dimensional volume occupies a space often shared with ornaments, lamps, furniture and even people. This bears little resemblance to the meticulous lie the painter tells us, with its illusion of space and volume, and with the image concentrated and its authority increased by the isolating effect of the frame. These paintings would certainly justify some theatrical contrivances on the part of the flower arranger, such as a dark, false back to an alcove which might be used occasionally.

Now the mention of darkness suggests the importance of light, and of course all descriptive painters, whatever their subject, paint light, some more obviously than others. Thus, in the flower pieces, the one great unifying factor for disparate forms and colours is the controlled light which commonly reveals them. All these painters use the formula

Flowers in a vase by N. van Verendael
Fitzwilliam Museum, Cambridge

of setting off their white blossoms against the dark, so that they break on the eye like stars against a night sky; by this means they create patterns or directional paths for the eye to follow through a composition. This must surely raise interesting possibilities. Again the problem arises of translating what is shown on a flat, two-dimensional surface into a complete three-dimensional concept which will hold interest from whichever angle the arrangement is viewed. Clearly a path of pale blossoms, used as visual stepping-stones to create a low diagonal in a painting, might best be interpreted as a spiral motif in the arrangement proper: verticals and horizontals would need to be envisaged as sections of an elliptical or circular hoop motif. A striking composition by J. M. Picat (1644–1721) uses white flowers in a tall, tight cross shape, with yellow flowers in the centre and low-toned reds at the four 'corners' of the arrangement.

From the 1630s onwards the later style of painting evolves. Early formality is replaced by an apparent casualness in design; this is most marked in the eighteenth century, and corresponds very closely to the developments in women's costume. Heavy, opulent fabrics hung in solid shapes are replaced by delicate silks and much lace, lighter in weight and colour. These materials, draped over a hoop, could move seductively to provide most provocative glimpses of feminine charms; hence the popularity of paintings of girls on swings, enamating from the French school. Indeed, just as the French were dictating costume fashion with their taste for *déshabillé*, so increasingly French fashion in painting influenced the flower piece, resulting in exceedingly ornate works.

However, initially the change in composition which takes place after 1630 is typified by far fewer individual flowers being presented in a more loosely knit arrangement, in which leaves and stems play an important part. The containers for these arrangements are now more sophisticated, being of porcelain, metal or glass. In particular, glass allows the painter to show his skill in rendering transparency whilst at the same time emphasizing the new visual importance of stems; the latter can be revealed continuing inside the vessel, so completing their rhythmic contribution to the whole design.

A carefully controlled but apparently casual fluidity, suggestive of movement, together with an asymmetrical arrangement, is the essence of this later style. In order to achieve this rhythmical quality the painter is now at great pains to describe the whole pose or stance of a blossom on its stalk, together with the curve of every leaf edge. Often the flower, in a wayward mood, is presented with its face turned

A vase of flowers by Elias van der Broeck
Ashmolean Museum, Oxford

Flowers in a glass beaker by follower of Jan Bruegel the Elder
The Fine Arts Museums of San Francisco, a gift of Mrs Herbert Fleishhacker

Jacob van Walscappelle, a painter of fruit and flowers
The National Gallery, London

away or hung in three-quarter view, so that the emotion conveyed by these paintings is one of elusiveness. There is now too a much greater use of the illusion of space within the painting, with great caverns appearing between and beneath leaves, whilst stems snake in and out of the light, taking the eye into and through the depth of the composition. For maximum effectiveness, obviously flowers which have a tendency to a sinuous pattern of growth were frequently incorporated, foremost amongst them being the tulip. Rather surprisingly, while the whole gesture of the flower, stalk and leaf is most closely observed, the flower head itself is occasionally less than botanically correct, so that accuracy is now subordinated to an overriding decorative concept.

In the same spirit colour too is now more considered; it is no longer the random kaleidoscope produced by scores of mixed flowers, but rather a chosen, limited scheme. Sometimes the composition contains just varying tones of two basic colours, as in a work by Simon Verelst in which he only uses coral pinks and sea greens, even subduing the irises to a deep blue-green hue. This more subtle and sophisticated use of colour reinforces the elusive emotional content of the painting, leaving an image which lingers in the memory like an unusual flavour or haunting tune.

For a strictly limited and unusual scheme, Rachel Ruysch, in a painting from the Broughton Collection, shows an arrangement and its accessories set against a stone niche. Before this basic, sombre stone colour she displays a range of greens, including a wonderful blue-green thistle, various insects, a bright green lizard and some rocks, in which accents of warmer earth colours complement the cold greens. Together with the crispness of delineation this painting affords a feast for the eye. Of all the possible means of adding an arresting ingredient to a flower arrangement, surely carefully controlled colour can be the most rewarding – and even the most easily achieved through a careful selection of material. However, a highly developed and creative colour sense to use with flair and confidence is an additional talent.

There is a category of flower painting of this period, as yet unmentioned, which is not concerned with an arrangement in the sense of flower arranging. There is no container for water, and the relationships between the flowers seem totally haphazard. These are usually small paintings, portraying a little posy, such as might just have been gathered and put down for a moment; the blooms have slightly tumbled from the bunch, and in this captivatingly innocent state their portrait has been painted. Once again we are being shown by consum-

Flower piece by Rachel Ruysch
Cheltenham Art Gallery and Museums

mate skill a group of flowers that could not have stayed fresh for longer than to allow the painter to sketch in the shapes and positions required, the painting itself being realized only gradually. The concept, however, is quite remarkable, and seems to underline the potent emotional and sensuous content that flowers have of themselves, through appearance and association, without any additional artifice. Indeed many studied arrangements reduce this impact, though they may in its place achieve one of a different quality. Can there be a place for such ephemeral delights as fresh flowers tossed down for their scent and colour, unsustained, a complete sacrifice to the senses? A flower-strewn place setting at a table can be a rare pleasure, or a blossom-trimmed plate for a sweet dish. Though beware the emerging caterpillar or beetle, which may be desirable in a Dutch painting but won't be enjoyed in reality!

This use of flowers as a decorative subject without their being in water occurs in two other types of painting. First there is the flower-decked shallow *tazza* (bowl). It would seem this was a favourite subject of Jan Bruegel the Younger; there are two examples painted on a panel in the Prado Gallery, Madrid, and a line and wash drawing in the British Museum, London. A variation on the theme can be found in the Musée Royal des Beaux Arts in Brussels, known as *Still Life with Garland of Flowers* and showing a garland balanced on a *tazza* with jewels. A further charming example comes from the collection of Rudolf Pallamar in Vienna.

Secondly, there are numerous occasions when a painter scatters a garnish of flowers through a still life painting. Probably the finest examples are by Jan van Huysum (1682–1749), who was as much a painter of fruit as of flowers. A dish of peaches, their bloom unblemished, resting on a bed of leaves with flowers scattered in disarray above

Bowl with flowers. A line and wash drawing by J. Bruegel the Younger
The British Museum

and around them, is a very choice sight indeed and surely can provide ideas for anyone with a garden.

So far this chapter has dealt only with flower pieces of a particular period, which incidentally also saw a great blossoming of Dutch and Flemish painting in all its genres. For very sound reasons this is known as the Golden Age of Lowland painting; were the subject of this book painting in general, much would again be written of Rembrandt and Rubens, Ruisdael and Hals, Steen and Vermeer, to name but a few of the greatest exponents of their art. However, concerning flower painting it must be legitimate to ask what the background was which produced so great a skill in such a specialized field. Surely such expertise could not have come into being merely to accommodate a new fashion or taste, though, as has been shown, this is largely what the flower piece was. It is therefore necessary to look at the degree of concern with flowers in the times prior to the seventeenth and eighteenth centuries.

The most striking evidence of close investigation into plants and flowers is to be found in the illustrated herbals, first compiled in monastic medieval Europe. In a way these themselves can be considered as windows through which we may look back, probably for many centuries. As collections of accumulated knowledge they combine sound learning with many an old wives' tale, and point to the basic terms in which flowers and plants can be approached. From earliest times flowers were appreciated as much for their essential oils and fragrance as for their appearance, and for these attributes were considered as elements suitable for sacrifice; an obvious continuing example is the burning of incense. Or again they were employed in spells and incantations in the occult sense, irrespective of any medicinal application. It is, however, something of a combination of these two approaches which gives rise to the use of the flower as a talisman, usually of a protective nature and so carried or worn as a charm. Flowers then were in extensive use in medieval Europe, being employed either superstitiously, religiously, medicinally as ingredients of many a potion and poultice, or practically for culinary purposes or as much needed nosegays in a stinking environment.

It is at this time also that certain flowers acquire a symbolic role, again as a part of religious thought. Obviously the flowers involved are those most widely grown in the monastery garden – rose, lily, columbine, iris and violet being the foremost selection. The outstanding symbolic use of these flowers is their association with the Virgin Mary, and here contemporary paintings provide information as well as pleasure. The Virgin shown in an enclosed garden, usually hedged about by a briar rose thicket, is a fairly common medieval image and seems to develop with the cult of the Madonna as a subject for meditation. Indeed, in literature Mary begins to be referred to as a rose, as in the German carol 'Es ist ein Ros entsprungen'. The rose more than any other flower is loaded with emblematic meanings, all of which have been documented; sufficient perhaps here to mention the rosary, the term *sub rosa* and, of course, the Wars of the Roses as being indications of this great preoccupation with that flower. Again the lily is widely used as a symbol of the Virgin Mary, and is shown particularly in paintings of the Annunciation from early medieval times onwards. In the seventeenth century it can still be found, when, for example, Jan Bruegel collaborates with Rubens to paint an elaborate garland around a representation of the *Virgin and Child*, and in so doing gives pointed emphasis to the spray of lilies on a level with Mary herself. Indeed the lily is that frequently grown in old-fashioned gardens and still known as the Madonna lily (*Lilium candidum*).

The iris too comes to be a symbol of virginity. It is interesting to see it transferred from the religious sphere to the secular when in Elizabethan England it is shown as an attribute of Queen Elizabeth I, as in the *Armada Portrait*, where the iris figures prominently on her gown with other symbolic motifs. The violet, symbol of humility, can also be comfortably associated with Mary the Handmaiden, and is often so employed. The foreground of an important masterpiece by Hugo van der Goes, an *Adoration of the Shepherds*, is occupied by two vases: one is ceramic, holding irises and a stem of lilies; the other is of glass and contains aquilegia, which from their dove-like form become symbols of the Holy Spirit. The ground here is strewn with violets, whilst a sheaf of wheat lies behind the group.

It is apparent then that, prior to the Renaissance, there was a strong tradition of including flowers in religious paintings, often as symbols, but occasionally for their therapeutic or medicinal association; a representation of the *Martyrdom of St Sebastian* may include plants known for their healing properties. Moreover, though every medieval painter was well aware of their purely decorative function, it may be that each flower-strewn meadow we see in painting or tapestry has more hidden meaning in it than is generally realized.

The coming of the Renaissance, with its rediscovery of the learning of classical antiquity, provided a new, more scientific attitude to investigation in many fields. Yet even so the sphere of Nature was not entirely neglected; someone of the stature of Leonardo da Vinci, concerned as he was with matters as diverse as the invention of machines and an analysis of human anatomy, could still fill a page in his sketch book with studies of an individual flower. For searching scrutiny and immaculate technique the watercolour studies by the great German Renaissance painter Albrecht Dürer, of grasses, weeds and flowers, cannot be surpassed; these were made for their own sake, with no overtones of special meaning. On the other hand, when commissioned to paint religious works, Dürer retained in his oil paintings traditional flower symbolism, if anything intensified in impact through his exact knowledge of the plant involved. This objective representation of the physical world particularly appealed to northern European painters, and to those of the Netherlands most of all, especially in the fine details of a painting. Whether they are portraying jewels, porcelain, glass, fur or fabric, there is the intense delight in rendering them in all their tactile reality, and this holds true of their descriptions of flowers. This then is the springboard from which the flower piece of the seventeenth century is launched, when the special circumstances of horticultural expertise made the Netherlands a centre for the wealthy gardener and collector.

Finally, it is worth noting that a form of symbolism is present even

Studies of flowers. A drawing by Leonardo da Vinci
Photo: O. Böhm, Venice
Accademia Gallery

Wild columbine. A water colour drawing by Albrecht Durer
The Albertina, Vienna

in some of the flower pieces themselves. In Jan Bruegel's *Small Bouquet of Flowers in a Ceramic Vase* in addition to the flowers he has chosen to depict, scattered on the ledge on which the vase stands, several rings, coins and precious stones. Adding nothing to the overall design of the composition, they surely are included as reminders of vanity and greed. Once given this direction of thought it becomes apparent that the flowers themselves, in all their ephemeral loveliness, symbolize the transitory quality of life. Such an interpretation is well supported by the Dutch *Vanitas* type of still life, with its *memento mori*, its emphasis on the uncertainty and fleetingness of life; the same theme is here transferred to a flower piece.

Bibliography

Grant, M.H. *Flower Paintings Through Four Centuries. A descriptive catalogue of the Collection formed by Major the Hon. Henry Rogers Broughton.* Leigh-on-Sea: F. Lewis, 1952.

Nash, J.M. *The Age of Rembrandt and Vermeer.* Phaidon, 1972.

Rose, Barbara. *The Golden Age of Dutch Painting.* Praeger, 1969.

Salinger, Margaretta. *Flowers: The Flower Piece in European Painting.* New York: Harper, 1949.

Salinger, Margaretta. *Early Flower Paintings.* The Metropolitan Museum of Art Bulletin, No. 8, pp. 253–61, May, 1950.

Van Guldener, H. *Flowers: The flower piece in painting.* London: Longmans, 1950.

Van Puyvelde, Leo. *Flemish Painting: The Ape of Rubens and Van Dyck.* Weidenfeld and Nicolson, 1971.

Winkelmann-Rhein, G. *The Paintings and Drawings of Jan "Flower" Bruegel.* New York: H.N. Abrams, 1969.

Wright, Christopher. *The Dutch Painters.* Orbis, 1978.

French Rococo
AD 1715–1760

PAMELA SOUTH

THE GRACEFUL, LIGHT-HEARTED, FLOWING ASYMMETRICAL lines and double curves of the Rococo style were a reaction to the heavy classicism of Versailles. The overlong reign of Louis XIV, the Sun King, had stifled artistic change. On the accession of Louis XV the aristocracy started building smaller, less formal residences in Paris. These had more intimate rooms and were furnished in the new style in the height of elegance and luxury. Swirling asymmetrical forms and the subtle play of curves were introduced into furniture and panelling. Commodes and cabinets were *bombé* or outward curving, or had serpentine-shaped fronts and sides. Ornamentation evoked the curves of waves, and scallop and other shells were used as motifs. Leaf forms, especially the acanthus, were used decoratively but not in their natural growth patterns.

The style was called Rococo, a name that stemmed from the French words *rocaille* meaning rock-work and *coquilles* meaning shells. Rocks and encrusted shells had long been used to decorate artificial gardens and in association with water and fountains. Ancient Rome was also one of the main inspirations of the Rococo style. Painted stucco decorations of murals were discovered in 'grottos' when Roman tombs and villas were excavated, and were thus called *grotesques*. Nero's Golden House provided examples which influenced applied decoration.

The French at this time were importing oriental works of art, especially lacquer panels and Chinese vases of the highest quality: *famille rose, famille verte* and *famille jaune*. They were particularly fond of the willow green celadon ware, and vases and ewers were mounted in elaborate ormolu in swirling Rococo style. The French made their own excursions into chinoiserie, creating European works of art in the Chinese manner and often adding Rococo flourishes.

This was an era of style, grace and wit. Pleasure was pursued by a wealthy aristocracy tied to the formal constraints of court life. Music, opera, dance and amorous dalliance added gaiety and purpose to idle hours. The acceptance of arranged dynastic marriages led to the rise of powerful mistresses, who exerted a tremendous influence over the King. Because the most famous of these, Madame de Pompadour, was a cultivated woman of great taste and a great patron of the arts, the fine arts flourished.

The predominantly feminine influence affected the colours of the decorative style. Delicate pastels of palest pearl, rose, turquoise, blue

Ewers of Chinese celadon procelain with French gilt-bronze mounts
The Wallace Collection, London

Worktable 1783 made by Martin Carlin
The Wallace Collection, London

green, apple green, silver grey, warm apricot, orange, pale yellow and glowing golds were flattering, subtle and harmonious. The flower motif gracefully danced and curled across painted panels, upholstered furniture, wall hangings, tapestries, curtains and women's dress. It appeared at perhaps its most delightful on inlaid panels of porcelain on table or commode.

Decoration was light-hearted, and often divorced from reality or useful purpose. It was an unreal world for the ordinary populace, evoking as it did a fairy-tale vision of youth and beauty. This was epitomized in many Rococo paintings of Watteau, Fragonard and Boucher, which showed intimate boudoir scenes and a gaily elegant society in Arcadian settings. Imagine relaxing in intimate feminine rooms with the new emphasis on comfort, reclining in padded chairs and drinking from eggshell porcelain, beneath glittering chandeliers whose lights are reflected in carved gilt mirrors. All around is the scent of flowers selected for their fragrance: single and double hyacinths, jasmine, roses, lillies of the valley, tuberoses, gardenias, lilacs, carnations, pinks, narcissi and honeysuckle.

Flowering plants were set in porcelain plant holders, and there were special porcelain bulb holders. On a grander scale, orange trees flourished in marble urns or silver tubs. Flower bricks and large oblong vases, with covers studded with holes to support stems, produced low massed designs with space between the divided stems. Artificial porcelain flowers on stems were made at the Sèvres factory (first at

Cupid à Captive by Francois Boucher
The Wallace Collection, London

Vincennes and then near Versailles), and were placed in similar low vases or in taller bouquets in *caisses-à-fleurs*. At Bellevue, one of the royal residences, Madame Pompadour created a winter garden of porcelain flowers, scenting them to heighten the illusion of reality. The

King was said to be deceived by this artifice. However, the enormous cost of this fanciful deceit shocked even that spendthrift court.

Flowers especially selected for interesting form or colour, to add to the chosen scented flowers, were poppies, peonies, tulips (both streaked and parrot), auricula, clematis, *Viburnum opulus* 'Sterile', cornflowers, nasturtiums, calendula, bluebells and forget-me-nots. To supply all these cut flowers, in addition to those grown in French *jardins fleuristes* (cutting gardens), large quantities of flowers were imported at considerable expense from the Haarlem florists. To give an example of the scale of plants needed for the garden and outdoor bedding, at the Trianon alone there were said to be two million pots grown. Flowers in the garden were renewed daily when necessary, labour being so cheap.

In the interior settings, to heighten the already scented air, pot-pourri was used extensively in the most exquisite porcelain pot-pourri vases ever made. The vases had pierced holes to release the scent. At the top there were clusters of porcelain flowers, and the side decoration often featured romantic scenes. Urns on classical lines of all sizes were popular flower containers. Many had handles, and their own plinths were usually incorporated. These urns could be of metal, marble or porcelain, and were frequently made in pairs which were then placed on mantels or matching console tables.

Flowers were worn extensively for adornment. Garlands were placed diagonally across the chest from shoulder to waist, or encircled the upper arm. Small wreaths or chaplets were worn on the head with

Pot-pourri vase in the form of a gondola, Sèvres porcelain 1757
The Wallace Collection, London

Mademoiselle de Châteaurenaud
by Jean-Marc Nattier
The Wallace Collection, London

a tiny central posy. Children sometimes wore small posies at the back of the head. The fashion was for a low *décolletage*, and a glimpse of a gently heaving bosom could be highlighted by a small cluster of flowers.

Flower baskets also were popular, and appear as a frequent design motif. Reed baskets would be more appropriate in an outdoor setting. In paintings, the low oval or round open-work basket is shown being carried full of flowers. Tall upright handled baskets are depicted standing on plinths, which are often garlanded. Alternatively, the baskets are shown somewhat improbably swinging from blue-ribboned bows. The idea of swinging or indeed movement adds to the light-hearted rhythmical flow of Rococo, akin to music. The style is especially in sympathy with the enchanting operas of Mozart; their elegant artificiality was in harmony with the highly cultivated taste of the era. Decorative musical instruments were often grouped with flowers.

The King's two principal mistresses both loved roses. Madame de Pompadour had a richly fragrant Gallica rose, 'Belle de Crécy', named after one of her houses. This rose starts as a rich cerise pink and turns to a soft Parma violet. Madame Du Barry also loved roses, and had her bedroom decorated with them. The bed pillars held up a canopy of roses from which hung embroidered silk curtains – extravagant, frivolous, but probably enchanting.

When seeking to conjure up the spirit of this age and emulate its style, perhaps think first of that delightful painting by Fragonard, *The Swing*, in the Wallace Collection, London. In a romantic sylvan setting with graceful trees and wandering pink shrub roses, an enchantingly attired young lady swings high above her lover standing below and carelessly kicks off her shoe, affording him an appreciative glimpse of her leg. The work is elegant, *risqué* and fun!

To capture the Rococo mood, your arrangement of mixed flowers, though massed, should have a lightness of touch and a delicacy of harmonious colouring. A hint of waywardness – a curving tendril, a wandering stem – will add gaiety, charm and wit.

Bibliography

McIntyre, James. *The Story of the Rose*, Ward Lock, 1970.
Mitford, Nancy. *Madame de Pompadour*, Hamish Hamilton, 1954.
Victoria and Albert Museum. *Rococo Ornament*. V & A, 1984.

Places to visit

The Wallace Collection, Manchester Square, London W1. Finest eighteenth-century collection of Sèvres porcelain, furniture and paintings in Great Britain.
Victoria and Albert Museum, London.
Lady Lever Collection, Port Sunlight, Liverpool.
The Frick Collection, New York.
The Louvre, Paris.
The Hermitage, Leningrad.

The flowers of colonial America

JULIA S. BERRALL

THE SEVENTEENTH-CENTURY WOMEN OF COLONIAL AMERICA led lives of daily toil and hardship, and their responsibilities were many. One marvels at their strength and admires their faith in the future. They had unceasing work within their households, and one of their most necessary chores was the planting and tending of kitchen gardens which they started from the seeds and the cuttings they had carefully brought from England. In these gardens grew the useful plants which provided medicines, balms, flavourings, pest repellents, fragrances and dyes, all necessary in every household. This was women's work; the men and boys had to clear fields, build enclosures, plant the crops and start the orchards.

With the beauty of the land and the plant life it supported, one has to believe that eyes were opened to the new flowers and blossoming trees never before encountered. All along the Atlantic seaboard settlers found the native dogwood (*Cornus florida*) with its showy white flowers (actually bracts) which bloomed in May under the light shade of woodland trees. In the south grew the magnificent evergreen *Magnolia grandiflora* with shiny leaves and large creamy-white blossoms. Interspersed among them was the native pink-flowered redbud (*Cercis canadensis*). Northerners found rosy-flowered mountain laurel (*Kalmia latifolia*), and in the woodlands there was the delicate pink azalea (*Rhododendron nudiflorum*, or Pinkster flower).

Summer brought a variety of sunflowers (*Helianthus*) and the black-eyed Susan (*Rudbeckia hirta*), soon to be followed by the autumn goldenrods (*Solidago*) and the many asters which were named Michaelmas daisies. These were all flowers which grew in the fields. Bittersweet vines (*Celastrus scandens*) clinging to stone walls unfolded their orange berries. Could any sensitive person fail to take pleasure in such discoveries? Might not a branch or a few blossoms have been picked to admire and possibly enjoy indoors? If a girl or woman went to a brook or spring to draw water, might she not have been entranced by a group of delicate trout lilies (*Erythronium*) or by a spectacular pink lady's slipper (*Cypripedium acaule*) which was also called moccasin flower?

Within the herb gardens, peonies, roses, hollyhocks and calendulas were planted, all of which provided very necessary essences. Each also added colour, fragrance and foliage variety. Of great interest is John Josselyn's small book *An Account of Two Voyages to New England Made during the Years 1638 to 1663*, in which he recorded the 'Garden herbs as do thrive there.' They were those with which he had been familiar at home. They included 'Marygold [*Calendula officinalis*], French Mallowes, Fether-few [feverfew: *Chrysanthemum parthenium*], White Satten [*Lunaria annua*], Gilly Flowers, Hollyhocks, English Roses and Tansie'. In another passage he listed 'Native Lilies'.

About 20 years later Adriaen Van der Donck wrote his *Description of the New Netherlands*. In this he listed 'the flowers in general which the New Netherlanders have introduced'. He was describing the flora which he noticed in the small gardens of New Amsterdam at the lower tip of Manhattan Island. His list included white and red roses, sweet William, rocket, violets and pot marigolds (calendulas). Among the bulbs were tulips, crown imperials (*Fritillaria imperialis*), white lilies (*Lilium candidum*), and the guinea-hen flower (*Fritillaria meleagris*). Also of great interest is his statement that the clove tree (*nagelboomtjes*) was being grown by the Dutch. *Nagel* is the Dutch word for clove, and of course the tropical clove tree could not have thrived in what is now New York City. What he was referring to was the common lilac (*Syringa vulgaris*) which has individual florets resembling cloves.

Let us suppose that gradually the newcomers to a strange land took a great interest in the plant life of their adopted country, that they took pride in their successes with the seeds and bulbs brought from home, and that gradually the women were freed of some of their chores as indentured servants arrived. By the end of the seventeenth century a few luxury items began to appear from England. One must not forget, however, that the settlements had different ties to 'home' which were reflected in their lifestyles. The New Englanders came as religious dissenters and were quite cut off from the mother country for a number of years. They only received news and goods as new settlers arrived. The Dutch of New Amsterdam who settled on Manhattan Island and along the Hudson River valley achieved fairly comfortable lives more quickly, for their climate was more equable and they traded through the Dutch East India Company. In Virginia and other southern colonies the Church of England was clung to and the colonists remained loyalists. Tobacco plantations were developed, slaves were brought from Africa and by the eighteenth century comparatively comfortable and wealthy lifestyles were achieved. Wealthy plantation owners had agents in London who arranged for shipments of furniture, silks, wallpapers and other luxuries.

Among the imported items which the housewife treasured were silverware, ceramics and articles made of brass. Some pieces were potential containers for flowers. Very highly prized among the imports were English gardening books, which were important additions to a gentleman's library. In 1629 John Parkinson had written of daffodils which 'perfumed a whole chamber', and he wrote of other flowers which were used 'to deck up a room' (*Paradisi in Sole Paradisus Terrestris*: the first three words are a play on the author's name). Probably the most useful book, and the most revered, was Philip Miller's *The Gardeners Dictionary* (1731-9). Some of the editions had hand-coloured engraved plates. In 1730 Robert Furber had published his *Twelve Months of Flowers*; there were 25 American plants listed and eleven species had the appellation 'Virginian'.

Portrait of Elizabeth Paddy Wensley. Artist unknown
The Pilgrim Society, Plymouth, Massachusetts

Portrait of Mrs Davenport by Joseph Blackburn
The Brooklyn Museum, a gift of the Dick S. Ramsay Fund

Visual documentation for the enjoyment of flowers indoors is very scarce for the seventeenth century, but one unique example exists in Plymouth, Massachusetts. It is an oil portrait of a young woman in unusually fine apparel who stands beside a glass vase which holds roses, tulips and a striped clove pink; it was probably painted in Boston between the years 1670 and 1680. There is some speculation that the roses were used symbolically, the red roses for love and the white one for virtue. *Elizabeth Paddy Wensley* was a woman of substance, as her dress and accessories indicate.

The eighteenth century does bring rewards in a search for pictorial clues to the enjoyment of indoor bouquets, or for the display of several treasured flowers, but at no time can it be said that 'flower arrangements' were made as we use the term today. It is natural to believe that the women who gathered flowers grouped them informally in bouquets, and it is also natural to suppose that some women were more adept than others in displaying them. Perhaps some had natural colour sense and others could achieve a graceful effect more readily than some. A portrait of *Mrs Davenport* painted by Joseph Blackburn in the mid eighteenth century shows the sitter proudly holding a blue and white Chinese vase in which are displayed three large tulips. Another portrait of the same period by John Singleton Copley shows

Left *Portrait of Mrs Benjamin Blackstone by John Singleton Copley*
Mead Art Museum, Amherst College, bequest of Herbert L. Pratt

Right *Portrait of Catherine Brower by MacKay*
National Gallery of Art, Washington, a gift of Edgar William and Bernice Chrysler Garbisch

Mrs George Watson also holding an oriental vase. Hers contains a parrot tulip and two chequered lilies or guinea-hen flowers (*Fritillaria meleagris*). Both women were seemingly very proud of their flowers. And well they should have been, as the bulbs had travelled all the way across the Atlantic Ocean from Holland to be planted in their gardens. Another Copley portrait, that of *Mrs Benjamin Blackstone*, includes a small glass tumbler, possibly a 'flip' glass, which holds a few simple flowers.

The flower holders that came by shipboard included five-fingered posy holders or quintals, crocus pots and true flower vases from many of the English ceramic factories. There was Spode, Wedgwood, Worcestershire, Bow, Crown Derby, Leeds and Chelsea to name a few. Some vases had perforated removable tops which held the flowers in place. Blue and white Delft from Holland was introduced by the trading ships, and Chinese wares came to the colonies by way of England until American ships finally reached China after the Revolutionary War. American ceramic wares were all made of coarse local clays, for there was no porcelain manufacture until several deposits of fine white clay, or kaolin, were discovered in the nineteenth century. Glassware was manufactured locally, and utilitarian shapes such as bottles, tumblers and pitchers were available and useful.

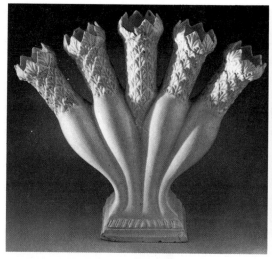

Five-fingered posy holder
The Colonial Williamsburg Foundation,
Virginia

18th century Chelsea porcelain vases
The Metropolitan Museum of Art, bequest of John L. Cadwalader, 1914

**A small Pennsylvania German
earthenware flower holder**
The Metropolitan Museum of Art, a gift of
Mrs Robert W. De Forest, 1933

**An 18th century Stiegel type flip
glass**
The Metropolitan Museum of Art, a gift of
F. W. Hunter, 1913

China trade porcelain bowl
The Metropolitan Museum of Art, a gift of
the members of the committee of the
Bertha King Benkard Memorial Fund,
1946

Ships' captains were accustomed to advertise in the newspapers of the large port cities the articles which they had for sale. Not infrequently these included 'rootes from Holland'. During the pre-Revolutionary period there were many exchanges of seeds, bulbs and cuttings and much is known about the available plant materials. The most rewarding reading is found in the letters of John Bartram, farmer, naturalist and plant explorer of Philadelphia, and Peter Collinson, horticulturist and wealthy Quaker wool merchant of London. For some 38 years the two men corresponded and exchanged plant materials. Bartram sent over 150 American species of trees, shrubs and wild flowers in the form of seeds and seedlings to Collinson, who in turn sent bulbs, perennial plants and rose cuttings. One of Collinson's letters which accompanied a shipment reads:

> Dear Friend, inclosed is the Mate's receipt for a box of bulbs, directed for thee. Make much of them for they are such a collection as is rarely to be met with all at once: for all the sorts of bulbous roots being taken up this year, there is some of every sort. There is above 20 sorts of Crocus – as many of Narcissus – all our sorts of Martagons and Lilies – with Gladiolus, Ornathogalums, Moleys [*Allium moly*], and Irises – with many others I don't remember, which time will show thee.

In all likelihood the gladiolus was the European cornflag, either *Gladiolus communis* or *Gladiolus segetum*; the South African species had not then been discovered. Bartram also received tuberoses, gas plant (*Fraxinella*), a double yellow rose, a moss rose, China asters and carnations. Many shipments lacked proper care during rough ocean voyages; the imagination is stirred by Collinson writing to Bartram, pleading that wood slats be nailed over the boxes of seedlings to prevent the cats from scratching. And it is heart warming to read Bartram's letter describing 'a glorious appearance of carnations ... the brightest colors that ever eyes beheld'. These were probably clove pinks which he had succeeded in growing from seed.

While the writers tell us a good deal about the flowers which the colonists grew, there are only a few scattered references to their use indoors. Peter Kalm, the Swedish naturalist and explorer, in his *Travels in North America* (1750) mentioned that 'the ladies were much inclined to keep flowers all summer long about or upon the chimneys, upon a table or before the windows, either on account of their beauty or because of their sweet scent.' Kalm also reported that the women often gathered bunches of 'life everlasting', also known as 'pearly everlasting' (*Anaphalis margaritacea*), saying that they were 'put into pots with or without water amongst other fine flowers which they gather in the gardens and in the fields and place them as an ornament in the rooms'. Lady Skipworth of Virginia, who kept careful garden records, wrote of drying purple statice to ornament her mantelpiece in the winter.

Other garden flowers which were dried for the winter were the celosias, both crested and plumed, strawflowers, globe amaranths and honesty or satin flower. The fields and marshes provided sea lavender, cat-tails and bayberry. Philip Miller noted that he placed his straw-flowers in vases filled with sand.

Often writers let us know where floral bouquets were placed in the rooms. Very frequently the 'chimney' or mantelpiece was mentioned, and the fireplace itself was used in the summer when heat was unnecessary. Bouquets placed on the hearth were called bough pots. Peter Kalm mentioned 'flowers at the window', probably referring to the windowsill. Peter Collinson suggested to John Custis of Virginia that dried globe amaranths would 'make a pleasant Ornament to Adorn the Windows of your parlor or study all winter'. Since furniture was not overly abundant during these times, and every piece had a truly functional use, tables were probably often reserved for the serving of meals or tea, and floral bouquets took their places elsewhere.

In essence it cannot truthfully be said that 'the art of flower arranging' existed in the American colonies. But with an abundance of flowering material readily available, and with vases and other containers at hand, flowers did brighten the parlours. We know this from both the writers and the artists. Mixed bouquets were probably the norm, for there were so many lovely flowers to gather and it was the very English thing to do.

Bibliography

Bartram, John and Collinson, Peter. *Correspondence, c.1730–1768.*

Berrall, Julia S. *The Garden: An Illustrated History.* Viking, 1966.

Fisher, Louise B. *An Eighteenth Century Garland.* Colonial Williamsburg, 1951.

Furber, Robert. *Twelve Months of Flowers.* 1730.

Josselyn, John. *New England's Rarities Discovered in Birds, Beasts, Fishes, Serpents and Plants in that Country.* 1672.

Kalm, Peter. *Travels in North America,* 1750.

Leighton, Ann. *American Gardens in the Eighteenth Century.* 1976.

Miller, Philip. *The Gardeners Dictionary.* 1731–39.

Parkinson, John. *Paradisi in Sole Paradisus Terrestris.* 1629.

Van der Donck, Adriaen. *Description of New Netherland.* 1650. (for complete translation of flower list cf. Berrall, *The Garden – An Illustrated History.* New York: Viking Press, 1966.

Modern Italian flower design

PAOLA BURGER and LOLI MARSANO

IN ITALY, FORMAL INSTRUCTION IN FLOWER ARRANGING began only recently. Being such latecomers, it is therefore natural that Italian arrangers should come to the art with a fresh outlook, influenced by modern Italian living and design. Modern styles therefore appeal in Italy more than elsewhere, and many who have attended international flower arrangement competitions in recent times have been struck by the quality of the work of Italian arrangers. It is accepted that they have made a significant and influential contribition – so much so that a distinct Italian style is now recognized. We shall try to explain how it has developed.

Along the coast from the French Riviera and across the border into Italy, you pass through a wild landscape with steep hills and red rocks. The vegetation is Mediterranean scrub and the occasional majestic pine tree. Now and again, through gaps in the hillside, you catch a glimpse of the snow-capped Alps. As the landscape becomes less wild you will see how the hillside has been terraced by man many centuries ago in order to plant olive trees and grow basic crops and, later, to establish vineyards, market gardens and pleasure gardens. As you near San Remo you will notice how whole hillsides are covered with greenhouses, and the reflection of the sun in the glass will blind you. Valuable produce such as asparagus and artichokes is grown there out of season, as well as orchids and violets for northern European markets at Christmas time. There are also whole hillsides with extensive cultivation of carnations, which have been successfully exported since the end of the nineteenth century.

Of course, the climate plays an important role. Winters are generally mild and most trees are evergreen, but gales often carry salt spray from the sea, and the branches of bushes are twisted into the strangest shapes. This part of Italy has therefore a vegetation both native and imported, consisting of agaves, aloes, palm trees, chamaerops, phormium, geraniums and many plants with grey leaves. It is natural that, in such surroundings, interest in flowers should be great and a desire to arrange them in one's home widespread.

The fact that the late Princess Grace of Monaco and her Garden Club started organizing annual competitions obviously heightened interest in a more systematic study of flower arrangement. The enthusiasm and flair of the Princess in encouraging as many arrangers as possible to come to her competitions from all over the world gave an impulse

Photos: A. Cassan

'Footlights' – a modern interpretative mass arrangement by Loli Marsano. It consists of trimmed chamaerops leaves in the shape of wings with two masses of white carnations. Branches of tropical lianas give tension and rhythm

(*Note*: The photographs on pages 109 to 112 are taken from *Scultura Floreale* by Paola Burger and Loli Marsano (Idea Books))

Interpretation of 'underwater fantasy' placed on a perspex stand. It appears as if suspended in midwater. Kelps are used to give movement and seafans are placed horizontally to give depth. Coral like celosia cristata and shells form the central core. Arranged by Paola Burger

An abstract arrangement of clear and neat design. The main emphasis is on the vertical line which is enhanced by the inclusion of perspex rods. Loli Marsano has used two palm leaf stems and bilbergia flowers

Photos: A. Cassan

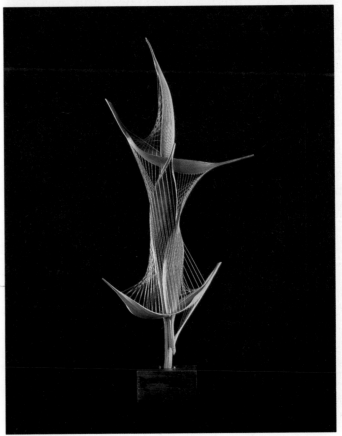

A decorative abstract arrangement by Paola Burger. Intersected palm spathes are linked by a network of cotton thread. The arrangement can be viewed from all sides with changing aspects

to flower arrangement in the whole area. All the well-known demonstrators have been in turn to Monte Carlo as a part of the competition events and helped to create interest in flower arrangement.

The moving spirits in the foundation of the Italian School were Rosnella Cajello of San Remo, Carla Crosa di Vergagni of Genoa and Camilla Malvasia of Bologna. Rosnella Cajello created the Italian modern mass arrangement, which has a strong line and grouped masses of flowers as an integral part of the design. This was the starting point. It has helped the Italians to evolve other designs and ideas. As mentioned previously, the plant material which grows in this part of the world has strength and is unsuited to delicate and romantic designs, and this has encouraged the pursuit of modern styles. Another advantage which the Italian School has is that because it is so young it does not have to pay homage to older models; it is therefore much freer to experiment in other directions. There is therefore less risk of the movement becoming ossified.

Flower arrangement courses in various parts of Italy have all been structured on the lines laid down in the manuals issued by the San Remo Flower Arrangement School. During the five years of the courses, traditional flower arrangement is taught, and the basic lines which are so elegant and have given so much pleasure over the centuries play an important part. However, from the third year onwards a considerable number of lessons are dedicated to modern arrangements.

It is undeniable that modern flower arrangement owes much to Japan. The disciplines which ikebana teaches through its strict rules, stylization of line, and sophisticated manipulation of plant material have played an important part in the culture of modern flower arrangement. In Italy there is an active branch of the Ohara School founded by Jennie Banti, and there has been a lot of contact with them. But we must not equate ikebana with modern style. When considering suitability of plant material, or conceiving a design, modern style requires respect for the fundamental rules of western visual arts rather than the strict academic and philosophical eastern ones.

In Italy there are everywhere works of art and artefacts of various kinds, representative of all the styles of the last 2000 years. Italy has produced many famous painters, sculptors and architects. The best they have created survives, and anything that is good can provide inspiration for modern work. Painting helps us to choose colours and to organize the design. Sculpture helps us in the positioning of the various masses, and provides the principles for the three-dimensional aspect of a work. Architecture is the frame within which every arrangement will need to be placed.

But it is obviously modern art which will exert the greatest influence on the modern Italian flower arranger. In this connection it is today's frequent major art exhibitions that will have the most influence. To mention but two, there has been an important Henry Moore exhibition in Florence and the first major Futurist exhibition in Venice. Abstract art enjoys great popularity; consequently most advanced arrangements tend to be abstract in style and are becoming more sculptural

Photos: G. Cajello

Left *A striking modern mass arrangement by Rosnella Cajello. Masses of amaryllis and carnations are exalted by the contrasting chamaerops berries. Admirably shaped variegated agave leaves wind in and out of the arrangement, which rests on a metal tripod*

Right *A sophisticated modern free form arrangement by Rosnella Cajello. The texture of the ceramic container is repeated with slight variations of rhythm in the plant material which ranges from shaped aspidistra leaves contrasting with asparagus miriocladus to crushed phragmitis comunis and topped by an anthurium leaf and bamboo nigra*

all the time. In fact it can be said that they are sculptures created with plant material. It is not considered that to create in abstract means to go against nature. On the contrary, it means trying to get to the core of things and to isolate the essential, so as to achieve an effect of simplicity or to express a particular feeling or mood. The arrangement will tend to be outlined in pure, almost geometrical forms, where the flower is merely a spot of colour and the strength of the lines play the main role.

As it has been relatively easy to take part in international flower arrangement competitions (particularly in Monte Carlo), more and more Italian arrangers have been able to make friends with arrangers from other lands and to compare work. Every country has its characteristics, and the differences between the various styles can be appreciated. One can admire beautiful arrangements made with foliage from rare plants, and with refined colour schemes or elegant monochromes. Italian competitors use the material which they have near at hand, such as early vegetables from the Riviera; masses of wonderful carnations; chamaerops, sometimes trimmed but so Mediterranean; and anthuriums, spatiphillums, strelitzias and so on. Another important point is that the Italian arranger will only rarely alter or paint plant material. It is felt that what nature has created should, as far as possible, be left intact, and that it is the structure of the design which gives strength to an arrangement. To alter plant material is often to diminish, if not destroy, the beauty of what nature has created.

The decisive break that modern style requires from tradition can cause difficulties for arrangers who are not familiar with the modern idiom. Sometimes this becomes hostility and even refusal; however, to be relevant to the period in which we live, we have to adapt to its language. In all periods artists and artisans have caught the spirit and created in the style of their time. The same applies to flower arrangers. In the creation of an arrangement flowers and leaves are the raw material, just as stone is for the sculptor and colours are for the painter.

Having established the need to arrange flowers in the modern style, we will consider what conditions are required in order to promote such work. It is obvious that anybody having natural gifts of good taste and creativeness will find it easier than others, but it is our view that an environment capable of nurturing such gifts can be created. In Italy such an environment seems to exist. The successes of many Italian arrangers in the modern style have encouraged newcomers to have a go. Modern arrangements, especially when they require an interpretation of a theme, require thought and planning; they also require full rein to be given to one's imagination so that the hobby of arranging flowers in a pleasing manner can become real sculpture. In this context things have been made easier by the many new materials becoming available for containers or stands. Perspex is relatively new and has helped arrangers to make stands unobtrusive. Oasis has made it possible for arrangers to produce work much less constrained by technical limitations. Italian artisans such as carpenters and blacksmiths, and the many small workshops producing objects in perspex, are generally very helpful and even find themselves stimulated by the demands some of our arrangers make. After all, they are used to working for Italian designers who by general consent are at the forefront of design. With these premises things have been much easier for Italians than for others. There are groups of keen flower-arranging friends. By working, comparing and competing together, they have been able to inspire each other not only in competition but by example.

Italian arrangements can be recognized by economy of material and importance of line. However, the concern is not only to simplify, synthesize and remove the superfluous, but also to try to analyse all that surrounds us in nature, and to make use for our arrangements of the roundness or the spikiness of objects. The design must be original in its lines, rhythm and colour. We try to analyse its essential features and to discover the qualities of our material, to understand its significance in the particular context. Nature offers an immense variety of shapes and colours, and it is up to us to find the one which is best suited to our design. Inspiration can be sought in many ways: the direct observation of plant material, the world of primitive or contemporary art, the shapes and patterns present in nature. The only limitations are the basic principles of design, namely proportion, balance, rhythm and contrast:

Proportion The complex systems of proportion governing classical design, of which the most famous and important is the Golden Section, cannot be applied strictly. In contemporary flower arrangement these criteria are more flexible, and traditional aesthetic laws, whilst understood, are applied with more daring. Experiments are made with contrast, elongation and foreshortening in order to obtain a certain degree of dominance.

Balance Balance consists in the placing of weight and mass in relation to a vertical axis. Two similar objects placed at each end of a vertical axis produce static balance. Balance may be related either to the real weight, or to the visual weight, of the arrangement. However, balance can also be created between dissimilar objects. In fact in this case the eye is attracted all the more and moves among the various elements, which are therefore in dynamic balance. Modern flower arrangement is often based on asymmetric design, and balance is of fundamental importance. Solids and spaces must be in correct proportion; the projecting lines must be visually counterbalanced. A typical example is Calder's sculpture, where balance is achieved by the combination of creativity and the strict application of the rules of gravity.

Rhythm All existence is based on rhythm, and all natural phenomena are controlled by recurring rhythms such as the changing of the seasons and the ebb and flow of the tides. In traditional flower arrangement, rhythm is created through the apparent movement of the lines, which guide the eye to the focal point of the arrangement and then back again to the exterior. Modern arrangements do not necessarily have a focal point and may have more than one centre of interest. Rhythm is achieved by the flow of lines and the repetition of shapes, volumes and spaces.

Contrast Contrast gives interest to life and to nature: night and day, heat and cold, rough and smooth, and so on. In traditional flower arrangement, contrasts of texture are subtle and restrained, and the use of many different elements is a fundamental feature. Modern arrangements rely on fewer elements and contrast is essential, involving the shape and texture of materials, the space/volume relationship, and colour. To give contrast and to rest the eye, rough and spiky elements may be alternated with wide smooth surfaces such as leaves, stones or fruits. Contrast should be decisive.

In addition, colour is obviously extremely important in all flower arrangement. To achieve a successful design, much thought has to be given to the colour scheme, and fashion plays an important role. At times subdued colours are favoured, and at others strong ones. It is very difficult to understand all the emotions and sensations that colour arouses. It has a very precise language and a very definite message. Much research has gone into its significance. All this must be understood in order to use colour effectively, especially in interpretative arrangements where it may be of primary importance, and where contrast of colours may be fundamental to the theme of the design.

This chapter has tried to show how modern Italian flower arrangers are trying to achieve economy of material and purity of line. The designers are as conscious as anybody of the transience of flower arrangements. They last but the space of a few days, but will change subtly in shape and colour. Even the best of them can give pleasure for only a short time but, like a good performance in the theatre, they linger in the memory.

Bibliography

Burger Paola and Marsano Loli. *Scultura Floreale*. Idea Books, 1984.

5

Britain: tradition and empire

Ritual and remedy: herbs and flowers in tradition

VALERIE FORD

FROM EARLIEST TIMES FLOWERS AND HERBS HAVE BEEN USED throughout our lives, symbolically, decoratively and for practical purposes, on private and public occasions, to invoke good and repel evil, to express joy and assuage grief, to embellish and protect the person and the home.

Herbs in folklore, magic and medicine

Fear of witches and their evil craft was the basis for much folklore, but there is often a confusion between good and evil. Many plants connected with witches were at the same time endowed with beneficent power; for example hawthorn, with which witches were alleged to hedge their gardens, keeping out all light, was also revered as a holy plant used for Jesus's Crown of Thorns. Foxglove (*Digitalis*) and belladonna are well known as poisons, but when used with discretion can have healing effects. Dill, a favourite with witches as an opiate, was (and still is) used to lull children to sleep; the herb's name is said to come from a Saxon word meaning 'to lull', and the lullaby 'Lavender's blue, dilly-dilly' may have the same derivation.

As antidotes to witchcraft, holly (the 'holy' tree), witch-hazel and wych-elm were planted. The holly and also rowans were additionally well regarded because they bear red berries – the colour of blood and therefore of life. Elder too was planted as a defence in cottage gardens, as it was thought that eyes anointed with juice from its berries could see witches from far off, and its white flowers were a symbol of purity and goodness.

Herbs have been sampled for food and experimented with medicinally for centuries. We can only guess at how many poor wretches died before it was found, for example, that the oil from the beans of the castor-oil plant taken in small amounts is useful medicinally, but to *eat* two or three of the beans is fatal.

Interest in herbs and their prophylactic powers increased in the fifteenth and sixteenth centuries. Culpeper, Gerard, John Parkinson and others wrote their great Herbals, where gardening and folk medicine are inextricably mixed. Some of the 'vertues' they claim for plants are valid: comfrey or 'knit-bone', whose grated root mixed with water is recommended for supporting fractures, is still used for external wounds by pharmacists today. It is doubtful though whether anyone still believes with Gerard that Solomon's Seal 'seals' (i.e. heals) wounds or that it 'taketh away in one night ... any bruise ... gotten by women's wilfulness in falling on their husbands' fists'.

However, it had long been believed that plants showed in themselves how they could be used medically. Wild parsley and saxifrage, whose roots could break through stony ground, were held to have the power to break up kidney stones; all plants with red petals, leaves or sap were said to be good for the blood and to cure nose-bleeds. Such theories were developed in the Doctrine of Signatures or Sympathetic Magic proclaimed by Paracelsus and Giambattista della Porta in the sixteenth century. There it was propounded, for example, that a walnut kernel, looking so much like the brain, must be good for ailments of the head; sundew, whose sticky liquid never dries up and so was believed to be the elixir of life, was prescribed for longevity; and pansy, with its heart-shaped leaves, was said to be good for the heart. The Doctrine led to the naming of plants according to their use: clary and eye-bright, for example, being good for sore eyes.

Although centuries later Kipling was to write 'Anything green that grew out of the mould, Was an excellent herb to our fathers of old,' many of these old remedies are still used by homeopathic doctors, for there are good pathological bases for their alleged curative properties. Willow (*Salix*) was prescribed for rheumatism because both were connected with damp conditions, but there are sound medical reasons for its efficacy: salisylic acid, a main constituent of aspirin, can be obtained (as its name shows) from willow bark. The customs of earlier times were retained right up to the eighteenth century, when it was still held that the growing, drying and distilling of medicinal herbs for simples was an essential part of the training of young women of every degree.

It is often hard to divide custom from folklore, and when considering herbs and gardening this is especially the case. Parsley is sown on Good Friday to counteract the evil influence of the devil, to whom the seed is said to descend seven times before rooting as an explanation for the difficulty experienced in getting it to germinate. Parsley and sage are said to grow best for he (or she) who rules the house; sage also grows best, as one would expect, for the wise. Tansy was said to be good for fertility; it flourishes where rabbits abound, but is this cause or effect?

How straightforward life would be if we could all still believe, with the old herbalists, that 'to gather sweetbriar in June promoteth cheerfulness'; that 'to comfort the brain' all that was needed was to smell camomile; that 'bugloss confermeth and conserveth the mind'; and that powdered betony and wine would help 'at the time when fere cometh'. In that case perhaps there would be less need for tranquillizers.

Scents and savours

In times gone by when sanitation and personal hygiene were virtually non-existent, there was a great need for sweetening of the air and herbs, spices and scented flowers were used for this purpose. Herbs had been strewn on stone and clay floors at least since the time of King Stephen (twelfth century) to keep houses, churches and other public buildings warm and dry underfoot and to offset the stuffiness of unventilated rooms. A list of 21 strewing herbs in 1577 includes basil, balm, marjoram, tansy, germander, hyssop, camomile, sweet sedge, meadowsweet, bay, wormwood, juniper and myrtle.

In the Middle Ages aromatic flowers and herbs were strewn to ward off fevers, and they were used as disinfectants during the plagues. Later the burning of fragrant herbs was advised in hospitals to banish flies and smells from stuffy wards. However, it is pleasanter to dwell on the Elizabethan 'sweetening of the house' when, in their equivalent of our spring cleaning, they renewed the dried leaves and rushes used instead of carpets and to give off fragrance. There is evidence too that sweet herbs were strewn at coronations, at least until the reign of George IV. In 1560 a visitor praised 'sundry sorts of fragraunt flowers' about the rooms of English houses, with 'wallflowers and the greater flag . . . used in nosegays to deck up the house'; this was an early example of the flower arranging we do today! But the decoration of the house was only one art practised by the Tudor housewife. Every house from cottage to palace had its stillroom. The stillroom books are a link between the Herbals and the cookery books of modern times, containing as they do a practical blend of recipes for medicinal, cosmetic and culinary purposes.

The perfume trade was scarcely in existence in England before the

Herb-woman and her six maids strewing herbs at the Coronation of King George IV by Sir George Naylor
East Sussex County Library

time of Elizabeth I; even as late as 1860 there were only 40 manufacturing perfumers in the whole country. However, in the fifteenth year of her reign the Earl of Oxford brought sweet bags and perfumed clothes from Italy, and at Court both sexes made use of every kind of aromatic for perfuming the body and clothes. All such luxuries were banned under the Commonwealth but were restored by Charles II. Indeed their use clearly became widespread, for an Act of Parliament in 1770 made it an offence 'to betray into matrimony by scents, paints or cosmetic washes'.

To obtain the necessary ingredients for the pomanders and pot-pourri used for scenting rooms and clothes, sweet-smelling flowers were planted in gardens, in addition to the mazes, labyrinths and knots all made of herbs. Pomanders (the name comes from the French *pomme d'ambre*) were originally simple pastes of herbs and spices; the one carried by Cardinal Wolsey was merely 'a very fair orange whereof the meat or substance was taken out and filled up again with part of a sponge whereon was vinegar and other confection against the pestilential airs'. Pomanders were developed during the sixteenth and seventeenth centuries into luxurious articles of fashion among people of rank; many of the delicate and beautiful containers used for them may be seen in the Wellcome Galleries of the Science Museum in London. They were worn round the neck or on a chain from the waist (Elizabeth was given a 'fayre girdle of pomander'), and the scented herbs, spices and essential oils they contained were thought to possess prophylactic virtues against plague and typhus as well as masking unsanitary smells. The author of *The Dialogue against Pestilence* (*c.* 1564–78) urged his readers to 'be not without a good Pomeamber'. The Queen's favourite fumigant was a mixture of ginger, cinnamon, aniseed, caraway and fennel seeds, and it is interesting to note that a combination of similar spices was still used in India in 1962 to make a pomander nosegay for important guests.

Pomanders from a collection in the Wellcome Galleries
The Science Museum, London

Pot-pourri (literally meaning 'rotten pot') was made from fresh or semi-dried scented leaves and petals layered with salt to cure and ferment them. Their popularity increased in the sixteenth century when essential oils for fixing the scent were imported from the East. By the eighteenth century most country houses had their own recipes, and they were called, more prettily, 'sweet jars'. A recipe dated 1750 quoted by Vita Sackville-West in *Knole and the Sackvilles* gives precise instructions:

Photo: John R. Marr

Pomander-nosegay presented to VIPs at official function in Tangore, India, 1962

Gather dry, double violets, rose leaves, lavender, myrtle flowers, verbena, bayleaves, rosemary, balm, musk and geranium. Pick these from the stalks and dry on paper in the sun for a day or two before putting them in a jar. This should be a large white one, well-glazed with a close-fitting cover; also a piece of card the exact size of the jar which you must keep pressed down on the flowers, and keep a new wooden spoon to stir the salt and flowers before you put a fresh layer of salt above and below every layer of flowers. Have ready plenty of cinnamon, mace, nutmeg, pepper and lemon-peel well pounded. For a large jar, $\frac{1}{2}$ lb orris root, 1 oz storax, 1 oz gum benjamin, 2 ozs calomino aromatico [sweet sedge], 2 grains musk and a small quantity of oil of rhodium. The spice and gums to be added when you have collected all the flowers you intend to put in. Mix all together, press it down well, spread bay salt on top to exclude air. Keep the jar in a cool place until the following January or February.

Such sweet-smelling mixtures were used to scent not only drawers and cupboards but also writing paper. Mrs C. W. Earle, in *Pot-Pourri from a Surrey Garden* (1897), further suggests filling little bags made of thin Liberty silk and placing them under and behind chair cushions to the delight of her visitors.

These same scented plants were reduced to 'sweet pouthers', distilled into 'sweete washing waters' or used for washing balls. In the Middle Ages soap was unknown and soapwort was used for cleansing. In Tudor times the nobles and merchants imported rich, white Castile soap from Spain, and washballs were made from it by mixing in herbs, spices, fixatives and bark to give a coarse-grained ball which acted like a loofah. This was used until the early nineteenth century, when the Victorians' insistence on cleanliness led to a lifting of the tax on soap and the home-made product became widely available.

Cosmetics have been closely linked with flowers since the first century, when a Greek physician mixed wax with oil of roses to make the first cold cream. An Elizabethan pomade was prepared from hogs' fat and fresh rose petals or elder flowers. Little refinement had been achieved by the end of the seventeenth century, when Ninon de Lenclos affirmed that she kept wrinkles at bay into her seventies by using a cold cream concocted from houseleeks. In the first half of the twentieth century there was a move away from natural products as chemists learnt to synthesize perfumes, but in the 1980s there has been a strong move back to using 'the real thing' for body lotions, shampoos and all types of cosmetics.

In the kitchen too there is a revival of interest in old recipes for herbal teas and tisanes, drunk for many centuries before the clipper ships brought tea from India and China, and in home-made wines using rose-hips, dandelions, cowslips, blackberries, elderberries and numerous other flowers and berries. Spice ropes (just another name for sweet bags) are used today as they were in Tudor times to sweeten drawers and cupboards. Lavender bags, always so popular at any village sale of work, remind us of the old custom of hanging washing to dry on lavender bushes and putting freshly washed linen into drawers scented with lavender; from this practice may derive the twelfth-century word for a washerwoman, 'lavanderess', corrupted in time to our 'laundress'.

Customs and festivals

From birth to burial, the events of our lives are closely linked with flowers. Babies are soothed with dill water. Children blow dandelion clocks, laugh at pansy 'faces', make daisy chains and test each other's fondness for butter by holding a buttercup under the chin. They play ring-a-roses unmindful of the origin of this nursery rhyme in the plague years, when the 'posies' were prophylactic nosegays and 'all fall down' referred to those stricken with the disease. Daisies feature again in teenage years when petals are removed to see if 'he loves me' or 'he loves me not'.

Wedding customs have always been particularly linked with flowers. Orange blossom denotes fecundity and white is the colour of purity, but the bride in Tudor times sometimes wore, instead of flowers, a wreath of ears of corn. Vaughan writes in 1606: 'When the marriage day was come the bride was bound to have a chaplet of flowers or hearbes upon her head.' The *Origins of Ancient Customs* (1672) affirms that 'No-one questions the propriety of a chaplet of roses for newly-married people, seeing that flowers in general and roses in particular are sacred to Venus, to the Graces and to Love.'

As late as the nineteenth century the bridal path on the way to church was strewn with rushes, wheat, rosemary and flowers including marigolds and broom. Broom was also used in the bride's posy ('When the furze is out of bloom, kissing's out of fashion'), as was a sprig of myrtle, a symbol of both fertility and purity; this was given to the bridesmaid, just as today's bride throws her bouquet, and it would have been planted to bring good luck. A bush grown from a sprig of myrtle from Queen Victoria's bouquet has provided a sprig for every royal bride since. Wheat and later rice (later still, rose petals) showered the pair after the ceremony, echoing a Greek and Roman fertility rite.

Rosemary, sometimes dipped in scented water, was often included in the bride's posy, worn on the sleeve by a boy attendant or, as in the case of Anne of Cleves, wound into the bridal wreath. This herb indeed has a place at both weddings and funerals. As Robert Herrick sang in 'Lines on rosemary': 'Grow it for two ends, it matters not at all, Be't for my bridall or my buriall.' At funerals the mourners would often be given a sprig of rosemary before they left for the church and they would throw it on to the coffin as it was lowered into the ground. Rosemary bushes were planted on graves, as were white roses for virgins and red on the graves of persons of good character. Sage, the assiduous use of which was said by John Evelyn to render man immortal, was also planted on graves, perhaps to symbolize the immortality of the soul.

On happier occasions, particularly in Victorian times, flowers were worn on the person. 'Beautiful flowers for the hair and bouquets for evening wear are now the rule rather than the exception', and although readers should 'carefully avoid using too many flowers', family photographs of grandmother's wedding bouquet and the drawings of a corsage and buttonhole of the period indicate that scant notice was taken of this advice.

A simple spray of flowers and a buttonhole bouquet
From *Domestic Floriculture* by F.W. Burbidge (William Blackwood and Sons, 1875)

All through the year flowers are used as part of civil or church festivals. Mothering Sunday was celebrated at least 300 years ago, being well established in the seventeenth century. Apprentices and servants were given a day off in mid Lent to visit their families, and would gather primroses and violets on their way home; 'Go a-mothering and find violets in the lane' runs an old saying. The special service to bless these offerings is a newer practice. On Palm Sunday, palm crosses are still given out, especially in rural parishes. In olden days, branches of palm (or more often willow) were brought into the house in Holy Week and were believed to give protection for several months.

May Day is a revival of a Roman spring festival. Youngsters in the fifteenth and sixteenth centuries would go off into the woods to select a tree for the maypole; sometimes it would be so heavy an ox was needed to pull it, and the beast too would be decked with flowers and herbs. Everyone joined in the fun – even Henry VIII and Catherine of Aragon in the early years of their marriage. Instead of a maypole, sometimes a may garland would be made and carried round the village by young men and girls, asking for coins. It could take the form of single posies of garden or even wild flowers on a pole, or a more elaborate flower-decked hoop with a doll inside.

Well-dressing, with its echoes of another Roman festival, the Fontanalia, is recorded first in Derbyshire where Tissington twice had cause to celebrate. In 1350 the Black Death passed the village by, and in a period of drought in 1615 it was the only well in the district which did not run dry. Today the decorations of fresh and dried flowers, mosses and herbs are works of great artistry. Flower shows, so much a part of English life, were in fact introduced into England in the seventeenth century by Huguenot refugees from France.

But it is at Christmas that most time is spent decorating our homes and churches. The laurel, bay, rosemary and pine we use date from pre-Christian times. Holly, ivy and mistletoe are strong life symbols, being evergreen and bearing fruits in winter. The holly is also considered to have connections with the Crown of Thorns; ivy, with its

A May garland with doll
From *Folklore and Customs of Rural England* by Margaret Baker (David and Charles, 1974)

divided leaf, represents the Trinity. Mistletoe, the Sacred Bough of classical legend, is not normally allowed in churches, but paradoxically has long been used in the house as a protection against evil. The custom of kissing under the mistletoe dates back at least to the seventeenth century, when 'social' kissing in England was much more customary than it is today.

The language of flowers

The language of flowers is 'A pleasantly useless subject with no political, social, academic or commercial *raison d'être*. It exists purely for fun to enable us to pick a bunch of flowers which contains a poem ... a private code with great style.' Each flower in a Greek garland has a meaning, but without the key it is impossible today to unravel it. The Persians, Chinese and Indians all used flower language in a symbolic way. In 1716, when Lady Mary Wortley Montague accompanied her husband to Istanbul where he was Ambassador at the Turkish Sultan's court, she became fascinated by the idea and was the first to bring the language of flowers to England.

The Oriental Love Letter by Henry William Pickersgill, R. A.
The Royal Academy of Arts

The Language of Flowers by G. D. Leslie
Manchester City Art Gallery

In Victorian times this symbolic language offered the perfect vocabulary to the tongue-tied young lady further inhibited by propriety; a small bouquet could be used to start a spirited conversation which could be carried on without a word being spoken. Books were compiled, many of them beautifully illustrated, containing over 800 domestic and wild flowers with their meanings; these offered a method of communication to both men and women. A volume, *Le Langage des Fleurs* by Madame de la Tour, appeared in France, and although the text was somewhat racy for the Victorian miss the idea caught on. In 1847 Thomas Miller wrote *The Poetical Language of Flowers* which gave precise information as to the composition of bouquets and the manner of presentation. Great care was needed, for the message to be conveyed could be reversed by placing a flower upside-down and the material used to bind the bouquet could denote either negation or a query. The position of flowers worn on the person was a matter of great importance too; a marigold in the hair bore witness to mental anguish, while pinned to the bosom it conveyed indifference.

We may perhaps today regard these coy exchanges with amusement, but to some at the time, both sophisticated town and simpler country dwellers, they were a matter of the utmost importance. However a poet of the period, Leigh Hunt, in his *Love Letters made of Flowers*, pokes gentle fun at the idea:

> An exquisite invention this
> Worthy of Love's most honeyed kiss.
> This art of writing billets-doux
> In buds and odours and bright hues.
> In saying all one feels and thinks
> In clever daffodils and pinks,
> Uttering (as well as silence may)
> The sweetest words the sweetest way.
>
> How charming in some rural spot
> Combining love with garden plot
> At once to cultivate one's flowers
> And one's epistolary powers.

Ceremonial flowers

The distribution of money by the Sovereign at the Royal Maundy Service on the Thursday before Easter dates back to the thirteenth century, and the carrying of posies by the principal people taking part was originally a precaution against possible infection from the recipients. As the centuries passed, so the shape and composition of the posies has changed. An eighteenth-century print shows members of the procession carrying very small sprays of wild flowers and herbs; by the end of the nineteenth century more formal flowers had been added. Photographs of the Royal Family in the 1930s show them carrying quite large, loose bouquets of mixed flowers and herbs.

Today's posies are tighter and have a dome-like shape; they are made by Mrs Valerie Bennet-Levy, Supplier of Nosegays to the Queen since the 1950s. They include daffodils, white stocks, narcissus 'Cheerfulness', violets, primroses, rosemary, thyme and cupressus (this last representing eternal life), mostly collected from friends' gardens; sweetly scented and colourful, they are indeed true 'nose-gays'. The posies, made during the night before the service, are carried by the Queen, Prince Philip, the Lord High Almoner, the Sub-Almoner, the Secretary and the Assistant Secretary to the Royal Almonry, the Clerk of the Chapels Royal, the bishop and dean of the cathedral where the ceremony is being held, and any visiting bishops. Smaller posies are made for two girls and two boys from a local school; originally these would have been 'children' of the Almonry, that is to say two old men who were paid £1 per year to sweep out the chapel.

Just as members of the Royal Maundy procession carried posies to ward off infection, so too did judges. However, theirs were originally mainly composed of rue, which 'was supposed to be anti-pestilential, hence they were "regaled" with its unpleasing odour'. This practice too continues to the present day, although the nosegays now are

Photo: Tim Graham

Maundy posies. The Queen and the Duke of Edinburgh with Royal Almonry Officials, Worcester Cathedral 1980

composed of sweeter-smelling mixed herbs and garden flowers – no doubt to the relief of the judges.

Posies are also presented, by the Keeper of the Guildhall, to the new Lord Mayor of London at his election on 29 September each year, and to members of the Civic Procession: the Recorder, the Sheriffs, the Aldermen and Officers. They carry their posies (these days made of garden flowers) in procession to a service at the nearby Church of St Lawrence Jewry and return to Guildhall still carrying them. This ceremony dates back to the election of Richard Whittington in 1406, when flowers and herbs were regarded as a protection against infection and the evil smells of the streets. For the election of the Lord Mayor and also on 24 June for the election of the Sheriffs, the dais in Guildhall known as the Hustings and the adjacent Livery Hall where the Court of Aldermen is held, are strewn with camomile, mint and rose petals.

The Lord Mayor attends the first and second days of the May, June, July and September sessions at the Central Criminal Court, and on these occasions too he carries a posy of flowers, preserving the ancient custom when such posies were carried to conceal the smell of the unwashed bodies of the prisoners. As late as the eighteenth century three Lord Mayors died from gaol fever caught from the prisoners at the Old Bailey sessions, and it was probably at about this time that herbs were strewn in the courts and around the docks, as they still are today on the specified days. Nearly two centuries earlier Culpeper tells us that rosemary was placed in the dock 'to comfort the heart and help a weak memory', but that of course was for the benefit of the prisoners.

On Remembrance Sunday (the Sunday nearest to 11 November) a service is held at the Cenotaph in London, and poppies are worn by the highest and humblest in the land in memory of the dead of two world wars. A Canadian doctor, John Macrae, after the first Battle of Ypres in 1915 wrote the poem which begins 'In Flanders' fields the poppies blow' and ends with the bittersweet lines: 'If ye break faith with us who die, We shall not sleep though poppies grow In Flanders' fields.' After the war a Frenchwoman, Madame Guérin, first had the idea of making artificial poppies. In 1921 they were made in France and sold in England, and in 1922 the Royal British Legion factory opened to raise money for the disabled and to provide work for them making the poppies we wear with pride today.

In 1977, as part of the celebrations to mark the Silver Jubilee of Her Majesty Queen Elizabeth II, the National Association of Flower Arrangement Societies of Great Britain (NAFAS) was privileged to place beneath the cloisters of Westminster Abbey an arrangement of spring flowers, 165 mm tall and 190 mm wide, standing in a silver dish on a base with a collage of more spring flowers. In order that the flowers should retain their bright colours, after being picked at the Royal Horticultural Society's Garden at Wisley, Surrey, they were taken at once to the natural history section of the British Museum, where they were freeze dried by a special process developed by the Department of Zoology. The arrangement, together with messages written by the officers of NAFAS and packets of seeds chosen in part for their interest to twentieth-century flower arrangers, was then encapsulated in a gas-filled container designed at Reading University. It is hoped that if

An arrangement of freeze-dried flowers by NAFAS for the Silver Jubilee of Her Majesty Queen Elizabeth II and opposite the message from the NAFAS Founder President enclosed with the arrangement
NAFAS Ltd

NAFAS

21a Denbigh Street, London SW1V 2HF Tel. 01-828 5145

As founder of the National Association of Flower Arrangement Societies of Great Britain, I, Mary Pope of Dorset, write this message in the year of the Silver Jubilee of Her Majesty Queen Elizabeth II – 1977.

Enhancing the beauty of sacred places with flowers has been a rewarding part of the work of the members of our Association.

Therefore it is with gratitude these flowers are placed with this message in the glorious Abbey of Westminster on behalf of one hundred thousand members.

Their united wish is that you of our future will continue to enjoy the beauty of flowers and the pleasure of flower arranging with the same love and enthusiasm that we experience today in Great Britain.

Wrackleford.
Dorchester.
Dorset.

The National Association of Flower Arrangement Societies of Great Britain
Affiliated with the Royal Horticultural Society

perhaps it is uncovered in time to come, the lovely arrangement and the thought behind it will convey to future generations our sense of beauty and gratitude – and that flowers will still be used in many ways to enrich their lives.

Bibliography

Back, Philippa. *Herbs about the House*. Darton, Longman and Todd, 1977.

Bairacli Levy. Juliette de *The Illustrated Herbal Handbook*. Faber and Faber, 1974.

Baker, Margaret. *Folklore and Customs of Rural England*. David and Charles, 1974.

Baker, Margaret. *The Gardener's Folklore*. David and Charles, 1977.

Bockee Flint, Martha. *A Garden of Simples*. Nutt, 1901.

Brentnall, Margaret. *Old Customs and Ceremonies of London*. Batsford, 1975.

Brownlow, Margaret E. *Herbs and the Fragrant Garden*. Darton, Longman and Todd, 1978.

Burbidge, F. W. *Domestic Floriculture*. Blackwood, 1875.

Burbidge, F. W. 'Fragrant leaves and scented flowers'. *Journal of the Royal Horticultural Society*, 1899.

Ceres. *Herbal Teas, Tisanes and Lotions*. Thorsons, 1981.

Coats, Peter. *Flowers in History*. Weidenfeld and Nicolson, 1970.

Coleman, Vernon. *The Language of Flowers*. Chilton Designs, 1973.

Conway, David. *The Magic of Herbs*. Cape, 1973.

Duff, Gail. *A Book of Pot-Pourri*. Orbis, 1985.

Eagle, Robert. *Herbs, Useful Plants*. BBC, 1981.

Friend, Rev. Hilderic *Flowers and Flower Lore*. Swan and Sonnenschein, 1892.

Gordon, Lesley. *Green Magic*. Ebury, 1977.

Grieve, M. *A Modern Herbal*. Cape, 1931.

Grigson, Geoffrey. *A Herbal of All Sorts*. Phoenix, 1959.

Hole, Christina. *The Dictionary of British Folklore and Customs*. Hutchinson, 1976.

Jacob, Dorothy. *A Witch's Guide to Gardening*. Elek, 1964.

Lehner, Ernst and Johanne. *Folklores and Odysseys of Food and Medicine*. Harrap, 1973.

Le Strange, Richard. *A History of Herbal Plants*. Angus and Robertson, 1977.

Leyel, C. F. *The Magic of Herbs*. Cape, 1926.

Macleod, Dawn. *A Book of Herbs*. Duckworth, 1968.

Northcote, Lady Rosalind. *The Book of Herb Lore*. Dover, 1971.

Ohrbach, Barbara Milo. *The Scented Room*. Sidgwick and Jackson, 1986.

Poucher, W. A. *Perfumes, Cosmetics and Soaps*. Chapman and Hall, 1932.

Powell, Claire. *The Meaning of Flowers*. Jupiter, 1977.

Stevenson, Violet. *The Encyclopaedia of Christmas and Festival Decorations*. Collingridge, 1963.

Woodward, Marcus (ed.). *Gerard's Herbal*. Bracken, 1985.

Georgian elegance

MARY SMITH

THROUGHOUT THE COMPLEX TAPESTRY OF HISTORY, flowers and plants have been enjoyed and used, their perfume captured and their beauty transported to the canvas or trapped in precious metal by craftsmen and women. To understand their relevance to daily life, in either a humble house or royal court, it is wise to look beyond at the framework of society, and to feel the penetrating fusion of past and present. The Georgian period, with its extremes of poverty and great wealth, its bitter political conflicts at both home and abroad, was also an age of superb craftmanship and gaiety, an age of elegance, an age of art.

When George I inherited the crown, he arrived in England, a foreigner speaking only his native German, to govern a turbulent country. Despite his ability to create complex alliances and his loyalty to the Whigs throughout his reign, he was disliked by his subjects who resented his long absences in Hanover. Yet following unsuccessful

Queen Charlotte by J. Zoffany
The Royal Collection, London

(*Note*: The photographs from The Royal Collection in this section are reproduced by gracious permission of Her Majesty the Queen.)

George III, Queen Charlotte and their six children. Detail including vase by J. Zoffany
The Royal Collection, London

Charlotte, Princess Royal and Prince William, later Duke of Clarence by J. Zoffany
The Royal Collection, London

attempts to restore the monarchy to the Stuart Pretender, James Edward, in 1715 and 1745, the house of Hanover was secure and its dynasty ensured by the succession of George II on the death of his father in 1727, to be followed by his son George III in 1760.

This period of our history, above all others, reflects the growing prosperity of both wealthy landowners and middle classes, with the more fortunate artisans and workers beginning to enjoy the benefits of better standards of living. England had become more settled in her domestic politics, less austere in her religion, and generally a more secular society.

Likewise in France there was a relaxation from the heavy Louis XIV Baroque style, and as court life became infused by a previously unknown gaiety, the arts became expressive of a lighter and more frivolous mood. Clearly, since the English were followers of continental style, this new 'modern' French was soon to be imported and to make an important contribution to changing Georgian taste.

An interest in both Chinese and Gothic styles became evident by the middle of the century; a combination of these was often to be seen in garden design. There had also been a return to Classicism by 1760, since it had become increasingly popular to study the antiquities of Italy and Greece on the Grand Tour. Britain was now playing a more important role in Europe; as travel had become more practical, the Grand Tour became an educational necessity for gentlemen of means. Archaeological discoveries at Herculaneum and Pompeii added to increased knowledge in this area, and inspired the reproduction of artefacts to sell to a public in England eager to share this enthusiasm. The publication of a number of volumes of engravings made the styles accessible to craftsmen and designers and enabled the vogue to spread more easily.

Enthusiasm for early Greek design led to the important contribution of Robert Adam (1728–92) to the architecture of the period. The son of an architect in Edinburgh, Robert Adam set up practice in London

Left *Queen Charlotte by T. Gainsborough*
The Royal Collection, London

Right *Queen Charlotte by J. Zoffany*
Holburne Museum, Bath

following a tour of Italy. His instinctive use of elegance in decorative design gave him great popularity amongst wealthy landowners anxious to design or improve their houses. One of the main features of Adam style was the design of everything in the house from the smallest detail in order to achieve complete harmony. His use of colour in interior decoration made an important change, using light backgrounds with white stucco ornamentation, and also red, yellow and black based on Pompeiian houses. The decoration of early Greek vases, mistakenly believed to be Etruscan, were a source of inspiration and his use of these designs is often to be seen.

Josiah Wedgwood, the Staffordshire potter, anxious to please public taste, was decorating his ware in classical style with encaustic colours. In the search for better paste he was able to produce a white stoneware of great delicacy eminently suited to the newer vogue for Adam decoration.

The transition of styles during the late eighteenth and early nineteenth centuries led to some conflict in the combination of style. This however was not evident out of doors, as houses were also built and specifically designed to blend into the landscape. The close relationship of house and surrounding land began to emerge as landscape gardeners (see later) and architects strongly influenced the popularity of this cult. The partnership of John Nash and Humphry Repton embraced this aspect of the picturesque. John Nash, more concerned with exteriors, developed much of the Crown farmlands at the beginning of the Regency period, building Cumberland Terrace and part of Regent Street in London.

Part of the confusion of Romanticism led to the design of the most bizarre of Regency buildings, the Royal Pavilion in Brighton. The house, Brighton House, was enlarged by Henry Holland for his patron the Prince of Wales, later to become George IV. Henry Holland had been closely linked to Lancelot 'Capability' Brown, landscape architect, by both profession and by his marriage to Brown's daughter. This liaison introduced him to an influential circle of friends and eventually to royal patronage. The interior was decorated to suit the Prince's taste for chinoiserie. Later, in 1815, John Nash was engaged to transform and extend the Royal Pavilion in the Indian style adopted for the picturesque qualities. The association of building and landscaping was a considerable achievement, and the unique decoration used in the interior was most exotic. Opulent and dignified, the Royal Pavilion stands today as the perfect monument to the stately dream of the King who cried for joy on contemplating its splendour.

The City of Bath is a further monument of all that Georgian society represented. Its Palladian architecture is considered one of the finest achievements of the period. The Royal Crescent was built between 1767 and 1775 by John Wood the Younger. Many wealthy and distinguished visitors travelled to Bath to 'take the waters' of the hot mineral springs. The rich and aspiring were devotees of the social rituals promoted by Beau Nash, who had succeeded in making Bath a centre of wealth and fashion. Cultural life also prospered, with leading actors and musicians of London entertaining during the busy winter season. Many artists found wealthy patrons anxious to indulge their

Captain William Wade by T.
Gainsborough
Bath Museums Service

vanities and boredom in portraiture. Bath was transformed from a
provincial spa town to a pleasure resort of international repute. The
Assembly Rooms, also designed by John Wood the Younger and
completed in 1771, were the setting for social assemblies of all kinds;
dancing, card playing, tea drinking and concerts could all be accom-
modated concurrently.

Meanwhile the influence of European design was frequently seen as
well as exotic oriental influences. The English love of flowers, massed
or individual, was characteristic. Flowers were used in both soft furnishing and fashion design in abundance. By the middle of the century
design had reached an increased elegance. Floral design became
daintier, with sometimes single scattered flowers or posies linked by
curving stems or ribbons. Bright colours were heightened by a white
background, often lively with naturalistic forms.

From 1824 striped chintz, usually associated with the period,
appeared with alternating vertical stripes and sprigs of flowers.
Towards the end of the period it became fashionable to copy accurately
large botanical drawings. It was only after 1820 that chintzes printed
entirely by machine were found in quantity. The indiscriminate use of
new mineral and chemical dyes such as antimony orange, Prussian
blue and cochineal pink often marred the high standard of draughts-
manship of these designs. The silk weaving industry of Spitalfields had
profited by the skills of French refugee weavers and was extremely
prosperous during the early period. Many original designs of patterned
silks are preserved in the Victoria and Albert Museum.

Development of the English garden

The eighteenth century in garden history heralds a shift from a strict formality derived from European influences over several hundreds of years towards the unrestricted stylized landscape usually associated with the period. Early attempts to break with the constraint in formality were made by William Kent, a versatile artist whose career ranged from architect, interior decorator and furniture designer to book illustrator and gardener. Kent opined that gardening was landscape painting and that nature abhorred a straight line. His contribution to the beginning of the new relaxation in garden design is considerable. His major achievements were the management of water to allow its natural beauty to dominate, and the release of the rigid boundary between building and garden. Walls disappeared to allow unrestricted viewing of the landscape, apart from those surrounding the kitchen garden, which was usually sited at some distance from the house. Trees were planted in small groups, and neo-Palladian buildings placed strategically around the garden emphasized his arcadian dream.

An important estate at Stowe in Buckinghamshire became much visited and was an influence on other landowners anxious to adopt the new style. Conventional enclosed gardens with parterre and terraces had been altered early in the century by Charles Bridgeman, whose work showed French influence. Changes were later made by Kent and finally by Lancelot Brown, who worked under Kent as head gardener. Brown, having been trained in practical gardening, eventually practised as a professional landscape gardener; he won acclaim for his further developments at Stowe and became the most fashionable landscaper of the day. He claimed he could always find 'capabilities for improvements' for his clients, and it was said that he would be least remembered when his genius was at its most creative since 'so closely did his works resemble nature that his works will be mistaken'. His concept of the idealized garden were that it should be totally unified into the landscape. Parkland with easily managed grazing areas soon replaced labour-intensive formal planting, with ha-has constructed to prevent cattle from straying into the ornamental lawns which led to the house itself. The planting of trees and the alteration of natural obstacles were all important factors in Brown's 'capability' plan for naturalizing the English country estate. Other gardeners were adopting the vogue for simplification of the landscape. One outstanding example is Stourhead in Wiltshire, largely created and developed by its owner Henry Hoare in the middle of the eighteenth century. Stourhead is considered to be one of the earliest and most perfect examples of picturesque landscaping. Small classic buildings, temples, grottoes and a rustic cottage set amongst woods and lakes with superb planting and views combine to delight the eye. Wilton House, owned by the Earl of Pembroke, is yet another garden epitomizing taste for the naturalistic.

Following Brown's death in 1783, Humphrey Repton, who had turned to landscape gardening in mid career, became a natural suc-

Josiah Wedgwood and his family in the grounds of Etruria Hall by G. Stubbs
Josiah Wedgwood & Sons Ltd

cessor. Repton's influence began to emerge as the garden with specialized effects was gradually brought back nearer to the house. The art
of flower arrangement in the garden was an important element of his
design. Parkland now became a background for the growing of the
newly acquired plants becoming available through explorations
abroad. New information was beginning to circulate more easily, with
books and catalogues distributed through horticultural societies. The
Gardener's Dictionary, published in 1772 by Philip Miller, the curator
of the Chelsea Physic Garden, was an important source of education
for a public now interested and aware of botanical and horticultural
changes. Miller described himself as 'Gardener to the Worshipful
Company of Apothecaries in their Botanick Garden in Chelsea'. The
Botanical Magazine, published in 1787 by William Curtis, provided a
valuable reference for porcelain decorators at a time when accurate
botanical decoration was the vogue. Engravings were copied by
eminent decorators from the magazines, which were sent by request
to the factories.

The development of the royal lands between Richmond and Kew led
eventually to their amalgamation and the beginning of an important
centre for plant research, made possible by the Princess of Wales,
Princess Augusta. Court had been held at Richmond Lodge by Queen
Caroline, wife of George II, whose interest in following landscape
fashion led her to employ Charles Bridgeman to lay out the garden in
a more natural style. Her son, Prince Frederick, later made a significant contribution to the modernization of the adjoining White House
estate, employing William Kent to do so. Prince Frederick's long friendship with the Earl of Bute, a keen botanist, led to the beginning of the
royal plant collections. The Prince and Princess Augusta were both
passionately interested in gardening, and following the Prince's death

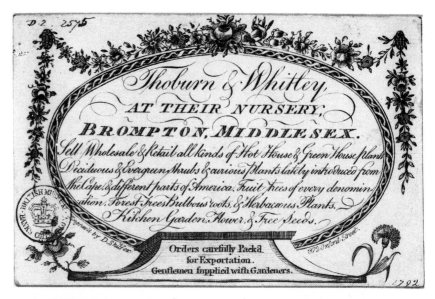

Tradesmen's cards
The British Museum

in 1751 the Princess continued the development of her garden. Sir William Chambers was employed as architectural adviser; his interest in oriental design led to the building of several Chinese buildings there, the most important being a pagoda which stands today as a monument both to chinoiserie and the royal influence in the development of the gardens at Kew.

An orangery was built to provide shelter for the tender exotics imported and bred, as well as for oranges grown in tubs for use in the court. The botanic garden flourished and, following Princess Augusta's death in 1772, the direction of it was given to Sir Joseph Banks, recently returned from a voyage of exploration to the South Seas with Captain Cook. The two estates were unified and became regarded as Kew Gardens, with George II and Queen Charlotte spending many years enjoying and developing their horticultural interest in their family home at Kew.

The popularity of plants

The wonders of plants introduced during the eighteenth century continued to inspire both amateur and professional alike. Sir Joseph Banks was instrumental in the formation of a society, the Horticultural Society, which first met in 1804 and whose aims were devoted to the improvement of breeding and cultivation of both useful and ornamental plants. The name became the Horticultural Society of London following the granting of a Royal Charter in 1809, and later the Royal Horticultural Society.

Amongst the many plants introduced and popularized for garden use were magnolias, camellias, lauristinus, weeping willow, wisteria, halesia, witch-hazel, hypericum, ceanothus and arbutus. Listed in Thomas Fairchild's nursery catalogue of 1722 are an extensive range of plants grown in his Hoxton nursery. Spring-flowering plants included stock, gillyflowers, wallflowers, tulips, anemones, ranunculus, polyanthus, primrose, auricula, fritillaries, lady's smock, Solomon's seal, geraniums, Persian lily, sweet William and monkshood. The vast multitude of summer blooms included scabious, day lily, columbines, lady's mantle, cytisus, iris, Canterbury bells, honeysuckle, lilac, Spanish broom, lupins, spiraea, golden rod, myrtle, passion flowers, mallow, chrysanthemum and antirrhinum. Winter flowers, greatly limited in number, included hellebore, snowdrops, aconite, hyacinth, cyclamen and mezereon.

A wave of enthusiasm for the raising of new plants often caught the popular imagination. The auricula was such a plant; new varieties were avidly collected as they emerged. They were displayed in auricula 'theatres' – tiered and sometimes velvet-lined showcases.

Over many centuries confusion had arisen over the naming of plants, with many names being given to the same plant. Clearly some form of classification was necessary. A binominal system of logical grouping of plants was introduced by a Swedish botanist Carolus

Linnaeus in 1753, and a refined form of the Linnaean system is in use today.

The most outstanding botanical illustrator of the era was George Dionysium Ehret (1708–20) who, after travelling widely, spent much of his life in England. He became popular with wealthy and influential patrons and contributed to important publications. Franz Bauer (1758–1840), an Austrian-born artist, illustrated many of the newly acquired plants at Kew where he had been appointed botanical draughtsman by Sir Joseph Banks. In 1730 the famous *Twelve Months of Flowers* was published by Robert Furber, a nurseryman. It was intended as a catalogue from which seeds, plants and bulbs could be ordered. The original paintings were done by a Flemish artist, Pieter Casteels; they show large, colourful massed arrangements which provide the clearest insight into the available plant material at the beginning of the Georgian period.

Flowers and their uses

The rapid growth of interest in gardening during the eighteenth century was soon reflected indoors by the decorative use of flowers and plants. Cultivated plants imported or brought back from continental visits made it necessary to invent ways of displaying and caring for them. Ranges of flower and bulb containers in new shapes were manufactured to be suited to every room. Myrtle pans and hooped pots were produced to suit evergreen plants and shrubs; many of these were situated in the corners of the large halls of country houses. Bough pots were for use on the hearth or under tables. Vases, often in garnitures of three, were used to furnish the chimney-piece. Flowers were not often used there, and more generally the vases were merely furnishings. Containers for flowers were preferred when designed to support the stems by perforated holes or spouts. Josiah Wedgwood, the distinguished pottery manufacturer whose wares won royal patronage and popularity, wrote that 'Ladies find they prefer those things with spouts … they say that sort keeps the flowers distinct and clever'; the spouts possibly referred to five-finger vases or to pyramidal tulip vases. The symmetry of the chimney-piece, influenced by the Adam brothers' designs, did not allow for flowers to destroy the overall effect.

Flowers were used extensively from drawing room to boudoir. They were fresh, dried or artificially made from silk, paper, straw, glass, ormolu or even shellwork. Out of season, thousands of women were employed making expensive but exquisite artificial flowers, and bouquets of dried flowers became popular.

Baskets of fresh flowers – geraniums, pinks or rosebuds – were a popular decoration for any room. Flower vases rested on stands, referred to as pedestals, candelabra, termini and monopodia; they were often of carved and gilded wood. Low pedestals were referred to as *table de marbre*, and taller ones as candelabra. The reservoir of such a stand, often assembled in stages, was lined with thin lead to contain water, over which thin silver network was placed as support. Flowers were

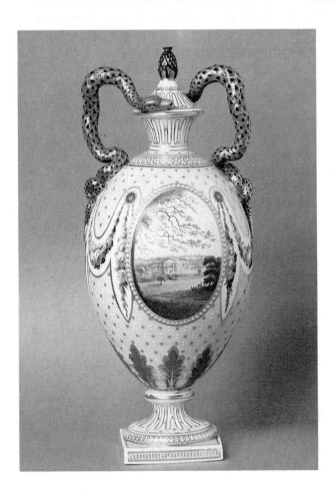

Left *One of a pair of rare cornucopia*
Derby City Museum

Right *Bough pot*
Derby City Museum

The Kedlestone Vase painted by James Banford, Zachariah Boreman and William Billingsley
Royal Crown Derby Museum

often taken off with the cover to change the putrefying water. Moss or sand was also used for support. Towards the end of the century flowers were arranged naturally with freedom and charm, having become an important feature of interior decoration. Previously only the occasional vase had been in use about the house, arranged in a more solid asymmetrical style or festooned on formal occasions.

The dining room often featured an elaborate table centrepiece, perhaps with fruit arranged pyramidically and decorated with leaves in low *compote* dishes. Mrs Hannah Glasse, in the *Art of Cookery* (1753), recommends 'a high pyramid of one salver above another ... these salvers to be filled with all kinds of wet and dry sweetmeats in glass and little knicknacks and bottles of flowers prettily intertwined'. *The Complete Confectioner* (1765) suggests 'centrepieces ... high flowers, images etc. dressed with grass, moss or other ornaments according to fancy'. A vogue for the indoor showing of bulbs led to root or bulb pots being used; the new designs were eagerly sought after.

Flowers were worn extensively by ladies of fashion and to some degree by men. Towards the latter part of the century, hair-styles had reached extremes of height and elaboration. Ornaments of every description were added to the mass of powdered and frizzled hair, including bunches of flowers, fruit, vegetables and even models of complete gardens and baskets of flowers. However, by the early nineteenth century elaborate trimmings had been discarded and a shorter classical style had become more popular. Flower ornaments, a French fashion, were worn in the evening to dress the curls and ringlets. By the mid 1820s the top-knot had developed into a skilfully dressed arrangement using wire frames and special pins. To suit this style

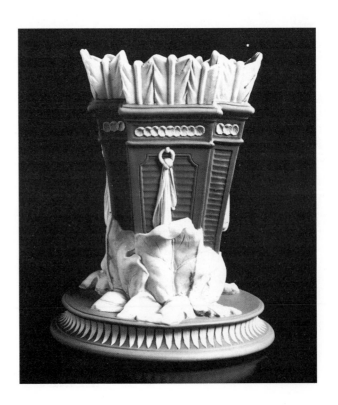

Solid blue and white jasper quiver or arrow vase
Josiah Wedgwood & Sons Ltd

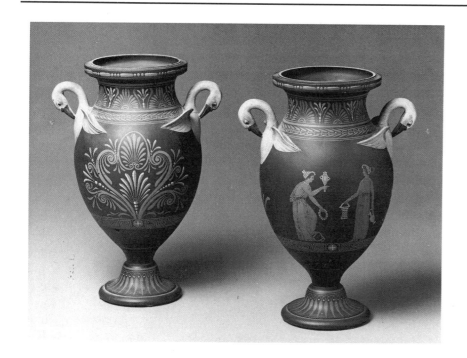

Top left *Pair of black basalt vases.* **Bottom left** *Pair of black basalt vases decorated with encaustic enamels.* **Bottom right** *Caneware vase in the form of four bamboo tubes*
Josiah Wedgwood & Sons Ltd

Collage by Mary Delany
The British Museum

flowers were added, wired in order to stand erect and often with ears of wheat.

Flowers were worn pinned to the shoulder of a dress or bodice, and are often seen used in this way in portraits. Men were also seen to wear flowers as buttonholes. Evidence of the use of flowers in paintings is limited in this period owing to the fashion for backgrounds of a landscape or classical scene in portraiture. However, a number of paintings of conversation pieces exist, showing flowers arranged in vases or baskets or other containers in use in the home.

Flowers were of course used as inspiration in many other ways, enhancing and enriching life for gentlewomen. Leisure hours could be profitably filled by painting, embroidery and other crafts. The art of paper cutting at its most skilful is to be seen in the work of Mary Delany, born in 1700; later in life she created a thousand specimens of paper mosaics, being botanically accurate records of plants of the period and now housed in the British Museum. Domestic needlework characteristic of the turn of the century was the embroidered picture, imitating in stitchwork the paintings of both old and modern masters. A collection of work by Miss Mary Linwood, a renowned worker in the style, is to be seen in the Leicester Museum.

Japanning, an English equivalent of oriental lacquer, became a popular pastime for women of the upper class. Hundreds of designs intended primarily for use by the amateur, but often used by the porcelain manufacturers, were published in *The Ladies Amusement* (1763). Designs included flowers, fruit and shells, and many can be seen in the Japan Room at Frogmore, decorated by Princess Elizabeth the daughter of George III.

The Georgian period, having begun under continental influence, has ended with a golden age of craftsmanship and a new longing and enthusiasm for horticultural knowledge. Plants and flowers have inspired and charmed their way into the fabric of history's page, an elegant reminder of an elegant age.

Bibliography

Ackermann, T. *Regency Furniture and Interiors.* Crowood, 1984.

Fisher, J. *The Origins of Garden Plants.* Constable, 1982.

Halliday, F. E. *An Illustrated Cultural History of England.* Thames and Hudson, 1967.

Harris, L. *Robert Adam and Kedleston.* National Trust, 1987.

Harvey, J. *Early Nurserymen.* Phillimore, 1974.

Hayden, Ruth. *Mrs Delany: Her Life and Her Flowers.* British Museum, 1980.

King, R. *The World of Kew.* Macmillan, 1976.

Plumb, J. H. *The First Four Georges.* Spring Books, 1974.

Ribeiro, A. *A Visual History of Costume.* Batsford, 1983.

Thomas, G. S. *Gardens of the National Trust.* Weidenfeld and Nicolson, 1979.

Thornton, P. *Authentic Decor: the Domestic Interior 1620–1920.* Weidenfeld and Nicolson, 1984.

Places to visit

Interiors, furniture, sculpture.
Kedleston Hall, Derbyshire
Bowood, Wiltshire
Victoria and Albert Museum, London
John Soane Museum, London
Kew Gardens, London
The Royal Pavilion, Brighton
Wilton House, Wiltshire
Saltram House, Devon
Arbury Hall, Warwickshire
Paintings
Kenwood House, London
Burghley House, Lincolnshire
National Gallery
National Gallery of Scotland
National Portrait Gallery
Holburne of Menstrie Museum, Bath
Porcelain, Jewellery, Silver
Nottingham Castle Museum
Ashmolean Museum, Oxford
Dyson Perrins Museum, Worcester
Wedgwood Museum, Barlaston, Staffordshire
Royal Crown Derby Museum, Derby
Derby City Museum
Gardens
Stourhead, Wiltshire
Lacock Abbey, Wiltshire
Wimpole Hall, Cambridgeshire
Cliveden, Buckinghamshire
Melbourne Hall, Derbyshire

The Victorians' flowers

DAPHNE VAGG

AT NO OTHER TIME IN HISTORY HAVE FLOWERS AND foliages been used in such abundance, or copied and adapted in so many ways, as in nineteenth-century Victorian England. Flowers were painted on furniture and china; modelled in metal, pottery and glass; carved in wood on tables, sofas and sideboards; moulded in plaster on walls and ceilings; modelled in leather and wrought in iron; inlaid in mother-of-pearl and marquetry; shaped for tulip glasses; cast as arum lilies for gas brackets and candle sconces; embroidered on bell-pulls and rugs in the fashionable Berlin work; painted on mirrors and articles of papier mâché; and festooned as ivy and convolvulus on wrought-iron gates. Even the lavatory pan did not escape, for the bowl was often decorated with elaborate roses, chrysanthemums or sprays of ivy.

Indoor plants and the fern craze

No Victorian home would have been without its quota of plants grown indoors in pots. The potted palm and the aspidistra were ubiquitous, and in the end became a joke, considered by the twentieth century as outrageous pieces of Victoriana. But ivy was even more popular, and yucca, agave, the rubber plant and the kangaroo vine almost as widespread.

Ivy, the symbol of persistent life amid death, lent itself to being trained in many ways, both indoors and out. It was used to outline arches over doors, windows and the frames of mirrors, and to swing in long garlands from brackets or to drape around statuary and busts. It could be encouraged to climb stairways and banisters, or to make a complete arbour round a sofa or alcove. When planted outside near a door or window it could be persuaded into the house to be trained in any desired manner. A white cross wreathed with snowy ivy was a much admired parlour ornament.

Equally ubiquitous were the ferns, popular throughout the whole of the Victorian era, but especially in mid-century when no home was complete without a display of fern plants. Quantities of common wild ferns were dug up in Wales and the Lake District of England and sent to the London markets, so that eventually even the poorest home could afford them. Although the plants were not happy indoors in the atmosphere of coal fires and gas lighting, they were soon found to thrive in a parlour or fern case. This sealed glass case had been developed in the 1850s by Doctor Nathaniel Ward, and became known as the Wardian case. In it, plants would live for a long time without watering, and this discovery was much used by plant hunters and botanists who were travelling the world in search of new plants. Their treasures could then be sent back to England, on long sea voyages through changing climates and temperatures, in comparative safety.

It also meant that decorative versions of the botanist's Wardian case could be made to house displays of plants in the home. Large and elaborately designed fern cases quickly became status symbols. They ranged from small table-top models to vast structures that were virtually conservatories. A modest version was to be found in almost every home, often fixed outside a window, so that the plants could be tended from inside, but enjoy as much light as possible and provide a living curtain against the gaze of passers-by.

Mignonette was another favourite indoor plant because of its sweet smell. Jane Loudon recorded that 'whole streets of London were quite oppressive with the odour of mignonette in early Victorian times; Mrs Beeton, when planning the garden of her new house, wrote: 'I have no partiality for anything but mignonette.' Many potteries, including Minton, produced attractive mignonette boxes in terracotta ware, often decorated with relief patterns of classical figures.

Floral decoration indoors

In grand houses it was the duty of the head gardener and his staff to arrange the flowers indoors, and this custom continued well into the twentieth century. They would bring indoors the treasures of the greenhouse and the cutting garden to decorate the rooms and the dining table and to impress their master's guests. In smaller homes the mistress and daughters of the house undertook this task of 'doing the flowers', and it was regarded as a very suitable occupation for young ladies.

A marked feature of indoor flower decoration at this time was the number of flower vases or bowls dotted about among the knick-knacks in the parlour or drawing-room. They often held bunches of just one type of flower, such as pansies, roses, lilacs, lilies of the valley, primroses or violets. As most vases and ornaments came in matching or complementary pairs, asymmetrical grouping or arranging did not come naturally to the Victorians and almost all flower arrangements were symmetrical.

Flower holders were of every conceivable (and inconceivable) shape and size. Glass vases or bowls were very popular, whether cut, blown, etched, moulded, milk, coloured, painted or gilded. In china or porcelain tall vases usually had narrow necks, but they could also be in

Girl in Interior. Photographer unknown, c. 1860. The photograph shows the contemporary fashion for a clutter of ornaments and vases of flowers dotted about the room
Victoria and Albert Museum

the shape of jugs, hands, baskets, shells, boots, boats, birds (swans in particular), heads, figures or animals. Spelter (a zinc alloy imitating bronze or pewter), silver, silver plate, copper and brass jugs and bowls were also used. Ladies often made their own containers from china mosaic work – small fragments of broken china of all sorts, patterns and colours were pressed into glue or a thin coating of plaster to decorate a clear glass vase or bowl. More painstaking was potichomanie, where coloured paper scraps and cut-out pictures of birds, flowers and scenes were glued, jigsaw-fashion, *inside* a clear glass vase, then coated with enough layers of varnish to become absolutely waterproof. A gilt rim was usually added to resemble Sèvres or Dresden china.

Flower vases almost invariably stood on a mat or doily made of crochet, lace-edged or embroidered fabric, velvet or plush with fringe or bobbles, or even crocheted in green and brown wools to simulate moss.

The flowers available for cutting at the end of the nineteenth century were almost as varied as they are today, but the Victorians had a special liking for bell-shaped flowers (lily of the valley, lily, campanula, convolvulus, gladiolus, gloxinia, bluebell and snowdrop) and curious forms such as antirrhinum, sweet pea, calceolaria, fuchsia and violet. Roses, of course, continued to be popular, and so were carnations, pinks, stocks, tuberoses, camellias, daisy-type flowers of all sorts and spring bulb flowers, especially any variety that was two-coloured, striped, streaked, blotched or picotee edged. Fussy flowers like gypsophila, viburnums, hebes, Michaelmas daisies and grasses of all types, whether wild or cultivated, were all used in season.

Much evergreen foliage from the shrubbery was used (laurel, yew, box, myrtle, cupressus and *Viburnum tinus*) and, of course, ivy and ferns, including smilax and asparagus. In their leaves also the Victorians favoured variegation if it was available, and grey-leaved plants, much used for garden bedding, were popular.

In the winter months, dried and pressed leaves, and immortelles or everlasting flowers, were much used for indoor decoration. The immortelles strictly comprised those composite flowers of papery texture which retain their colour when dried, such as helichrysum, rhodanthe and acroclinum, but pampas grass fronds (*Cortaderia selloana*) and other grasses, love-lies-bleeding (*Amaranthus caudatus*), Chinese lanterns (*Physalis franchetii*), silver honesty pennies (*Lunaria annua*), yellow heads of achillea, pressed fern and bracken, dried palm fronds and the seed heads of love-in-a-mist (*Nigella damascena*), iris, crocosmia and acanthus were also included.

Glass domes or shades, used to protect fragile bouquets of artificial

Interior at the 'Chestnuts', Wimbledon, 1867 by J. L. Dyckmans. The rounded bouquet of summer flowers and grasses in a glass vase would have been found in many homes
Victoria and Albert Museum

Photo: John Webb

Northwest Passage by Sir John E. Millais. The blue and white jug on the table holds a casual arrangement of daffodils, narcissi and lilies-of-the-valley
The Tate Gallery

flowers made of shells, wax or feathers, bowls of fruit or other intricate hand-crafted ornaments, were also used over dried flower arrangements and even over fresh ones.

Dressing the table

About the middle of the nineteenth century the way of serving meals in Britain changed completely, and it became fashionable to dine *à la russe*. It had long been the custom to set out all the food dishes on the table, spread with a white cloth, at the beginning of the meal. The dirty dishes accumulated through the courses until they and the (no longer white) cloth were 'drawn' by the servants after the cheese course. The dessert was then served without the white cloth. When the continental habit of dining *à la russe* was introduced, each course was served from

Photo: John Webb

The Empty Purse by James Collinson. Church bazaars became popular in the mid-nineteenth century and were crowded with examples of ladies' handicrafts. This picture includes a vase of fresh magnolias and their leaves under a glass dome or 'shade'
The Tate Gallery

a sideboard and then cleared by the servants, and it was no longer necessary for the cloth to be drawn.

Flowers and fruits could now be arranged on the tablecloth before the meal and did not need to be disturbed. Imagine what an opportunity this presented for increasingly elaborate and ostentatious display, as society hostesses vied with each other to produce more and more eye-catching decorations!

Soon great banks of greenery or pot plants supported towering palms; swans glided over pools of looking-glass; shrubs emerged from swathes of gauze or silk; fountains jetted up from blocks of ice; and to honour a special guest a jungle or desert scene might be created. Garlands of flowers and foliage were looped over wire arches or curved between individual place settings; trails of smilax linked the centrepiece with pyramids of fruit and patterns of overlapping geranium or ivy leaves swirled between the guests and the serving dishes. These patterns, even for breakfast, were shown in *Floral Designs for the Table* by John Perkins, published in 1877.

Dinner table à la russe
From *Mrs Beeton's Book of Household Management* (Ward Lock, 1895)

The epergnes used in grand houses in Georgian times were usually of silver and held sauces, pickles, sweetmeats and fruit. In the nineteenth century the many-trumpeted epergne, usually in glass with metal mounts and sometimes with baskets hung on barley-sugar curls, became the centrepiece for even quite modest table decorations. (The origin of the word 'epergne' is not known, but it is not French as one might expect.) The glass was either clear or shaded with colour – a rosy red, a rather harsh grassy green or a 'Vaseline' yellow.

There is also some confusion over the exact difference between an epergne and a March stand, named after T. C. March, a head gardener, who wrote *Fruit and Flower Decoration* in 1862. This stand was described as having 'a glass dish as a base with a slender glass stem from

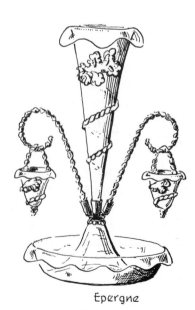

March stand and epergne

March stand   Epergne

twelve to fifteen inches in length, on top of which rests a smaller glass dish and from the centre of this a cornucopia or trumpet-shaped vase'. Miss Maling, writing in *Flowers and How to Arrange Them* in 1862, favoured the 'single cornucopia', a glass trumpet stemming directly from a glass dish base. Her book gives much information on flower arrangements of the time. It was followed by Annie Hassard's *Floral Decoration for the Dwelling House* in 1870 and F. W. Burbidge's *Domestic Floriculture* in 1874, so there is no lack of contemporary information about the style of decoration and the flowers and foliage used. Every conceivable part of every centrepiece was filled with tightly packed stems arranged in moss or just supported by the sides of the container. Grasses or ferns often provided a top-knot, with trails of fern, smilax, ivy, honeysuckle or jasmine to soften the whole effect. Fruit was sometimes piled in the base dish, or arranged as formal pyramids on separate dessert stands or *tazzas*, usually with a frill of evergreens or a lace-edged doyly.

A number of subsidiary arrangements was usual even on a small dinner table. Sometimes there were posies piled in the centre, one for each lady guest, to be taken at the end of the meal. Menu holders also incorporated small containers for flowers, and on special occasions the cloth was swagged at the sides, looped with trailing smilax and caught up with posies of flowers.

In 1861 the Royal Horticultural Society held its first flower arrangement competition 'for the decoration of a dinner table ... Baskets of any materials, china vases, glass dishes or epergnes' could be used. The prizes were awarded by a jury including two countesses, two other titled ladies and one plain Mrs. The first prize went to T. C. March (mentioned above), though it was understood that his sisters actually did the arrangement! The three light, dainty March stands with maidenhair and other ferns, forget-me-nots, lilies of the valley, pansies, rosebuds and small bunches of grapes set a new standard for table decoration, which had previously been heavier and more solidly

A buffet for a wedding reception and an effective use of smilax, flowers and fruit as table decorations
From *The Art of the Table* by C. Herman Senn (Ward Lock)

massed, with large pineapples and huge bunches of grapes virtually obligatory.

Later in the century it became fashionable to have dinner and luncheon tables in matching colours, rather than the mixed colours previously preferred. Mrs de Salis, in her book *Floral Decoration à la Mode* (1891), is a mine of information on this, describing pink, green, yellow, old gold, lavender and primrose dinners. At the green dinner:

> The dining room was a bower of palms and tree ferns. Across the entire length of the white tablecloth was a broad strip of green plush thickly fringed with maidenhair fern. The centre of the table was a bed of ferns and lycopodium; in each corner were tall stem-glasses filled with green grass. Among the ferns and grasses were six fairy lights of pale green glimmering like fireflies. Before each guest was placed a bunch of lilies of the valley and maidenhair fern, tied with green ribbons. The soup was a purée of asparagus, the dinner service of green and white china, and the ices were also coloured. The menus were thick cards of bronze green stamped with copper, and the guest cards were in the shape of gongs. The glass service consisted of three shades of green.

This fashion was followed by theme tables, such as a Japanese table, an ocean flower table, a St Patrick's Day dinner, a hunt dinner and a wild flower table. The ingenuity was limitless, and 'the expense of the flowers amounting often to as much as that of the dinner itself' according to Mrs de Salis.

Personal adornment

The lady going out in the evening to dine, dance or attend the threatre would have felt quite improperly dressed without fresh flowers worn as a corsage, or in her hair, tucked in at the waist, pinned to her reticule or muff, as a wrist or arm band or used to catch up the flounces of her skirt. Bosom bottles – small phials to hold water – were tucked between the breasts to keep fresh the flowers worn with *décolleté* dresses. By day, she might have a spray of fresh flowers pinned to her hat or lapel.

She would also have carried a posy. Most often it would have been made of concentric circles, each of one type of flower, herb or leaf. A rose or a lily was fastened to a short stick for the centre, and then successive rings of flowers and leaves were tied firmly to the stick. A lace, paper or net doily, or sometimes a frill of leaves, was used as an edging. The flowers in the posy usually carried a message in the language of flowers. Although flower symbolism goes far back in history, never can so many plants have had a meaning given to them before. Scarcely a plant escaped the attention of the Victorians, and lists were so extensive that publishers brought out sign manuals or code books from which ladies could translate the message they received or compose one in the posy they were making.

Small posy holders, or *porte-bouquets*, were made to carry the posies. From about 1850 to 1875 they were highly fashionable; many were exquisite pieces of craftsmanship and are collectors' items today. The funnel-shaped holder was packed with wet sponge or moss to keep the flowers fresh and was secured with a long pin pushed through the holder and stems with a screw at the other side. Some had a ring to slip over the finger while dancing, and others a handle that sprang out into a tripod to hold the posy upright on the table during dinner or later, at home, on the dressing-table.

Cunning work for clever fingers

The title of this section is taken from a series in *The Art Journal* of 1898, and typifies the Victorian attitude to what was considered suitable for ladies to occupy their time with. Under similar titles all ladies' magazines of the time carried detailed craft items. Victorian women, with little chance of a career, or of leaving home until they married, were expected to be home-markers and to beautify the home as well as run

Photo: C. L. Patrick

A collage of dainty seaweeds arranged in a basket
Museum of Childhood, Edinburgh

it. Even quite modest middle-class homes usually had a daily maid, and a woman 'to do the rough', and as there might be several daughters of the house as well as the mistress, there were a number to share the task of home-making. As it was firmly believed that 'the devil found work for idle hands', wives and daughters were expected to occupy their hands and improve their minds throughout the day. Young women were encouraged to paint and draw, play the piano, embroider, study nature and generally concern themselves with making things. Flower arrangement and a host of handicrafts were among their accomplishments, and magazines were full of instructions and patterns so that even the least artistic could achieve something acceptable.

Handicrafts were wide ranging, and included many which used plant materials such as rustic twigs, seeds, cones, skeletonized leaves, seaweed and pressed flowers and leaves. Pressing was the simplest and most effective way of preserving botanical specimens brought home from walks or visits for further study, and albums of such pressings embellished with sketches, verses, recipes and the like made permanent attractive mementoes. Pictures and greetings cards soon became popular, and even quite large screens, firescreens and smaller items like table-mats were decorated with pressed flowers and leaves, then varnished over to preserve them permanently.

'Phantom' pictures and arrangements were made with skeletonized leaves and seedheads, laboriously (and somewhat dangerously) prepared in a solution of chloride of lime to dissolve the fleshy parts and leave the skeletonized veins. Washed, dried and pressed if necessary, they were then used for a picture in a deep, boxed frame or for an arrangement under a glass dome, or 'shade' as it was more commonly called.

The later Victorians had a passion for rustic work of all kinds. Not only were arbours, arches, tables and chairs made from poles and branches still with their bark on for use in the garden, but indoors too small tables, hat-stands, picture frames and the like were carried out in the same way, though with more carefully finished and polished 'rustic' wood. Ladies adopted this rustic work using fine twigs for frames for their pictures and cartes-de-visite (small photographic portraits mounted on a visting card about 90 by 65 mm), stands to hold goldfish bowls or plants, and fern baskets to hang or to stand on a table.

Many kinds of cones were carefully collected from the garden or on country walks to fill empty fire grates in summer and to decorate boxes, brackets or stands for plants. The cones were glued to the box or stand, then usually varnished, to create the effect of wood carving.

The garnishing of churches

It was inevitable that the devout, regularly church-going Victorians would tackle the task of decorating their churches with all the zeal they showed in arranging flowers on the table and generally in the home. Nor was it surprising that handicrafts, as well as flowers in vases, should play an important part. The interest in church decoration produced a number of books on the subject, often by clergymen who sought to guide their flock both in practical ways and in matters of taste.

In the middle of the nineteenth century, flower arrangements on the altars of Protestant churches were still a matter of some controversy. They were not approved by all churchmen, though floral decoration in other parts of the church was acceptable. Peter Anson comments in his *Fashions in Church Furnishing 1840–1940* that by 1850 'vases of flowers had not yet become popular', but by 1870 the placing of flowers on the altar had been proclaimed 'an innocuous and not unseemly decoration'.

At this time, following Catholic traditions, white flowers were generally preferred on the altar; the emphasis was on roses, eucharis and other lilies and narcissi in season. Daffodils were added at Easter and holly with its red berries at Christmas, so that by the time Mrs de Salis wrote her book in 1891 she could describe 'poinsettias, snowy eucharis lilies, maidenhair fern and holly' looking lovely on the altar.

On the font, too, white was preferred, and it was elaborately trimmed for christenings. White flowers such as lilies of the valley, Cape white flowers (chincherinchees? gladioli?), arums, lilac, azaleas, narcissi and hyacinths were pushed into banks of damp moss, laid over waterproof paper to avoid staining, to make a wreath at the top and round the base 'with white satin bows here and there'.

Windowsills and the base of the altar rails were treated in much the same way, also on waterproof paper described as 'two sheets of whitey-brown lining paper with a coating of india-rubber or gutta percha between'. Generally more colourful flowers were introduced here, especially with small, mixed spring flowers such as violets, primroses, crocuses and anemones, and with bright dahlias, chrysanthemums and Michaelmas daisies at harvest time.

The harvest festival provided a great opportunity for colourful decoration throughout the church, with sheaves of corn, loaves, coloured leaves, fruits, berries, vegetables and flowers as we do today. Contemporary writers also mention specifically the use of brambles, gourds, grasses, vines, red cabbages, teasels, capsicums, bulrushes and pampas plumes. Gas standards were 'wreathed and bunched with evergreens or decorated with banners' and pots of plants were banked at the foot of pulpit and lectern.

Much good advice was offered to church arrangers, such as being sure to obtain the consent of the churchwardens before decorating the church; to prepare and sort out the plant materials beforehand; and 'to ensure that all that have to use scissors should have them fastened by a string to the waist'!

Handicrafts, rather than flower arrangements as such, were employed in the form of 'devices', or emblems, which we should nowadays call collages. They were used as set pieces on the reredos behind the altar, above arches and windows and on areas of plain wall in the nave and chancel. The foundations for these banners, tablets and emblems could be bought ready-made from many church furnishers in a variety of shapes: all kinds of crosses, stars, circles, triangles, sheaves (for harvest), panels for the font or pulpit, crowns and religious insignia such as IHS. What could not be bought, the local carpenter or church handyman could make. Perforated zinc was often used, or wooden frames covered with wire mesh, or a strong millboard which was often preferred because it had the advantage that it 'admitted of a strong needle and thread being passed through it', whereas the zinc cut through the thread. In 1873 millboard could be bought at 4d (about 2p) for a sheet measuring 900 by 1500 mm.

On these foundations church decorators glued or sewed their designs, mostly in plant materials such as ivy and laurel leaves, fir, ferns, berries, silver honesty 'pennies', holly at Christmas, everlasting flower heads, moss and the heads of fresh flowers such as dahlias, garden daisies, camellias and other 'blossom work'. Trellis panels were very popular because the diamond pattern showed up well; W. A. Barrett, in his *Flowers and Festivals* in 1873, suggested that where no reredos existed, a screen of trellis-work should be made to stand round the back and two sides of the altar. The wood frame was to be 'covered with evergreens so as not to destroy the lines of the pattern, and at each intersection a small bouquet of flowers might be placed, the least valuable at the sides and the choicest on the dossal [back]'.

Other devices included patterns with texts and verses, the lettering and other decoration carried out in evergreen leaves, 'coarse Dunstable straw, sold for making bonnets', rice (to look like carved ivory), cork (hardly distinguishable from old wood carving), leather (like modern wood carving), honesty (like silver or mother-of-pearl) or white cotton-wool pasted on to paper strips. Mrs de Salis wrote that 'a little book of all church emblems, appropriate texts, designs for banners, etc. could be had gratis from a firm in the Strand', and alphabets could be bought ready to fix on chancel walls, where appropriate verses and texts could be attached. Red or blue cloth (velvet, baize or sateen) was favoured as a backing to show up the letters.

The decoration of pillars seems to have been far more elaborate than it is today. W. A. Barrett gave a number of different, mainly geometrical designs of leaves overlapped on tiling laths fixed to the pillars, or sprung to fit firmly between the base and the entablature. Flowers added to such decorations were in 'small invisible tubes that are sold for the purpose' and hidden in the greenery. One design shows long sprays of common bramble spiralled round a pillar.

The church decoration of the time did not meet with universal approval. Pugin, in his *Present State of Ecclesiastical Architecture* (1843), commented:

> Every reflecting mind must be both struck and pained with incongruous decorations of most of the modern altars; the chief aim of those who arrange them appears to be merely a great show ... everything is overdone. Candlesticks are piled on candlesticks as if arranged for sale; whole rows of flower pots mingled with reliquaries, images and not unfrequently, profane ornaments; festoons of upholsterer's drapery; even distorting and distracting looking glasses are introduced into this medley display; the effect of which upon persons who are conversant with ancient discipline and practice it is not easy to describe.

In church, as in so many other ways, the Victorians tended to overdo their floral decorations!

Bibliography

Barrett, W. A. *Flowers and Festivals*. Rivingtons, 1873.

Mrs Beeton's Book of Household Management. Ward Lock and Co, 1895.

Buczacki, Stefan. *Creating a Victorian Flower Garden*. Collins, 1988.

Burbidge, F. W. *Domestic Floriculture*. William Blackwood & Sons, 1875.

Earle, C. W. *Pot-pourri from a Surrey Garden*, 1899.

Elliot, Brent. *Victorian Gardens*. Batsford, 1987.

Geldart, Ernest. *The Art of Garnishing Churches*. Mowbray, 1882.

Geldart, Ernest. *A Manual of Church Decoration and Symbolism*. Mowbray, 1899.

Hibberd, Shirley. *Rustic Adornments for Homes of Taste*. 1856, 1870.

Lansdell, Avril. *Wedding Fashions 1860–1980*. Shire Publications Ltd, 1983.

Lasdun, Susan. *Victorians at Home*. Wiedenfeld and Nicolson, 1981.

Scourse, Nicolette. *The Victorians and their Flowers*. Croom Helm, 1983.

Taylor, Jean. *Flowers in Church*. Mowbrays, 1976. Chapter 13, p. 145.

Art Nouveau and the Edwardian era

PAMELA SOUTH

Art is the flower, life is the green leaf.
Let every artist strive to make his flower a beautiful thing.

Charles Rennie Mackintosh

THE END OF THE NINETEENTH CENTURY AND THE CLOSE OF Queen Victoria's long reign found Britain with a vast overseas empire and an expanding and prosperous middle class, both the results of wealth engendered by Britain's pre-eminence in the Industrial Revolution. Yet right across Europe there were already to be heard the rumblings of revolutions to come, the beginnings of socialism and a slow awakening to the need for society to make better use of women's talents. Artists and craftsmen were also rebelling against centuries of stifling classicism and traditional academic formulas. A new art was sought for a new age.

An early group of artistic rebels, called the Pre-Raphaelite Brotherhood, led the way under Dante Gabriel Rossetti, John Everett Millais and William Holman Hunt. Their use of a strong symbolic content, derived from legend and using flowers and fruit to establish this mythological connection, was to remain a profound influence on the emergent new style, called Art Nouveau in Britain. The Pre-Raphael-

A gold brooch enriched with translucent enamels designed by C. Desrosiers and made by Georges Fouquet of Paris
Victoria and Albert Museum

ites' love of muted colourings carried over into Art Nouveau paintings, epitomized by the mystic aura of a twilight dream world often associated with this *fin de siècle* period.

Britain was in the forefront of the Art Nouveau movement, with the influence of the writings of the art critic Ruskin and the artist designer William Morris being particularly significant. Morris deplored the general decline in true craftsmanship brought on by the Industrial Revolution, particularly castigating the mass-produced goods so proudly displayed at the Great Exhibition of 1851 in London as 'tons and tons of unutterable rubbish'. His aim was to encourage groups of artists and craftsmen, working through a revived form of the old medieval guilds, to produce objects of beauty that would transform the drab lives of ordinary working people. The Arts and Crafts Movement and the Century Guild embraced many of these laudable objectives. But sadly Morris had somehow overlooked the mundane practicalities; such objects, by virtue of their being hand made, were priced beyond the reach of the common working man.

Venus Verticordia by Rossetti
Russell-Cotes Art Gallery and Museum, Bournemouth

Photo: Harold Morris, photographer to the museum

The Woodpecker – high warp tapestry designed by William Morris and woven at Morris & Co., Merton Abbey 1885
The William Morris Gallery, Walthamstow, London

However, a felicitous result was that some truly beautiful individual objects were created in silver, ceramics and glass or as tapestries and furniture. Ironically, it was not until shops such as Liberty of London commissioned designs for mass production, from designers such as Archibald Knox and Rex Silver, that the new style became readily available and the overall standards of the mass market were thereby raised. Liberty sold distinctive vases in two series, called Cymric for silver and Tudric for pewter. The decoration might include enamelling or inset opals or *cabochon* turquoises or a linear decoration of Celtic *entrelac*. Ceramic vases much influenced by the Arts and Crafts movement were made by Royal Doulton, the Martin Brothers, William de Morgan, Moorcroft and the Poole Pottery, whilst Walter Crane designed for Wedgwood.

This Art Nouveau style swept in turn through Europe and North America, seeking to transform mankind's environment, whether it be via his buildings, his furniture, furnishings and ornaments, by vases, dress fashions, cutlery or jewellery. A comprehensive local variant developed in Italy called 'Stile Liberty'; in France 'Style Moderne' or 'Nouille' evolved, while in Germany the movement was called 'Jugend-stil' and in Austria 'Sezessionstil'. Thus, within the overall movement, there were wide local variations. Inate conservatism, however, ensured that the British Arts and Crafts Guild members never indulged in the wilder excesses of form or artistic decadence espoused by the European Symbolists.

The British painter and visionary William Blake had shown at the start of the century what could be achieved artistically through the use of extenuated line. Then through the medium of woodblock prints and with their flower arrangements the Japanese introduced other novel influences in the use of line and asymmetrical form. The distinctive classical Japanese form which had burst upon the world stage at the 1862 International Exhibition held in London was a complete revelation to European artists looking for new sources of inspiration. The emergence of Japan from her self-imposed 250 years of cultural isolation was in turn to play its part in shaping the Art Nouveau movement.

Japanese woodblock prints were collected and admired by artists such as Gauguin, Whistler, Toulouse-Lautrec and Van Gogh, and in turn subtly influenced their works. Van Gogh painted many studies of flowers direct from nature; movement of line and rhythm positively flowing through his canvases, causing him to observe that 'Painting promises to become more like music, less like sculpture.' The Japanese in their turn are now amongst the foremost admirers and collectors of Van Gogh's works.

Photo: Pamela South

Water lilies
From *The Theory of Japanese Flower Arrangement* by Josiah Conder (Kegan Paul, Trench, Trubner & Co. Ltd, 1935)

In 1889 Josiah Conder penned a very influential book, *The Theory of Japanese Flower Arrangements*, substantially introducing this art form into the mainstream of European artistic consciousness. He noted how Japanese flower arrangement stresses simplicity, asymmetrical form and the use of line to give vitality. In stark contrast to the prevalent European massed bouquet style of the time, where very little of the stems were visible and greenery only played a humble supporting role, the Japanese showed that flowers do not need to be of dominant importance in an arrangement.

In ikebana, or the art of Japanese flower arrangement (see Chapter 2), it is the lines of growth which give character and are emphasized by skilful selection, shaping and pruning. From such influences sprang the Art Nouveau convention of often using only one flowering branch of visually interesting shape in an Art Nouveau vase. There was no question of striving to follow Japanese rules slavishly; rather there was an appreciation of their simplicity and beauty of line. All the principal floral writers of this period drew attention to the Japanese style, with William Robinson finding that 'the Japanese ways of arranging flowers are extremely interesting and may sometimes be practised with advantage.'

Two shops, Siegfried Bing's La Maison de l'Art Nouveau in Paris and Liberty in London, acted as Meccas for artists, because these stores were importing the newly available and highly prized oriental objects, including fabrics and vases. At the same time they were encouraging and stocking the new domestic Art Nouveau designs. Liberty so aspired to influence public taste that not only would complete cohesive home interiors be created, but also the hostess would be freed from the constraints of her whaleboned corsets. The 'picturesque fashions' in the aesthetic mode featured graceful flowing dresses made of Liberty's soft draping fabrics, in which the mistress of the house could both retain her natural waistline and freely move her arms as she gently placed a bough of cherry blossom in her newly acquired Japanese bronze vase.

The Art Nouveau and Japanese influences led to simplicity of arrangement being associated with good taste. Simplicity of design, when executed artistically with some variation of material, came to be seen to be delightful. But with overpopularity a few stiffly arranged carnations and some sprays of fern in an upright glass vase were often passed off as artistic enlightenment. The Japanese influence also encouraged a restriction in flower arranging to the use of one or at most two kinds of flower with long, beautiful stems. Lilies were especially appreciated, being displayed in tall elegant vases simply to show the whole character of the plant and its foliage. People were urged to adopt this style for aesthetic reasons, not for economy. It was an age of conspicuous display, with the rising middle classes openly aping the aristocracy, often showing unrestrained vulgarity thereby. Somehow, some deep-seated need in the British psyche seems to require a mixed bunch of flowers, but even these began to be arranged more freely, with space between the flowers and a limitation placed on the number of forms selected.

In gardens, the combined influences of William Robinson and Gertrude Jekyll campaigned against the prevailing tyranny of labour-intensive carpet bedding. Their eloquent advocacy of the virtues of mixed herbaceous borders employing hardy plants, and of the wild garden, slowly led to more interesting foliage becoming available for use in the new more open style of flower arrangement. Robinson was a man of decided views, championing the humbler man against the prevailing pre-eminence of the professional formal gardener. He emphasized his dislike of gardens that were a sea of showy labels: 'There is no more need to speak of the plants in our gardens by their Latin names than to speak of the dove or rabbit by Latin names.' He also advocated leaving to stand in winter the stems of grasses and all herbaceous flowers, instead of cutting them down to expose a sea of tidy mud. He showed that careful groupings in the garden of stems with their greys and browns, when combined with the beauty of seedheads, could be an object lesson in the use of refined colour and beauty. Greyed foliage was particularly beloved of Gertrude Jekyll, who extensively planted *Stachys lanata*, *Cineraria maritima*, rue, santolina, echinops, lavenders, catmint and eryngium. Such colour sensibility epitomized the Art Nouveau appreciation of a subtle colour palette, one which did not favour sharp contrasts but rather appreciated soft harmonies of tints and tones.

It was from nature that the early themes of Art Nouveau received their inspiration, with their predominantly floral motifs characterized by strong asymmetrical line, flowing, curving, sinuously winding back

The whip lash – a silk embroidery wall hanging
Munich State Museum (the original picture is in the Munich City Museum)

upon themselves as in a whiplash or vanishing as in a plume of smoke. Floral designs predominated, with their tendrils, buds, flowers and leaves swaying on the stems of stylized plant forms. However, there were other motifs, including fantastic insects, particularly butterflies, dragonflies, moths and bats. From out of the oceans and swirling waves came fishes, seahorses, seaweeds and darting goldfish, swiftly changing direction. Yet it was a bird, the magnificent male peacock with its surrealistic 'eyes' adorning its tail feathers, which became almost a symbol of the whole movement. In his all-embracing decoration of the Peacock Room of a London House (1876), now preserved in the Smithsonian Institute in Washington DC, the noted contemporary artist Whistler provided a coherent but most expensive expression of the motif. He painted over the leather-embossed panels of the room and, because the border of the Persian rug clashed with his decoration, he cut it off!

The self-appointed arbiters of taste were the Aesthetic Group, led by Whistler, the illustrator Aubrey Beardsley, and the wit and playwright Oscar Wilde, who also lectured on decoration in the United States. Gilbert and Sullivan poked gentle ridicule at them in their light opera 'Patience':

> Though the Philistine may jostle
> You will rank as an apostle
> In the high aesthetic band
> As you walk down Piccadilly
> With a poppy or a lily in your medieval hand.

Certainly there was some conscientious posing amongst those of the artistic world. On one occasion Oscar Wilde was to be seen stepping backwards into a room in the path of the reigning society beauty, Lillie

Langtry, scattering roses in her path. At other times he was observed wearing a blue carnation, a daisy or a sunflower in his buttonhole. Sunflowers immediately appeared in all the smart drawing-rooms in imitation! The instantly recognizable statement of one's aesthetic sensibilities was to have a vase of peacock feathers waving across your drawing room, furnished in the Stile Liberty, to a tall upright vase of lilies.

Gradually the artistic stylization of plant forms moved off into the realms of pure fantasy, with artists such as Odilon Redon creating new flowers with a life of their own. Famous Art Nouveau artists produced pattern books and design manuals, such as Grasset's *La Plante et ses applications ornamentales* in 1898, *Combinasions Ornamentales* by Vermeuil, Auriol and Mucha in 1900, and *Das Weib in Modern Ornament* by H. Anker and J. Klinger in 1904.

The plant motif was everywhere, the winding stem being quite as important as the flower. The most favoured flowers in art were lily, poppy, rose (both briar and climbing forms), waterlily, iris and chrysanthemum. Other frequently depicted plants included honeysuckle, convolvulus, acanthus, narcissus, marigold, speedwell, pimpernel, nasturtium, tulip, echinops, onopordon, thistle, bullrush, and grasses and berries in great variety. Flowers which hang their heads, such as wisteria, fuchsia, snowdrops, lilies of the valley, Solomon's seal, cyclamen, bluebells and violets were also popular, together with the foliage of vitis, arum and palm and the seed heads of the poppy, honesty (*Lunaria*), Chinese lanterns (*Physalis franchetii*), ivy (*Hedera*) and pampas (*Cortaderia*).

Woman the siren, the temptress, was another dominant art motif, with her tresses flowing like seaweed or long noodles. Often she was bare bosomed and swathed in swirling draperies; at times her lower limbs metamorphosed into plant form. Reality and fantasy intermingled, with erotic overtones. A vast outpouring of Art Nouveau postcards and posters by artists such as Alfons Mucha helped spread the stylized image of this woman, often crowned with flowers and poppies.

The undoubted jewellery genius of the Art Nouveau period was René Lalique. His exquisite designs, taken from nature, featured unusual selections of plant forms such as willow, catkins, cow parsley, thistle, pine cones, pansy, wisteria, peaflower, berries, holly and raspberry leaf, as well as the standard poppy flower, so symbolic of sleep, dreams and narcotic images. The creations were stunningly executed with baroque pearls, opals, semi-precious stones and metals, often heightened by beautiful enamelling.

Art Nouveau plant selections caused Europeans to profoundly reassess what they considered to be beautiful in floral terms. Now not just massed brightly coloured floral bunches were considered to be beautiful. The scope of floral appreciation expanded to include the delicacies of bud, stem, berry and tendril in sensitive, muted colourings. This new perspective was to have a lasting effect on garden design, with the selection and grouping of plants for year-round beauty of form and leaf colouring. For the first time there was a general acceptance that foliage had sufficient beauty to stand alone. This new influence even extended as far as Court circles through Queen Alexandra who, whilst still Princess of Wales, took to having large vases of common beech displayed in the drawing rooms at Marlborough House.

Emile Gallé, founder of the Nancy school of design, was the leading French glassmaker with his own distinctive Art Nouveau style, one which had a great influence on very many others. He specialized in using two or more colours, a favourite combination being amethyst and grey. Decorations of flowers, foliage and insects flowed round his elegant vases, which often had elongated narrow necks. The Daum Frères, glassmakers also working in Nancy, evolved their own similar style.

In the United States, Louis Comfort Tiffany, son of the founder of the jewellery firm, was greatly inspired by William Morris. Tiffany established an interior decorating business, supplied in part by his own glassworks. He is particularly famous for his favrile glass, handmade and iridescent, with which he created beautiful fluid plant forms. His enchanting and highly prized floral lamps, with their shades of glowing jewel colours in opalescent glass mosaics, are amongst the most recognizable of all Art Nouveau objects.

Many of the glass vases made by these master craftsmen were beautiful in their own right. They proved easier to use as containers if they were not too heavily decorated. Yet, with sensitive selection of plant material, the line of almost any applied decoration could be rhythmically extended upwards through the selection of stems, ending with tendrils, curving seed pods or berries. Stiffness of added fresh material had to be avoided, or there would be disharmony with the fluidity promoted by the shape of the vase.

The Scottish architect, designer and painter Charles Rennie Mackintosh, leader of the Glasgow school of design, possessed a unique talent, greatly misunderstood in his own country, but widely recognized on the Continent. His place in history was at the forefront of the second wave of Art Nouveau style, one which promoted a far greater simplicity, combining predominantly straight lines with very gentle curves as well as intricate flat flower patterns, deriving their early Celtic entwining motif from ancient illuminated manuscripts.

All his life Mackintosh loved flowers, which he delighted to paint in watercolours. From these studies he abstracted delicate linear stem-like lines, with the flowers being translated into newly stylized abstract forms. His oriental approach to the handling of spatial relationships and his light but austere interiors are well illustrated by his drawings for a design competition in 1901. Included in the interior furnishings were a matching pair of tall slim vases holding long-stemmed roses and, in another part of the room, a separate tall slim vase, out of which arose an airy tracery of twigs. These arrangements, though but a small part of the whole, complemented the stylized floral-decorated panels and the starkly modern light fittings, with every object in the room balanced and meticulously placed in space. In the privacy of his own home Mackintosh even displayed bowls of coloured twigs – a unique and startling idea for flower arrangement at the time. In doing so he was moving away from the transient beauty of the flower itself towards a form of abstraction and an acceptance that abstract form

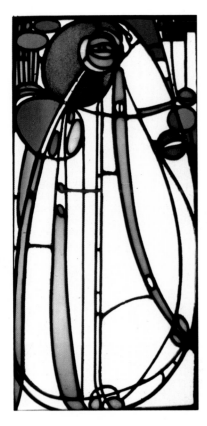

Leaded glass panel designed by Mackintosh for the Turin Exhibition in 1902
Hunterian Art Gallery, University of Glasgow Mackintosh Collection

C. R. Mackintosh's drawing room, Bath Street
T. & R. Annan & Sons Ltd, Glasgow

could possess a quiet beauty and distinction of its own. For as Mackintosh said: 'You must offer the flowers of the Art that is in you – the symbols of all that is noble – and beautiful and inspiring.'

As the Victorian age imperceptibly transformed into the Edwardian period, the elegant social life enjoyed by society increasingly came to revolve around the wanderings of the Royal Court. This hedonistic life centred on the London season, Derby week at Epsom, Royal Ascot, and yachting at Cowes, with the winter spent on the grouse moors of Scotland and recuperating on the French Riviera. True society enjoyed at least two homes, one in town and one in the country, the upkeep of which was made possible by an abundant supply of cheap labour. It was the era of 'upstairs, downstairs'; the servants operated out of basement quarters during the day, their domain separated from that of the main household by a heavy brass-studded green baize door.

To employ between five and thirty gardeners in such a world was nothing remarkable. The extensive use of cold frames, hothouses and conservatories ensured a continuous and copious supply of flowers for the house. Particularly favoured plants included carnations, chrysanthemums, lilies in great variety, water lilies, orchids, roses, and the foliage from asparagus, plumosus, caladium, croton, *Smilax phoenix*, ferns and palms. Chapter after chapter in books plus numerous articles in the magazines of the period were devoted to the skills required for the successful packaging of flower material to be sent by railway or post from the country garden to the town house. In addition to the packing, the head gardener was responsible not only for keeping a constant supply available but also for decorating the dinner table himself. Often he would be asked to match his floral decorations to the gown of the hostess as well as to make a daily change of flowers during house parties.

In his book *British Floral Decoration*, published in 1910, the society florist R. F. Felton observed: 'Conversation can never flag if there are beautiful flowers to talk about. Many an awkward break in the sequence of courses can be comfortably tided over if the guests have something upon which to feast their eyes.'

Banquets were commonplace. Although there had been some simplification from the wilder excesses of Victorian table decoration, epergnes were still in use, though often less ornate than formerly. Also, owing to increasing mass production, plate came to be more acceptable. A longer, much lower form of epergne made its appearance, featuring a lower central trumpet linked to smaller trumpets by lines of decorated vine or ivy leaf. Lighter, more open arrangements appeared which, combined with the new design, enabled the diner for the first time to see across the table and converse with the person opposite, as well as to see and hear the main speakers at a banquet. Formerly, table arrangements often had to be removed before the speeches started.

Felton still did not consider the revised arrangements adequate, so he designed his Ellen Terry stand. A central stack was painted green and embedded firmly in a solid flat pad of moss upon a saucer, crowned with another pad of moss on top. Both top and bottom were covered in greenery, whilst a long spray was entwined up the stem. Flowers were inserted directly into the moss, which when topped up daily acted as a most effective water reservoir. For formal dinners these Ellen Terry stands would be made at least 1200 mm high, so that the speaker when standing could be seen underneath the crowning flowers. For more intimate dinners, the crown would be much lower to enable seated people to see over them.

Gertrude Jekyll, in her 1907 book *Flower Decoration in the House*, favoured an even simpler style of table arrangement. A central bowl of flowers was linked to individual bowls or vases by sprays of foliage laid gracefully on the table. The whole was, of course, to be executed 'with artistic feeling and a sense of drawing'. According to *Cassell's Household Guide* Queen Alexandra, who was formerly a Danish princess, was particularly fond of using a three-legged ornamental clear glass basket filled with moss, flowers and fruit as a decorative accessory. In consequence this type of container came to be called a Denmark. They varied in size from that of an egg up to 225 mm across, being placed tastefully on the table, either amongst dishes or at the corners.

Meantime Gertrude Jekyll had introduced to Britain the simple Italian idea of heaping on a large metal dish an asymmetrical grouping of large and small fruits, the use of grapes and melons being particularly recommended. To this assemblage was added suitable sprigs of vine, fig, hop, Portugal laurel and *Skimmia japonica*, and over the whole a low arching spray of clematis might be placed. Another grouping favoured by Gertrude Jekyll was that where a tall vase was balanced asymmetrically by a lower bowl. She also designed her own plain Munstead glass vases of simple form, their shapes made to suit specific flowers. This stark simplicity contrasted with the intricately cut lead crystal vases and rose bowls which remained a wedding present status

Ellen terry stand
From *British Floral Decoration* by R. Forester Felton
(Adam and Charles Black, 1906)

symbol. Before becoming a gardener Gertrude Jekyll had been a painter and embroideress of some note. Her artistic friends included many of those within the Art Nouveau circle, and she favoured many of their muted colourings; their greys and silvers and their acid, limey and golden greens were transferred back from paint into living foliage in both vase and garden. Her strong sense of colour toning and combinations of harmonious colours has proved to be of lasting influence.

At this time much serious consideration was given by floral writers to the selection of the colours most suitable for use under differing lighting conditions, so that the greatest effect resulted either under daylight or during the evening. Lighting at night, when much entertaining was done, could be by candle, gas or electricity, all of which alter the tonal qualities of flowers. The receding colours of blue and purple were especially to be avoided.

In floral arrangement, bowls were particularly popular; silver was considered especially attractive for roses. The stems were supported either by a metal mesh fitted over the bowl or by a perforated glass or china block placed at the bottom of the bowl. Sometimes strips of lead were folded in a zigzag manner around a flower's stem to hold it steady in the bowl. This technique was also employed in upright vases. A naturalistic waterside arrangement with strong Japanese influence might be made in a large flat bowl, with a few waterside plants or spikes of iris being placed to one side, leaving an expanse of open water visible.

The slender glass vase, shaped as a cone or trumpet and ranging in height from a few centimetres to over a metre often perilously balanced on the floor, remained amongst the most popular of shapes, despite its practical drawbacks. R. P. Brotherston correctly observed that 'the stems of the trumpet shaped vases are not infrequently too slender and their capacity for water is too small for the requirements of flowers, the stalks of which are of necessity so close packed that, do as one may, flowers last fresh for only a limited period.' Daily topping up of these vases was essential. The physical balance of the flowers was often crucial to the maintenance of stability; the majority of the weight was concentrated near the flower-filled top, which was supported by a disproportionately small base. Dusting round these tall and slender vases was a daily hazard for the domestic staff – but at least the children were mainly confined to their own quarters!

To improve stability, much use was made of moss for water retention or of wet sand where weight was also required. Gertrude Jekyll devised a new form of scaffolding which employed 10–20 mm mesh galvanized wire netting in two tiers. She also promoted the use of stiff twigs of box or holly or 'bits of spray from an old birch broom' to hold stalks in place.

R. P. Brotherston, in his *Book of Cut Flowers*, made the delightful remark that 'All flowers that are loved rather than admired ought to be placed within easy reach, particularly common sweet flowers such as carnation, primroses, violets and lily of the valley.' The King himself was very fond of sweet peas and had them as floral arrangements on his birthday dinner table on at least four occasions. However, he did refuse to allow very strongly scented flowers, such as lilies, gardenias,

Lilies in a vase
From *The Book of Cut Flowers* by R. P. Brotherston
(T. N. Foulis, 1906)

tuberoses, hyacinths, jonquils and stephanotis in his personal rooms. Unfortunately, the growing enthusiasm of gardeners to display their hothouse varieties often meant that drawing-rooms became overcrowded and unbearably sickly.

Queen Alexandra loved violets and regularly wore a special violet perfume. One of the best varieties grown was called 'Princess of Wales' and featured large flowers with a long stalk. Many other varieties of violet, both single and double were grown for market, many coming from Devon and the milder south-west. A woman's favourite was to wear a bunch of violets tucked into her belt or sash. Wedding bouquets remained very large and, even though they were now much looser in form and often softened with trails of fern, they had to be wired to hold together the sheer bulk. Formal Court bouquets often contained 50 or more carnations, along with ferns and large bows of wide ribbon. When Lillie Langtry was first presented at Court she wore an ivory brocade gown with train, both garlanded with Marechal Niel roses. She carried an immense bouquet of similar roses sent to her by

Sprays of orchids in a court bouquet made for Queen Alexandra
From *British Floral Decoration* by R. Forester Felton
(Adam and Charles Black, 1906)

Edward, then Prince of Wales. Her beauty was so radiant and her reputation so great that people would stand on drawing-room chairs just to catch a glimpse of her when she entered a room.

Flowers were almost universally worn by women for adornment, at different times on the shoulder, at the waist, on the breast and in the hair. Many men sported a fresh buttonhole daily, and would have considered themselves improperly dressed without it. The flower was tucked through the lapel buttonhole into a tiny hidden glass or metal holder or phial, held in place by a pin.

Church decoration continued to be heavy and formal. Harvest Festival in particular was celebrated with great vigour. Festoons of flowers were draped over pulpits and galleries, along the base of screens and at the top and bottom of fonts, and garlanded round pillars. Copious sheaves of corn would fill every available corner. In his *Book of Cut Flowers* Brotherston suggested a Harvest Festival decoration made by first tying heads of corn to an upright pole, then adding tall-stemmed hollyhocks and gladioli on top. At the same time the American custom of decorating church porches came into greater usage, the floral bell being a popular motif.

Every period in history is seen in retrospect to have possessed particular social attributes uniquely its own. The turn of the last century, sometimes known as *la belle époque*, was unashamedly devoted to the cult of femininity. Due homage being recognized by the giving and receiving of flowers. Women were placed on pedestals and almost worshipped – for their beauty like Lillie Langtry (Jersey Lily) and William Morris's wife Janey, for their acting ability like Sarah Bernhardt and Ellen Terry, or for their dancing such as Loie Fuller and Isadora Duncan. The more pragmatic courtesans such as Lianne de Pougy, *la grande horizontale*, preferred the collection of jewellery tributes to merely temporal flowers.

A simple scene from *Pygmalion* or *My Fair Lady* could stand as a vignette for the entire Edwardian age. On a London evening, outside a theatre stage door, sits a humble Cockney flower seller with her large wicker basket. An aristocratic dandy in white tie and tails, sporting a newly purchased buttonhole, strolls past without a care in the world. He carries a tall upright presentation flower basket filled with roses. Attached to the large bow on the handle is an invitation to his favoured actress or chorus girl, requesting her to accompany him for supper at the Café Royal or Romanos.

Yet, all too soon, the luxury, style and wit of the Edwardian era, the floral fantasies of Art Nouveau, were to be swept away for ever by the distant thunder of cannon. Amidst the mud and blood of Flanders fields the poppy was to take on a new and far sadder symbolic meaning.

Bibliography

Art Nouveau
Amaya, Mario. *Art Nouveau*. London: Studio Vista, 1966.

Anscombe, Isabelle and Gere, Charlotte. *Arts and Crafts*. New York: Van Nostrand Reinhold, 1979.

Bossaglia, Rossana. *Art Nouveau*. London: Orbis, 1973.

Fanelli, Giovanni and Godoli, Ezio. *Art Nouveau Postcards*. Oxford: Phaidon Christies, 1987.

Fleming, John and Honour, Hugh. *Penguin Dictionary of Decorative Arts*. London: Penguin, 1977.

Hofstätter, Hans. *Art Nouveau Prints and Posters*. Omega, 1984.

Lucie-Smith, Edward. *Symbolist Art*. London: Thames and Hudson, 1972.

Walters, Thomas. *Art Nouveau Graphics*. New York: Academy, *Symbolism and Art Nouveau*. Oxford: Phaidou, 1979.

The Pre-Raphaelites (catalogue). Tate Gallery. Penguin.

The Jewellery of René Lalique (catalogue). Vivienne Becker, The Goldsmiths' Company, London.

Artistic Japan: A monthly illustrated journal of arts and industries. Conducted by S. Bing. Sampson Low, Marston, Searle and Rivington, London. First issue 1888.

The Studio. First issue 1893.

Edwardian period

Brotherston, R. P. *The Book of Cut Flowers*. Edinburgh: Foulis, 1906.

Cassell's Household Guide. London: Cassell,

Conder, Josiah. 'The theory of Japanese flower arrangements', paper presented to Asiatic Society of Japan, 13 March 1889. Reprinted by Thompson, Kobe and by Kegan Paul, Trench, Trubner, London, 1935.

Felton, R. Forester. *British Floral Decoration*. London: Black, 1910.

Jekyll, Gertrude. *Floral Decoration in the House*. *Country Life* and Newnes, 1907. Reprinted by Antique Collectors' Club, Woodbridge, Suffolk, 1982.

Langtry, Lily. *The Days I Knew* (autobiography). London: Futura, 1978.

Robinson, William. *The English Flower Garden*. London: Murray, 1883.

Liberty's 1875–1975 Exhibition Catalogue. London: HM Stationery Office, 1975.

Places to visit

Pre-Raphaelite Paintings
London, Tate Gallery.
Manchester, City Art Gallery.
Birmingham, City Museum and Art Gallery.
Liverpool, Port Sunlight, the Lady Lever Gallery.
Liverpool, Walker Art Gallery.
Newcastle upon Tyne, Laing Art Gallery.

Southampton, City Art Gallery.
Bristol, City of Bristol Art Gallery.
Bournemouth, Russell-Cotes Art Gallery and Museum.

Charles Rennie Mackintosh
Glasgow: Glasgow School of Art; Glasgow University, Mackintosh
   Collection; Hill House, Helensburgh.

Decorative
London, Victoria and Albert Museum.
London, Walthamstow, William Morris Gallery.
East Grinstead, Standen (National Trust).
Wolverhampton, Wightwick Manor (National Trust).

6

Britain: the twentieth century

The thirties

SHEILA MACQUEEN

THE THIRTIES BECAME THE WATERSHED IN FLOWER arrangement in England. Constance Spry was the prime mover in this amazing change, which revolutionized the methods and ideas of our generation. I became an apprentice trainee in her shop in Burlington Gardens in 1932 and worked with her intermittently until she died. I hope I may be forgiven if a personal note creeps into this section and this little bit of flower history.

After the profusion of plant materials, the over-ferned arrangements that often obliterated beautiful containers, and the banks of pot plants of the Victorian era, the use of pedestal containers of cut flowers was a welcome change, and gradually churches became transformed. The rather stiff brass vases on the altar, and the potted palms, hydrangeas, ferns and mixed house plants which acted as a feature either side of the altar on special occasions, were replaced with beautiful mixed flower groups placed either side of the chancel steps. Often as many as four pairs of vases strategically placed would be displayed, according to the grandeur of the occasion.

Although it had been recommended by Gertrude Jekyll in her book *Home and Garden* published in 1900, it was not until now that one of the greatest innovations in flower arranging occurred. It was recognized that the use of crushed 50 mm mesh wire netting pushed into the vases would greatly assist the placement of the flowers, and indeed many flower arrangers today still prefer the use of wire netting despite more modern aids.

In the thirties flowers were usually arranged by the head gardeners, or the young daughters of the house. There was a trend to put bright orange marigolds in a black bowl, or to float an open rose or dahlia in a shallow round bowl for the centre of the table. However, different materials began to be used. Fruit as well as simple garden flowers, so often neglected at that time, started off a great interest in gardening, and flowers of special interest were grown for flower arranging. This is of course a practice carried on to a greater extent today, but it was exciting when it began in the early thirties.

At this time there were four excellent flower shops in London: Edward Goodyear, by Royal Appointment to Buckingham Palace, Moysey Stevens and Feltons in the West End, and Longmans in the City. All were extremely efficient establishments with faultless floristry. Apart from one floristry school, the only training available was to become an apprentice trainee in the workroom of one of these establishments. School leavers aged 14 worked on mossing wreaths, dethorning roses, and cutting and putting flowers into water – probably the only way in two years that they ever handled flowers. It was a long hard grind, and they had to love the work to survive. These large well-established firms, who had the cream of the floristry work in London, were pretty formidable opposition for the small unknown firm run by someone with amazing artistic ability but little business sense. However, by the mid thirties Constance Spry had achieved a great hold on London society. Undaunted she battled on, influencing even the big florists, who gradually came to realize that large cut-flower pedestal arrangements were more effective. With this further interest in flowers, Mrs Spry opened a flower school in South Audley Street in 1935. To start with it catered more for the well-brought-up girl whose mother had ideas that her daughter should be usefully occupied. Its popularity increased because at this time there was little choice for the school leaver.

Constance Spry's influence was being felt more and more. She had a weekly contract with Atkinsons' perfumery shop in Bond Street, and this became her shop window. There were four beautiful windows to decorate every week, and she had a free hand to use any and all the flowers she wanted. This most elegant shop, designed by the late Norman Wilkinson, was the perfect setting for Constance's new look in flower arranging. Mirrored glass walls and cascading glass chains represented fountains of perfume. The flower arrangements were daring in colour, and so unusual; on one occasion an arrangement of red decorative kale and scarlet roses in the window facing Bond Street drew crowds to such an extent that the police were called to move on the traffic. Drages' large furniture store in Oxford Street soon followed Atkinsons, as did Elizabeth Arden and Hatchets' Restaurant. A special decorating department was established in the shop – an unheard of development at that time.

The off-white period

The small shop in Burlington Gardens, next door to Atkinsons, started the white vogue. Dull white surgical rubber sheeting pleated on screens divided the window from the shop. Vases became known as containers, and the use of bronze, malachite, alabaster and ormolu urns made them very collectable items. Soup tureens, vegetable dishes, *compotes*, wooden bowls and boxes were replacing the glass containers, in which the murky water was visible and needed to be constantly changed. Ceramic or metal saved a great deal of work and added interest to the flower arrangements.

Meanwhile an interior decorator known as Syrie Maughan was becoming increasingly popular in the West End. She had very artistic ideas, and often designed rooms in self or uniform colour. She and Constance began to work together. When a house she had decorated was complete, we were invited to add the final touch with flower arrangements. Her own house was enchanting and her all-white drawing-room became the talk of London. The white walls, white rugs on polished old York stone floors, white chair covers, cushions and lamp shades allowed for no colour at all. I was asked to prepare two alabaster vases with pyramid arrangements of white peonies, and these were to stand on a long refectory table in an exact position. I could not quite understand why they were so placed; however, when they were finished some lights were turned on which shone down from the ceiling exactly on top of them, and it was wonderfully effective.

Behind the scenes

The Flower Market at Covent Garden was changing too. Flowers bought there came back to the shop beautifully packed in wooden boxes. The boxes were chargeable, and in Constance Spry's early days of little financial backing the money recouped on the previous day's empties was immediately spent on flowers in the market. Everything was seasonal, and it was wonderful in the summer to buy scented sweet peas, grown out of doors, moss roses, delphiniums, foxgloves, eremurus and every conceivable garden flower. Camellias and gardenias arrived in boxes beautifully lined with cotton wool. In spring we waited patiently for the 'French stuff' (as we called it) to arrive, and then suddenly we were unpacking pads of mimosa, French ranunculus, anemones, eucalyptus and Parma violets. They came to England in French pads, which were slatted wicker baskets made like picnic hampers and very attractive. When they were stacked at the station or quayside, waiting to be sent to England, the staff would play hoses of water over them to keep them fresh for the several days they would be in transit. Flowers were not air-freighted to England until the time of the Queen's Coronation, and from then on the wooden boxes were replaced with cardboard and, later, polystyrene.

In 1933 there was great excitement when we were asked to decorate one of London's famous houses in Curzon Street. It was the first time that I had the fun of accompanying Constance Spry on a job of this kind. Many flower arrangements were made, all in delightful colourings to enhance every room; I stood by in wonder and admiration. It may be well imagined how shattered I was when the hostess returned to say she did not like anything we had done! Quick as a flash I was told to collect all the vases and call a taxi. Sitting surrounded by vases of flowers we made the short trip back to South Audley Street. Thinking of our very limited resources, I could not help suggesting that it might have been better had we done something she had wanted. Mrs Spry said firmly: 'No, I want her to have what she likes, but I do not want to be associated with carnations and asparagus fern. I want to bring the countryside to London.' Such was the courage of her convictions. Within two years we were back in the same house, and we arranged for every party held there after that.

The London season

Flower decoration was growing fast, and the interest in having unusual flowers for all occasions soon hit the London season. What a lovely time of the year, and what exciting parties and events there were! There seemed to be a great deal of money in London at that time – and also a great deal of poverty. Someone once asked us if we felt bitter that we were paid so little whilst seeing so much affluence. It is true we were paid little, and we worked hard, but I loved to watch the expansion of the firm and to become part of the creative art that was developing. Working with flowers and in such good company gave rise to a great deal of pleasure, laughter and companionship.

The Chelsea Flower Show was the start of our season, and from then onwards we were almost continually busy. The presentations of the year's débutantes at Court was a time of feverish excitement for us all. Each deb carried a bouquet as she curtsied to the Queen, and all gave coming-out parties or balls. We did the flowers for these parties, and found ourselves decorating marquees and ballrooms all over the country as well as in London. Flowers became more and more of a feature of these gatherings, and so our work became increasingly varied. I well remember doing the flowers for Lord Derby's Derby night banquet at Stafford House near Oxford Street, when we used his racing

Mantelpiece
(Note: The photographs on pages 184, 190 and 191 are from *Party Flowers* by Constance Spry (J. M. Dent & Sons))

colours for the colour scheme of the flowers down the centre of the table. I was fascinated when I was shown the underground world of the cellars by the butler and saw their own butcher's shop and dairy. The produce had been brought to London from their farms in the north of England. When I remember the buffet vases filled with fruits and flowers I can to this day close my eyes and smell the peaches, nectarines and grapes which had come straight out of the greenhouses and were still covered in bloom. We piled them on high *compotes* and tucked camellias, orchids and stephanotis in between them.

A marquee erected on the banks of the Thames was once hung with straw hats, filled with a profusion of summer flowers – cascading roses, sweet William, foxgloves and delphinium – and finished with ribbon bows with long trailing ends. On another occasion, the up-and-coming young designer Oliver Messel decorated a marquee with white plaster masks linked by formal garlands of laurel, and twisted garlands of evergreens ran down the muslin-covered poles. Sunderland House in Curzon Street was a popular venue for balls, and in one week I can remember decorating it on three nights in succession. We recycled any possible materials, and I recall overhearing one of our decorators saying to a stem of eremurus: 'Go in there, you really should know by now, you have been there three times already this week!'

Other memories I have are of the wedding in St Margaret's, Westminster, when we used white urns filled with cow parsley, and of the pyramids of white marguerites in St George's, Hanover Square. We would take the van from London down to Park Gate (Hants) where Constance Spry lived, and fill it with buckets of really hot water for 100 or more stems of philadelphus; this gave the flowers every chance to hold their petals long enough to be arranged the next day in huge vases and placed in the foyer, on the stairway and across the upstairs landings of the Royal Opera House. We picked large branches of lime trees in full flower and removed the outer leaves to expose the flowering bracts; the scent and the colour was superb. Some time later we decorated the Opera House again, this time for a gala performance attended by King George VI and Queen Elizabeth. On this occasion Oliver Messel had the most sensational ideas, which included one large and two smaller swags draped in front of the royal box. These moss-filled crescent shapes cut out of small mesh wire netting were filled with 900 camellia blooms, of all shades of pink and red with an edging of camellia foliage. The decoration took hours and hours of work, but the effect was breath-taking.

There was the occasion when we transformed the loggia in the then French Embassy into a garden. We placed 1200 mm baton frames covered with small mesh wire netting round the walls and threaded small pieces of cut box wood through it, which were then clipped. I have to admit you could have deceived anyone into believing they were rooted to the spot. It was a long, laborious, painful task but, with pots of white lilies placed behind the frames, the finished result was well worth it. Later we repeated this scheme for the newly built Highfield House in Regent's Park, to give the effect of a garden that had yet to be made.

The work goes on

This was all a far cry from what continued in the suburbs, where arum lilies were still used only for funerals. The moss-covered wreaths with tucks of spring flowers, primroses, grape hyacinths and snowdrops had not reached them, and floral tributes in the form of harps and 'the vacant chair' were still greatly in demand.

Our first all-green arrangement started in the strangest way. One of our valued customers arrived suddenly in the shop bearing two miniature porcelain tigers. These were to be a welcome-home present for a friend coming home after a safari trip in India, and we had to make a jungle for them. With a flat meat dish and a mixture of green plants and mixed foliage, bark and moss we achieved what was required. It was so effective that it gave us the idea to expand and experiment with all-foliage arrangements.

The highlight of the brilliant season of 1934 was the wedding of the Duke of Kent and the lovely Princess Marina of Greece. They took up residence in 3 Belgrave Square, and the fortnightly parties given for them by their neighbour, Lady Portarlington, enabled them to meet a varied selection of people outside the royal circle. These were wonderful parties with many flowers, a lovely setting, and personalities from the arts and theatre. After doing the flowers for one of these parties in the late summer, when we had used seed heads and beautiful large hydrangeas, we received a message not to dismantle the flowers in the hallway but to bring some more dried materials to add to them. It seemed that the hydrangeas had gradually dried off in the water, retaining their colour. With the addition of lotus pods from the East, dried 'gold plate' achilleas and some stems of green amaranthus we created our first dried arrangement.

We acquired our first royal client when HRH the Duke of Kent invited us to arrange flowers for their dinner parties. Pieces of the dinner service were used for the flowers on the dining table; a soup tureen was placed in the centre, then two vegetable dishes, and so on down the table according to the number of guests. Normally we used flowers which enhanced the beautiful Meissen and Sèvres services, but when Queen Mary came for luncheon the preference was for the conventional pink carnations. The Duchess enjoyed the flowers we did for her; only once did we have to make a change and remove a vase of lichen-covered branches and decorative kale before her brother arrived from Greece, as she felt he would not understand it.

When the Duke introduced Mrs Spry to his brother, the Duke of Gloucester, he gave her the order for the bouquets for his wedding to Lady Alice Montague Scott. The unusually delicate shadow leaves edged with gold made showering bouquets, with champagne-coloured roses complementing the bridesmaids' oyster satin dresses. It was shortly after this that the Dean of Westminster approached Mrs Spry to help the women of the Flower Guild with the flowers in Westminster Abbey. The Guild were asked to bring flowers from their gardens and we were to help arrange them. Two large lead garden urns were

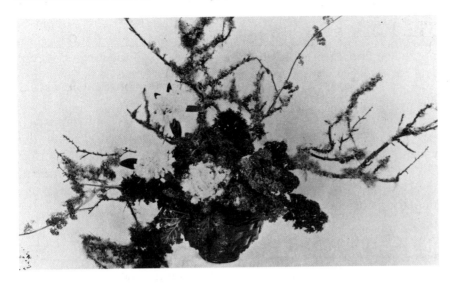

Kale and lichen
(Note: The photographs on pages 187 and
188 are from *Flowers in House and Garden*
by Constance Spry (J. M. Dent & Sons))

borrowed and placed ready for the arrival of the flowers. The few stems
of delphiniums, lilies and pink pyrethrums which arrived were a
disappointment, and it was soon realized that small gardens could not
supply the quantity of flowers required for such a vast building.
Constance offered to provide the flowers for the Abbey at cost price and
to arrange them on a voluntary basis, and this continued until 1975.
The National Association of Flower Arrangement Societies, with their
headquarters in London, then took over this most prestigious task,
which they fulfil to this day.

More and more contracts were received. One for which I was responsible on a twice-weekly basis was to arrange two glass accumula-
tor tanks in Bryanston Square in the home of Mrs Wallis Simpson. At
that time she was fairly unknown in London society but, as the
relationship grew with the Prince of Wales, so Mrs Spry herself came
to be introduced. There was an instant mutual liking and rapport, and
it was no time at all before Constance was asked to arrange flowers for
St James's Palace and weekend house parties at Fort Belvedere. It was
spring when we picked young green catkins from the silver birch in the
woods and added them to large vases of daffodils in the yellow drawing-room. The following week I was amazed to find a bundle of dead
silver birch branches on the dust sheet at Bryanston Court, and I was
told that these had been specially sent up from the Fort. I was viewing
them with horror when Mrs Simpson arrived, and said, 'Oh! I didn't
want those, I wanted the branches with the cute little green worms
on!'

Because of this close association, Mrs Spry and her assistant Miss
Pirie were invited to go to France and decorate the Château de Conde
for the Prince's wedding in June 1938. The salon in the château was
turned into a chapel for the occasion, and two large arrangements
were done on either side of the improvised altar. There were quantities
of madonna lilies and peonies together with syringa and cascades of
roses from Miss Pirie's home in Varennes. The groups must have
looked spectacular; the grandeur of the florist flowers was framed in
the rich informality of the garden flowers and foliage. In the turmoil
of this wedding I am sure the flowers brought sanity and reverence to

the occasion. It was remarkable that, through all the trauma of keeping the press from every country in the world away from the gates of the château, the Duke found time to ask one of the footmen to cut and pack a large wedge of wedding cake to send back with Constance for, as he put it, 'his girls' at the shop. It was typical of his kindliness. We all had a share of sleeping with it under our pillows; only Derby, our first pupil, kept hers in a box, and it now sids proudly at Longleat in Lord Bath's collection of the Duke of Windsor's artefacts.

Through Mrs Spry's friendship with the young South African dress designer Victor Stieble, and later Norman Hartnell, came the task of decorating their salons for their preview collections. Advice was given to débutantes and brides on the flowers they should carry, and thence more and more orders came to South Audley Street. There were times when we made as many as 40 bouquets for the courts, and then all hands were brought in to help. We made necklaces of fresh flowers, earrings of lily of the valley, and corsages. Bouquets were made of tulip tree flowers and gentians, on bound white or gold stems, and fern was replaced by delicate trails of variegated ivies. Pepperomia and tradescantia foliage, seed heads of clematis and berries were all incorporated in unusual and delicate bouquets. We made a point of delivering all our bouquets personally. We unwrapped the flowers and enjoyed seeing them held by excited débutantes in their beautiful dresses, made of exquisite satin, rich brocades, or simple tulle and lace, all crowned with the graceful feather plumes in their hair.

Frequently we did the flowers for the banquets at the Mansion House, Guildhall and many of the livery companies. The tall vases on the tables were now replaced with 450 mm narrow troughs which were made especially for narrow refectory tables. What a pleasure it was to see all the gold and silver treasures and trophies which were brought out from the vaults for these special occasions. Once when I

Old-fashioned roses

was fetching water to fill up the vases, I was fascinated to watch about 60 legs of succulent lamb slowly rotating in front of a wall of red-hot charcoal. There were so many wonderful occasions to look back upon in those years, when there were no thoughts of war.

In 1937 Mrs Spry went on a lecture tour of America. She amazed her audiences with slides of blackberries and hothouse roses, and she shocked them with her use of cultivated and wild materials together. She explained with patience that all things grow wild somewhere. However, the tour was an unqualified success and she enjoyed meeting some of the great American flower arrangers of that time. Adele Lovett was an arranger after Mrs Spry's own heart, making free-flowing arrangements, very different from the more stylized arrangements that seemed to be the vogue at that time. Mrs Ogdon Mills and Mrs James V. Forrestal banded together to persuade Constance to open a shop in New York, which they financed and to which Constance gave her name. These American women wanted to give her the scope to revolutionize American homes and gardens, and the New York business was envisaged as a fountain from whence her influence would flow. So as quickly as it had happened in London, it was becoming the 'in' thing in America to have flowers arranged by Constance Spry. The shop was expertly run by a young Australian, Pat Easterbook, who had run her own successful business and who came to London for a few months to get the feel of the way Spry's were doing flowers. Two of the staff from London went out for a year to help launch the shop.

The New York area had a notable Japanese arranger by the name of Madame Oria, a true artists. In San Diego, Gregory Conway was taking America by storm with lavish and interesting though formal arrangements; he was an excellent presenter who eventually made a visit over here. The west coast was deeply influenced by the Orient, and that type of arrangement was highly suitable for their modern homes. In the eastern states there tended to be a stiffness in the arrangements, partly due to the constant use of bought flowers, and as yet gardening and trying to grow to arrange was made very much more difficult because of the climate.

The war years

Sadly the war came and prevented travel between America and England; in fact, Constance never crossed the Atlantic again. The war brought a complete change for us all. The government urged that the shop should remain open at all costs, as they felt that the reopening of small businesses would be difficult once hostilities had ceased. The American Embassy in Grosvenor Square kept the workroom busy with a constant flow of GIs giving flowers and corsages to their various girlfriends. The shop was sadly depleted, and we relied on private growers for many of our flowers. There were weddings, of course, but they were much simpler; so too were the parties for the soldiers on leave, birthdays and so on. Most of the staff worked a night shift several nights a week in a small precision tool factory in Clapham, and their well-trained fingers were very welcome for as much time as they could spare. As I then had a small son, and was not eligible to be called up, I came in for special occasions. I found that I had acquired great speed, doing three or four arrangements in a matter of a few hours between visits to the air-raid shelter. My undying memory of those war days, when the blitz was at its height, was to arrive in the morning to the sound of the sweeping up of broken glass. The torn buildings – a bath and fireplace the only things hanging on the wall of a once beautiful house – are memories which can never be erased from one's mind.

The forties

After the war everything took a long time to settle down, but Constance Spry had very definite ideas as to what she wanted to do. She felt that instead of doing flowers for other people, *they* should learn to do them for themselves. A team was chosen to demonstrate flower arranging, to show the women of Britain how to make the most of the flowers and containers they had. In 1945 Winkfield Place, near Windsor, was established. Constance Spry joined forces with Rosemary Hume, and a combined flower arranging and cookery training school was launched. Winkfield became the finishing school of the post-war era, and hundreds of young people passed through its doors, learning to cook, dressmake and arrange flowers.

One of the most exciting post-war events was the wedding of Princess Elizabeth (now our Queen) to Prince Philip in Westminster Abbey in 1947. Because of the number of overseas visitors and the many guests, space for flowers was very limited. We were required to do only two large arrangements either side of the altar. The colour

Coronation lunch table

Close of crown arrangement

Lancaster House banquet table

scheme chosen by Buckingham Palace was white and pale pink, and we had wonderful camellia foliage, lilies, roses and variegated foliage of dracaena leaves. Looking back, it seemed so small in comparison with the Duke and Duchess of York's wedding 40 years later. I have a vivid memory of driving in a large Rolls-Royce, first to Buckingham Palace to decorate 'the' cake with a wonderful garland of white roses (I think there were seven cakes), and then down the Mall, which was closed to normal traffic, being cheered all the way to Westminster Abbey by the waiting crowds. Sitting nowadays in an inevitable traffic jam, I think what a unique experience it was!

For Constance Spry, the Coronation of Queen Elizabeth II was perhaps her greatest achievement. She was invited by Sir David Eccles to undertake and arrange all the decorations throughout London. She writes of it in her book *Party Flowers* with such affection and pride. She decorated luncheon tables in the Westminster City school, where Rosemary Hume did the food and produced the now famous Coronation Chicken dish. The school, with so much war damage still in need of repair, really was a challenge; a temporary ceiling and shrapnel-pitted walls filled one with horror. With a wave of a hand Mrs Spry said, 'We'll borrow tapestries from the V&A', and these made a magical transformation. The buffet tables were covered with white plastic tablecloths painted gold, and were extremely effective. For the dining tables, scarlet flowers were arranged in small crown vases on pale blue moiré silk tablecloths. France, Belgium and Italy all sent a marvellous collection of flowers – Baccarat roses, gladioli and carnations – all very much in the same shades and tones of red. When they were arranged they looked very dull, so we drove quickly to Wisley and picked armfuls of purple and deep-red rhododendrons and apricot and orange azaleas. The groups were then transformed; we learned so much at that moment of the value of mixing blue-reds and orange-reds together.

There was only one vase in the Abbey entrance, of scarlet flowers, and a lovely small sweetly scented vase of Blanc de Coubert roses in the Queen's retiring room. However, around the Commonwealth stand they made huge white troughs, and these were filled with the many hundreds of beautiful flowers which had been flown in from all over the world. Every country in the Commonwealth sent a collection of their native plants, and late on the night before the Coronation these were unpacked in the middle of Parliament Square, watched by fascinated crowds. Waratah, banksia, hibiscus, frangipani and tuberoses, with the heavy perfumed flowers of tropical lands, arrived by the plane load – the first time flowers had ever been air-freighted.

I will always be thankful for the day in 1932 when my mother and I looked in Atkinsons' window and saw some dried leek heads and old man's beard in a brown ceramic cylindrical vase. I felt that anyone who could make such a charming arrangement out of nothing was someone I must meet and learn from. How fortunate I have been to have done just that.

Bibliography

Macqueen, Sheila. *Flower Arranging from your Garden.* Ward Lock, 1977.

Macqueen, Sheila. *More Flower Arranging from your Garden.* Ward Lock, 1984.

Macqueen, Sheila. *Complete Flower Arranging.* Papermac, 1986.

Spry, Constance. *Flowers in House and Garden.* Dent, 1937.

Spry, Constance. *Summer and Autumn Flowers.* Dent, 1951.

Spry, Constance. *Winter and Spring Flowers.* Dent, 1951.

Spry, Constance. *Party Flowers.* Dent, 1955.

Spry, Constance. *Favourite Flowers.* Dent, 1959.

Thomas, Graham Stuart. *Perennial Garden Plants.* Dent, 1976.

Innovations and inspirations in the post-war period

JULIA CLEMENTS

WAR TORN AND WEARY, ALMOST WITHOUT HOPE: THAT was the state of many British women after the Second World War.

Although the war had been won in 1945 (and at what a price) the street and shop lights were not reinstated until October 1952, and rationing was not lifted until 1954. Houses were without roofs and windows; there were great chasms in streets over which temporary wooden bridges had been erected; buildings had not been repainted for seven long years; and there was a feeling of hopelessness everywhere. Gardens had been turned over to food growing, paper rationing was still in force, and few seed catalogues had appeared during the war years.

There was a great surge among women to help put the world right, but so much was met with frustration. Food was still rationed, and so too was clothing. Painting, knitting or creative sewing were out of the question, for necessary materials were not available. The devastation in the towns and cities only added to the gloom. It is not easy to pinpoint the start of a movement, it is in the air, and someone somewhere has to light the fire that will engulf others in flames of enthusiasm and positiveness.

At that time flowers were the only items that were not rationed or restricted, or even held back for export. They were free in the countryside and fields, and in gardens that still retained perennial plants and shrubs. Yes, it was flowers that could relieve this urge to do something positive. But how does one get this idea, and how does one pass the inspiration to other people? It was of no use to tell the women in bombed cities that they could create a beautiful flower decoration by using branches of *Cotoneaster horizontalis* with *Lilium martagon* when they had no hope of obtaining either.

In pre-war Britain women had always been accustomed to 'doing the flowers' in varying degrees of taste. In great houses the head gardener was often the chief decorator; the professional florists were called in for special occasions. Pre-war beautiful and lavish flower decorations were to be seen at banquets, society weddings and other special occasions. Many of the outstanding displays were created by Constance Spry, that innate artist with flowers. At the same time the average woman would pick or buy a bunch of flowers, place them in water, and then continue to discharge her other household chores. But now it was self-expression that was needed in a much simplified form, and giving the flowers a drink of water did not fulfil this pent-up desire.

And so flower arranging was presented as an art. No longer need the ordinary woman stand in awe before the flowers at a society wedding and inwardly feel it was not for her. It *could* be for her, the cry went up, but how could she learn about self-expression, how could she do something which enabled her to say 'I did it', 'That's me'? Of course she could do it, but leaders were needed whose own belief and inspiration would fire the latent abilities in others.

It was perhaps at this time that I first saw the need to step firmly into the public arena, to reach for the microphone, to deliver the message, and to find simple flowers to arrange in easy ways. I knew that we must bring a do-it-yourself method to housewives up and down the country. This mission, in which I believed passionately, began shortly after the war in the not very inspiring atmosphere of a Women's Institute meeting. I had recently returned from a brief visit to America, where I had toured the garden clubs giving thanks to the members for their generosity in sending seeds to England to help grow food. I still felt dazzled by the bright lights of the States, the food, the colour and the gaiety. When I looked out from the platform on to my audience in Britain I saw them as pale, dispirited and hungry – yet they were the so-called 'victors' in the bloodiest struggle in history. As far as any of life's graces and luxuries were concerned, they were severely deprived.

I was appalled as I witnessed this melancholy assembly, and I listened to the speeches which preceded mine in a kind of dream. The theme of the first was 'make do and mend', a self-explanatory phrase which even to this day must strike a chill to the hearts of all those British women who remember the greyness of the post-war days. After this there was a homily from an official who had been sent down by the Ministry of Agriculture to explain how to fill in the new chicken ration forms. In case there may be readers who have forgotten or never knew this gruesome footnote to the history of our times, they may be reminded that the object of these forms was to warn the owners of chickens that though they might receive permits to buy chicken feed, they must return to the Ministry any extra eggs that resulted from this munificence, keeping for themselves only the permitted ration, which was one egg per week.

Throughout these exhortations I watched as the audience became seemingly depressed. When I heard my name called I rose to my feet, and I realized suddenly that this was my opportunity to do something postive to help these women regain colour and expression in their lives. I spoke of flowers, which were the one natural source of beauty which England still had in abundance, the one unrationed commodity. I described how they could be woven into patterns of natural beauty. In the development of modern popular flower arrangement this event was historic; the enthusiasm engendered was immense, and many other meetings of WIs followed. Little or no cooperation was shown by the various horticultural societies, who were still enthusiastically promoting vegetable growing and discounted the somewhat frivolous art of flower arranging. And so it was that in 1952 I put pen to paper and wrote a pamphlet with the simple title 'How to form a flower club'.

That 'something in the air' was being recognized, and 'something' was being done. It was being done in other parts of the country too, for flower clubs and flower arranging societies were springing up all over the country. Demonstrations with flowers were given in department stores, or wherever an audience could be housed. For the women out of uniform, as well as those who had fought the war at home, there was a demand for colour and for beauty, and this had to be satisfied by opening the eyes of those who watched – eyes which had been closed for so long during so many restrictions.

One of the great problems during those early post-war days was the lack of necessary equipment to enable enthusiasts to pursue their interest. Vases were not being manufactured, as they were listed as not being necessary. Lamp bases *were* allowed as being part of household equipment, and so fixtures were made to go on top of lamp bases which made an elegant-looking 'vase'. With incredible ingenuity we melted old gramophone records, plugged their central holes with sealing wax and moulded them into the most artistic shapes and sizes. Casserole and oven dishes were very popular for the modern line designs, but pinholders were almost unobtainable. I recall cutting out a 75 mm disc of turf from the lawn, inserting nails with their head upwards into the soil, and later filling the indent with hot scrap metal. When set the device could be removed; with points upwards it served as a holder into which stems of flowers could be inserted. Wire netting was very scarce and was guarded preciously, but all kinds of holders were made and used with it. Petrol was still rationed, and so to spread the message the few teachers and demonstrators of the new art had to travel long distances by other means, carrying heavy bags of dishes and flowers. There was no colour photography or colour slides that could be shown to audiences and I recall the editor of the delightful magazine *My Garden* allowing his photographer to produce large 'magic lantern' black and white slides of arrangements that I made: The slides and script were then sent out to Women's Institutes, Townswomen's Guilds, Young Farmers' Clubs and newly formed flower clubs. Later, of course, pinholders were professionally made as the material became available, and colour slides are now being sent out on every main event to help members of flower clubs.

During my travels at this time I found it difficult to convey the full meaning of such an expressive art in the short space of an afternoon or evening if my audience was completely uninitiated. I did not feel the audiences were helped by watching intricate arrangements made by an expert. They were entertained, yes, and full of admiration for all they saw, but there was a need for more permanent guidance. The suggestions I made at that time proved to be good basic principles of flower arranging, and in 1953 I wrote a book called *101 Ideas for Flower Arrangement* (published by C. Arthur Pearson). It gave simple guidelines which may today seem very basic, yet at the time the need for some kind of advice was urgent, and the meanings of design, balance, scale, colour, line, rhythm and composition required explanation. The advice encouraged people to evoke their own ideas rather than to watch elaborate designs, for it is the sense of personal achieve-

Facing page *Iris pinholder, 1951*

Top right *Plants in a bottle, 1959*

Bottom *Primroses in Denby ware oven dish, 1950s*

Photos: Julia Clements

ment in creating a simple design that thrills a novice and urges her to attempt more ambitious arrangements later. And so at the risk of being assertive, I stressed that beginners should repeat to themselves the following basic rules: (1) outline, (2) fill in and (3) the main interest. That is, they should use points, fillers and dominants in the order of tall, medium and short.

The extremely simple arrangement of iris shown, using a casserole dish and a pinholder, is a perfect example of the designs I was trying, in 1950, to encourage people to do. They were economical and quick, yet pleasing to look at. Similarly the three forms of plant material arranged in a bottle make a delightful design. As an alternative, the woodland scene of primroses tucked into moss in a Denby-ware oven dish is a charming touch of spring, bringing the woods and hedgerows into the home.

Some at first thought that this simple approach to flower arranging would produce a nation of do-it-yourself, look-alike flower arrange-

Three forms and sizes of tall, medium and short, 1960

Photo: Julia Clements

Photo: Julia Clements

Mahonia, pine and heather on wooden base, 1950s

ments. Not at all; just as a student of the piano has to learn and practise scales in order to obtain flexibility of finger movement before moving on to creative work, so too does a flower arranger have to learn the basics before developing her own style of expression.

In the early fifties many people were developing their skills and their individual styles. Nurseries likewise began to recognize this new approach in the use of flowers, and quickly planned to supply more unusual plants, colours and textures. They were forerunners, no doubt, of the specialist nurseries of today who provide wonderful grey foliage, variegated shrubs and the ever-increasing varieties of hostas, euphorbias and hellebores.

Eyes were being opened in all directions in the early fifties. Weathered wood was introduced as plant material (it was later termed 'driftwood'), and this increased the awareness of those interested when they were walking in the countryside. When used with a few flowers these pieces of nature's sculpture helped to create artistic pictures. Accessories began to be used, and providing they were in keeping with the plant material they could enhance the display considerably. Many horticulturalists were appalled. On one occasion the weekly paper *Amateur Gardening* printed a photograph of an arrangement of daffodils on a wooden base, beside which stood a china figurine of Royal Doulton's 'Daffodilly'. The caption read: 'Is this flower arranging?' It is true to say that accessories, unless of natural plant material, fast faded from favour in the 1980s, and horticultural shows have always appreciated a very limited use of them.

It was about this time that the *Gardeners' Chronicle*, an esteemed paper for professional and head gardeners, sent an observer to a floral art show, and as a result wrote in an editorial, 'Let's get rid of this petticoat influence!' It was not understood that instead of a bunch of flowers placed in a bowl 'for effect', what they were now seeing was 'art', using living, dried and preserved plant material. It was pointed out that flower arranging was the end product of horticulture, but at that time it had not found its niche as a living art.

The drying of flowers and preservation of plant material was introduced in the fifties, or rather reintroduced, for the Victorians were

Plants, the basic materials with which the flower arranger worked was widely taught and discussed during the 1950s and 1960s

Photo: Julia Clements

adept at placing dry material in fireplaces and on landings. At that time the main items used were dried ferns, seed heads, teasels, bull-rushes and achillea. Now things were different; colour was needed, and new methods of drying and preserving were being sought. In March 1948, at an international flower show in New York, I was asked to display an orchid which had been sent to a friend by a guest at Princess Elizabeth's wedding; it was purported to have come from the top of the wedding cake. It had been preserved at the New York botanical gardens in powdered borax. It caused a sensation, and later I organized a course on the drying of flowers at the Royal Horticultural Society halls. Later still, in my book *101 Ideas for Flower Arrangement*, (1953), the four methods of drying and preserving plant material were set out. Treated in such ways, flowers retained their colours; drying

Photo: Julia Clements

Gold-coloured flowers and brown leaves in a gilded vase in St Paul's Cathedral by Julia Clements, 1966

became an expansion of the art, and all kinds of collages, pressed flower pictures, plaques and so on were produced. I recall at this time a whole house being decorated with dried flowers for charity. Seed firms also started offering packets of flower seeds suitable for drying. Later, the desiccant silica gel was introduced, and this not only facilitated the drying of flowers but quickened the process.

Much had still to be done. Looking back, I often used to ask myself who would have thought there was so much undiscovered talent among those early pioneers. Not only were they artistic with their flowers, but their administrative skills and knowledge of arranging shows would have surprised many of today's professional exhibition organizers. The post-war period of flower decoration in Britain, popularized as an art, was born of necessity. It was begun to help people become more aware of their natural surroundings, and to help spread love and goodwill through the silent lips of flowers. But all that is born must be kept alive; that depends upon those who follow.

Bibliography

Clements, Julia. *Colour Book of Flower Arrangements*. Pearson, 1964.
Clements, Julia. *Flower Arrangements in Stately Homes*. Newnes, 1966.
Clements, Julia. *The Gift Book of Flower Arranging*. Hamlyn, 1969.
Clements, Julia. *ABC of Flower Arranging*. Batsford, 1976.
Clements, Julia. *Flowers in Praise*. Batsford, 1977.
Clements, Julia. *Flower Arrangements Month by Month*. Batsford, 1978.
Clements, Julia. *The Art of Arranging a Flower*. Batsford, 1981.
Nichols, Beverley. *The Art of Flower Arranging*. Collins, 1967.

The formation of NAFAS and the years that followed

PAMELA McNICOL

THE BIRTH OF THE FLOWER ARRANGING MOVEMENT IN THE thirties and the post-war years has been eloquently described in the previous sections. Constance Spry brought her skills to grand occasions in palaces and stately homes, and Julia Clements crusaded to open horizons to everyone. Groups of women up and down the country welcomed the new art of flower arranging and an inspiration behind one of these groups was Mary Pope of Dorchester. During the war she had evacuated to Canada with her three young children. Her reputation as an artist with flowers had spread, and in the spring of 1942 in Toronto she gave a talk to the Hamilton Women's Art Association. The newspaper report of this event epitomizes her early work: 'She delighted her audience by arranging the flowers in unusual containers such as vegetable dishes and gravy boats ... she worked with colour as an artist does his paints.'

After her return to England at the end of the war, she lost no time in looking for ways of sharing these experiences with groups of friends, and they formed the earliest flower clubs in Dorset. By 1952 there were four groups of flower arranging societies in the country, namely the Colchester Flower Club, the Dorset Floral Decoration Society, the Leicester and County Flower Lovers' Guild, and the London Floral Decoration Society. In July of that year they combined to organize a flower academy which was held in the Royal Horticultural Society's new hall, and was the first exhibition devoted entirely to flower arrangements. The *Times Weekly Review* wrote:

> It is obvious that we are witnessing the emergence of flower arrangement into the realms of art. Hitherto it has been carried on quietly in thousands of British homes, but now it is coming out on to the national stage. Progress is inevitable; it may follow the symbolic school or the American school – a combination of the oriental and the traditional European schools; or a new school may evolve. The movement may continue for a long time to teach the technique of floral arrangement, or it may go forward to reach the stage of self-expression in floral art attained elsewhere. Its development in Britain will be watched with great interest.

Constance Spry with Mary Pope and Julia Clements with Lord Aberconway. The photographs were taken at the Flower Academy in London in July 1952 and appeared in an article in Sport and Country

Yes, it was watched – and watched with admiration and enthusiasm. It soon became obvious that an overall organization was required, and in 1959 the National Association of Flower Arrangement Societies of Great Britain was formed. Mary Pope was elected its first president, and Jocelyn Steward from the east of England (now resident in South Africa) its first chairman. A network of flower clubs and societies was formed all over the country and, owing to the enthusiasm of these founder members, a rapidly growing nation-wide organization came into being. As many of these early clubs sprang from established horticultural societies, the Association received knowledgeable help and encouragement from the RHS to whom, from its inception, it was affiliated.

In the section on the thirties, Sheila MacQueen describes the great innovation of that time in flower arranging as being the use of crushed wire netting pushed into vases. In 1960 an even greater development occurred, which was to revolutionize completely the placement of flowers in containers. A water-retaining foam-like substance known as 'oasis' was being used in America, and was imported in small quantities to this country. In 1963 it became available from a factory in Denmark and was brought over in what were known as the 'horseboats'; horses were sent to Belgium and Holland for slaughter, and the empty boats returned loaded with oasis. An observer at the time noted that the boxes arrived with a somewhat unsavoury odour, since the holds were not cleaned before the return journey! Later it was imported in a more conventional style from Denmark in container lorries, and today it is made in a purpose-built factory in Britain. A well-soaked block of oasis allowed flowers and foliage to be placed at angles above the ridge of the container, and no longer did one have to rely on curving stems to give a required shape.

In 1966 the first major flower festival was staged in Westminster Abbey to mark its 900th anniversary, under the banner 'One People'.

An arrangement by Mary Pope published on the front cover of The Flower Arranger Magazine in 1969

The first flower festival held in Westminster Abbey in 1966. Giant urns of scarlet flowers backed onto the pillars throughout the Nave
NAFAS Ltd

Festival of Flowers, St Paul's Cathedral 1969, which marked the 10th anniversary of NAFAS. Pedestal by Joan Newlyn, Chairman of the festival
The Flower Arranger

Skilled flower arrangers came from all over the country, and flowers were sent from the four corners of the world to help express the message of love to all people. Three years later a superbly planned festival took place in St Paul's Cathedral. Again experts foregathered and shared their skills, to the glorification of this masterpiece of Sir Christopher Wren's architecture. The Dean and Chapter were taken by surprise when 50 000 brochures were sold out long before the end of the festival and the National Association celebrated its tenth anniversary with the success of a second great festival.

The Association was now colloquially known as NAFAS and its emblem embraced the rose, the daffodil, the thistle and the shamrock.

NAFAS emblem

By the time it celebrated its silver jubilee it had 100 000 members, and there were flower clubs in almost every town and village in the country. It appeared to provide something for everyone. Older members enjoyed the relaxation of attending their flower club meetings and watching flowers being arranged for their enjoyment. They admired the skills of the demonstrator and went home inspired and determined to emulate in their own homes all that had been shown. But there was at the same time an increasing demand for evening clubs as more and more working women showed interest in this increasingly popular leisure activity. There was a growing urge to learn, and to learn at classes – evening classes in colleges, followed by examinations which provided City and Guilds qualifications.

Meanwhile similar organizations had become well established in other countries of the world. There was an important development in the history of flower arranging in the summer of 1981 when 20 countries met in London and formed the World Association of Flower Arranging (WAFA). Great Britain was elected the host country for the

WAFA emblem

first three years, and NAFAS agreed to organize a world show which would be held in Bath in 1984. Now, certainly, friendship through flowers would encircle the world in a way that perhaps nothing else could.

As the 1970s began, the accepted techniques used by the pioneers were being demonstrated to flower clubs, taught to students and developed in a great variety of ways. One of the most notable demonstrators at this time was George Smith from Yorkshire, a man who was, and is, truly an ambassador for Great Britain and NAFAS. He travelled the world illustrating his immense talents and superb artistry, and sharing his immeasurable knowledge of plant material. His performances developed more and more into a stage show, unequalled by any other demonstrator. His home and garden in Heslington, Yorkshire were a setting of beauty which was a joy to visit. He was pleased when once I described them as impeccable; there seemed no better word to use.

Flowers from my garden in a manner of Furber, the 18th century nurseryman. Arranged by George Smith
Photo: Allan Green

In 1975 an almost unknown demonstrator from Jersey brought an audience of 500 to their feet with a totally new concept of demonstrating. There were no words but simply music, a theatrical performance; it was given at Bournemouth as part of the National Festival of Flowers of that year. Graeme Audrain had made his name, and joined the ranks of notable flower demonstrators. Many men and women have swelled these ranks since then; all are dedicated and willing to teach, to entertain and to share their expertise.

During the 1970s festivals of flowers had become an integral part of the early summer and autumn programmes of events in cathedrals, churches and stately homes the length and breadth of the country. Many thousands of pounds were raised annually, and thus churches were reroofed, cathedral fabric preserved, lifeboats launched, guide dogs trained, and research furthered into a wide variety of medical problems. Members of NAFAS were proving that they were not just pretty faces under flowery or feathery hats; they used their talents to the best possible advantage, giving an enormous amount of pleasure at the same time.

These flower festivals were organized by a team of experts, who planned and designed each one with the precision of a battle commander. Details ranged from colour schemes and festival themes to car parking and refreshments. And in this team there was always the festival designer, chosen for her artistry and her powers of organization and administration. The artistry of the design must be the main consideration and, as the years pass, more and more ingenuity is required to think of new ideas and different ways of tackling old themes. Plans for a church festival are of course very different from those required for a stately home or a cathedral, but the basic rules are the same. A good designer gives herself time to sit quietly in the aisle of the church, the nave of the cathedral or the rooms in the stately home. This provides the opportunity for her to acquaint herself with the atmosphere of her surroundings, to visualize colouring which would best fit in with the existing fabric, and to feel the history which the centuries have given to the building.

I remember sitting in the nave of Winchester Cathedral; having studied its history, I could well imagine Cromwell riding through that mighty nave to vandalize its treasures. I pictured the pilgrims travelling through it hoping to reach the shrine, though some would fall exhausted on the steep stone steps of the transept; and I noticed the hooks on which hung the banners for the wedding of Mary Queen of Scots. Thus my ideas flowed, the ensuing designs interpreted them vividly, and the basis for an exciting and varied theme was established. When the festival began the stone steps were adorned with dried arrangements, which included a pilgrim's sandal, the shells they carried, and a tiny grey and black arrangement to indicate the pilgrim who was said to have died on the steps without reaching the shrine. Interpretation had become more and more a part of flower arranging.

Some years later I sat in another nave, that of the first and foremost church in the land, Westminster Abbey. We were planning a festival, and as I sat there very early one morning with my codesigners we became aware of the beautiful and varied blue glass in the stained glass windows. The idea was born for silk banners in shaded blues, which varied from deep royal blue at the west end through mid blues to a beautiful pastel blue at the east end. The sprays of flowers on each varied equally – dark reds on the dark blues, paler reds and orange on the mid blues, and pale cream, peach and apricot on the pale blue.

If in the past it had been enough to display beautiful pedestals, urns or columns of flowers at festivals, items of greater general interest were now required. Carefully planned set pieces were being staged in suitable areas, such as north and south transepts and small chapels. In Westminster Abbey in 1981, the 400th anniversary of the Nicene

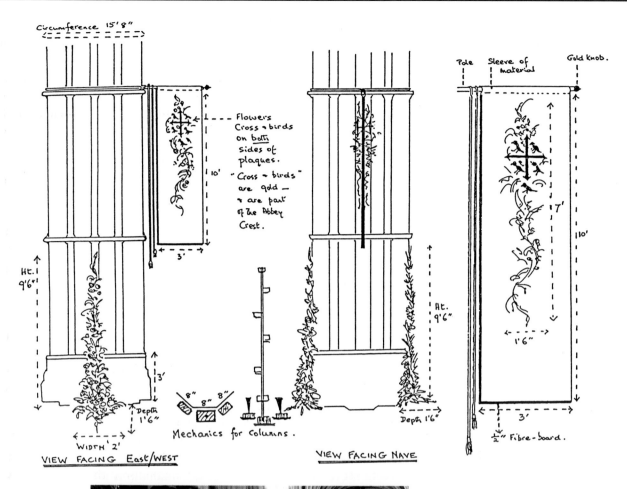

Circumference 15' 8"

Flowers
Cross + birds
on both
sides of
plaques.
"Cross + birds"
are gold —
+ are part
of the Abbey
Crest.

10'

3'

Ht.
9'6"

3'

Depth
1'6"

Width 2'

VIEW FACING East/West

8"   8"
8"

Mechanics for Columns.

Ht.
9'6"

Depth 1'6"

VIEW FACING NAVE

Pole   Sleeve of
Material   Gold knob.

7'

10'

1'6"

3'

½" Fibre-board.

The designs given to the arrangers who worked in the Nave in the Flower Festival in Westminster Abbey in 1981. The shaded blue silk banners bearing the Abbey crest and curving arrangements of flowers hanging above the Nave and complementing the varied blues in the stained glass windows

Creed in the established Church, the Guilds of the City of London, the Four Inns of Court, Westminster School, and the ancient and modern seats of government were honoured in dramatic set pieces staged in the transepts. The delightful photograph of HM Queen Elizabeth II, who visited the Abbey whilst the festival was being staged, shows her framed in the floral interpretation of the hammer-beam roof of Westminster Hall. This famous roof, which covers nearly half an acre, remains a masterpiece of medieval English carpentry, and by the time it was completed in 1402 the hall was the centre of the kingdom's administration and the home of the royal courts of law.

Careful notice began to be taken of wood carving, such as that of Grinling Gibbons, and corresponding swags were made in dried plant material and placed in such a way that it was often difficult to identify which was which! Similarly, carvings in the marble of tombs were echoed in natural plant material; a tomb in Westminster Abbey with a bishop's mitre, crook and open Bible carved on it was copied exactly with a silk mitre decorated with seed heads and a crook made in plaited corn. Bookmarks for Bibles resting on lecterns, and pulpit falls, were now invariably included in any festival, and they demonstrated the wide variety of skills within the art of flower arranging. This delicate and intricate work done entirely in natural plant material is in sharp contrast to the vast columns of flowers and flowing pedestals which remain an essential part of any festival. If variety is the spice of life, it certainly lends spice to a flower festival, and it has been well proven that a starkly modern yet exotic arrangement can find a place within the ancient fabric of any place of worship.

Festivals in churches need equally meticulous planning – perhaps more so since often the whole effect can be seen at a glance. Seldom are overall colour schemes used, but colours in the stained glass windows may be picked out and used in the flowers on the relevant sills. Often darker colours are chosen for the west end of a church,

Festival of Flowers, Westminster Abbey 1981. Her Majesty the Queen is framed in the interpretive hammer beam roof of the ancient seat of Parliament while visiting the Abbey on staging day
Press Association

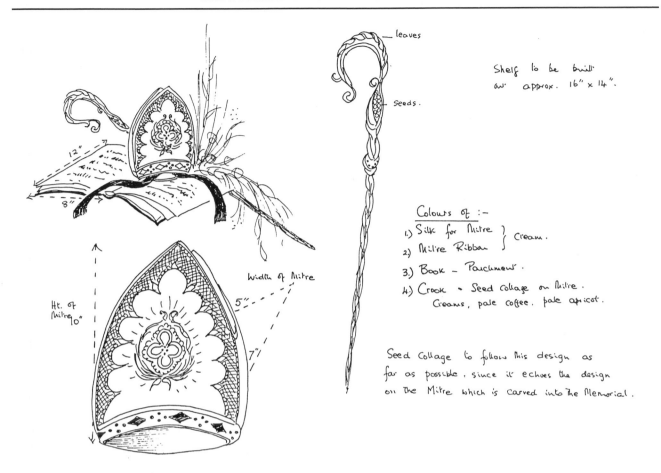

leaves

seeds.

Shelf to be built at approx. 16" x 14".

12"

8"

Ht. of Mitre 10"

Width of Mitre

5"

7"

Colours of :—

1.) Silk for Mitre ⎫ Cream.
2.) Mitre Ribbon ⎭

3.) Book — Parchment.

4.) Crook & Seed collage on Mitre. Creams, pale coffee, pale apricot.

Seed Collage to follow this design as far as possible, since it echoes the design on the Mitre which is carved into the Memorial.

Festival of Flowers, Westminster Abbey 1981. An example of the instructions which were given to the arranger, Constance Barnes, who carried out the design. The bishop's crook, mitre and open book were carved in the stone of the tomb
The Flower Arranger

becoming paler eastwards until the altar is adorned with cream and white flowers. Themes for church festivals are frequently chosen; well-tried ones are the Church's annual festivals such as Christmas, Easter, Whitsun and Harvest, and events such as christenings and weddings. Scenes from the Bible have often played their part, as have historical events that have taken place in the parish.

There may well be a set piece which depicts the charity for which the festival has been held. For example, a festival held in aid of the National Society for the Prevention of Cruelty to Children may contrast happy scenes from the lives of children – picnics, school and holidays – with a sad and stark set piece which highlights the lives of the deprived children cared for by the NSPCC. A set piece with organ pipes and music carries the message that the festival is in aid of the restoration of the church organ, and an exhibit which includes rafters and tiles tells of the need for roof repairs. Cleverly designed church festivals do not neglect the natural requirements of the fabric of the church. The choir stalls are best adorned with garlands and swags, the pulpit likewise; nothing need replace the traditional pedestal by the altar and/or by the lectern, and as a greeting at the entrance.

Not only were cathedrals and churches the settings for flower festivals, but so also were stately homes. They provided endless added interests; many housed magnificent collections of pictures, unique

A pedestal by Pamela McNicol at the Flower Festival in Romsey Abbey in 1979. It was admired by Lord Mountbatten who asked her to do a similar one at the wedding of his grandson the following summer. The pedestal was done but the wedding saddened since Lord Mountbatten had been brutally killed and his daughter attended the wedding in a wheelchair
The Flower Arranger

cabinets of china and glass, and priceless antique furniture. Dining tables were laid with beautiful china, glass and silver of the family, with a suitable floral table centrepiece. Invariably they had their own chapters in history which could be picked out and staged to create interest. For example at Bramshill in Berkshire, a Tudor mansion and now a police training college, there was the sad little story of the bride who, playing hide and seek on the eve of her wedding, hid in an oak chest and was unable to get out. It was assumed that she had run away from her prospective husband; the lid was not raised for many years, and then to reveal bones and dust. At a flower festival held at Bramshill in 1972, a charming bride's bouquet rested on the chest and her initials were done in seed collage on a velvet cushion.

Family crests were frequently seen displayed as plaques of seed heads and dried plant material. Indeed, at the dedication of the memorial to Lord and Lady Mountbatten in Westminster Abbey in February 1985, NAFAS provided two plaques, made entirely in plant material, of their cyphers, and these were laid on the memorial during the service by Countess Mountbatten and her sister Lady Pamela Hicks. The plaques were backed by black velvet with a raised oval covered in cream dupion, the initials were worked in red-dyed glixias, and the lettering in gilded lentils. Glycerined and gilded aspidistra leaves with fine gold braid were used to make the crowns. The service was attended by many members of the royal family, and the memorial was a fitting tribute to a well-loved man who had served his country well and had died so tragically.

There were castles also which lent themselves to exciting festivals. One with much romance and the most perfect setting is Leeds Castle near Maidstone in Kent. Many themes for many festivals have been used in this wonderful Tudor edifice, surrounded by its moat around which swim the black swans with their coral pink beaks. In recent years it has frequently been used for intergovernmental meetings,

The Mountbatten Cyphers done in seed collage by Beryl Greenslade
The Flower Arranger

since because of its moat it is deemed to be relatively secure. Obviously there have been floral themes to echo the building's history, and one's imagination has been inspired by the beautiful bedroom with its huge canopied bed and the rose-coloured crested silk wall coverings. It was the bedroom of Catherine de Valois, but the bed was only used by her for childbirth and in death. The castle's tiny chapel houses unique German woodcarvings, and the dungeon-like cellars held vast kegs of wine. It is a fairy-tale castle, and appropriately its most recent festival portrayed all the fairy tales. Romance and fantasy surrounded every flower arranged there, and it was well seen how flower arranging had indeed become an art to stimulate and inspire those who do it and those who enjoy seeing it.

If by the eighties flower arranging in festivals of flowers had progressed to this extent, likewise floral competitive work, organized by NAFAS and many horticultural societies, had progressed. Schedules produced for competitions became more and more ingenious and increasingly imaginative. There were classes for traditional styles, historical, modern, abstract, mobiles and stamobiles, dried pictures of seed collage, miniatures and petites, garlands and plaques, bookmarks and jewellery, all made from natural plant material, and there were the wide horizons of 'interpretation'. Some would say that the rules which accompanied the competitions were too many and too exacting, yet without them one would flounder amongst the unanswered questions. The national festival and competitions held by NAFAS every year in different parts of the country attracted more and more competitors and drew crowds in thousands from all over the country. Every year it was felt that the standards had increased; every year one saw advances in the art of flower arranging which were almost beyond belief. There was a 'new look' emerging – the transformation of nature into an art form. But was it flower arranging when there were so few flowers – or even no flowers? In 1986 the best-in-show award at the national festival at Rochford was won by a superbly artistic use of wood – a piece of wood in an almost bird form. It was severe, balanced and utterly pleasing to look at. Its flowers and foliage were minimal; it was a sculpture of nature, a wonderful use of natural plant material.

Meanwhile reports were coming from all over Europe of the new art form of arranging natural plant material. In Jersey in 1986 a German flower demonstrator produced a tangled mass of foliage which had a simple beauty of its own. At the world show in Brussels in 1987 was displayed a delightful, seemingly casual tangle of thin curves of wood. There too was a tribute to Queen Elizabeth of Belgium, founder of the world famous music competition which bears her name. It was done by a member of the Cape Province Flower Club in South Africa, and it won the best-in-show award. Again there were curves of wood, this time more tailored, but again with balance of colour, proportion, light, shade and design. These are the ingredients that an artist looks for when painting a picture; so also does a flower arranger. No matter whether the style is Flemish, Victorian, modern or abstract, those qualities need to be there, and indeed can be found in all the chapters of this book.

If today we are still uncertain how to describe or classify the new art

'Poised in space' by Kathy Mullins won the 'Best in show' award at Rochford in 1986. It was a triumph of simplicity and a meticulous selection of materials
The Flower Arranger

Photos: Rod Sloane

Pamela South's arrangement which won first prize in the Art Nouveau class at WAFA in Brussels, 1987
Garden News

Elize Oliver's 'A tribute to a Queen' won 'Best in show' award at WAFA, Brussels, 1987
Garden News

forms, and the sculpting of plant material, it may be of interest to note the foresight of our pioneers. Just over 20 years ago, in January 1967, Mary Pope wrote the following in a letter to Dorothy Cooke: 'It is so important that we should have a different approach to our "floral art" or whatever we choose to call it. I feel the modern and contemporary have come to stay, and therefore, as Sheila MacQueen suggested, it should have a special title: perhaps "Interpretative art with natural plant material".' How strange that, after all this time, this problem is still under discussion!

Whilst WAFA and NAFAS are looking ahead to these most exciting and stimulating ideas, there is a growing school of thought (largely promoted by coffee-table magazines) that calls for more simple presentations of flowers in basic containers, leaving them to fall naturally into place, often with the stems visible through the glass containers. It should be emphasized that there is a place in the history of flower arranging for every type, size and shape of arrangement which enhances natural plant material, and it should always be to one's personal taste. Members of NAFAS should not assume that they are the authority and that their rules must be followed by all who enjoy this art. But let us not minimize the place of NAFAS in the world of flower arranging, or the talents and skills of its members in producing such an immense variety of uses for plant material.

If I was asked to single out the things I have valued most through my association with a flower club, I have no doubt at all what I would choose. First, I learnt so much from the late Sybil Emberton (Association of Honour of NAFAS) about the use of foliage and how to grow it. Her superb coloured ink drawings won a gold medal at the RHS in 1973. Secondly, I began to appreciate the wonderful combinations of colours of flowers: the clashing reds, the soft pastel shades, the hint of pale pink which links the cream and peach and apricot, and the joy and coolness of a green and white arrangement. One of the many experts in this field is Lillian Martin of Edinburgh, now a Special Associate of Honour of NAFAS. The artistry at her fingertips gives a new dimension to colours in flower arranging and she has a subtlety which is indefinable. Thirdly, I now look at my garden, the hedgerows, the woods, the hillsides, the cliffs and the beaches in a completely new light, and find many treasures to use in my flower arranging.

It is reasonable to suggest that the flowers arranged by NAFAS in Westminster Abbey for the wedding of HRH Prince Andrew and Miss Sarah Ferguson on 23 July 1986 may well have a place in the history of flower arranging. They were totally different, and more ambitious and in some cases more precisely planned than any other flower arrangements yet undertaken. Both the Prince and the Abbey authorities were anxious that flowers should play an important part in the service. They asked that they should be spectacular, and well able to be seen not only by those in the congregation but also by the many cameras which would relay their pictures round the world. The Prince and his bride contributed many ideas of their own, not least that flowers should 'hang from the roof of the Abbey'. The resulting balls of flowers which were suspended between each pillar in the nave on double nylon ropes and hauled up from the triforium were the perfect

The designs for the pulpit for the Royal Wedding, 1985 by Mary Napper, and for the altar by Pamela McNicol and Mary Graves

answer. These and other ideas were suggested by the royal couple whilst I walked round the Abbey with them in late April. Miss Ferguson wrote down the colours of her dress and of the bridesmaids' and pages' clothing, and outlined the colours she would like for the flowers. Handing me the piece of paper on which this information was written, she confided that she wished it to be a secret even from Prince Andrew. I guarded the knowledge with immense care, despite the persistence of the media in the weeks that followed. The lovely soft colours she chose – apricot, peach, pale pink and cream – complemented the ornate decoration of Westminster Abbey to perfection.

Foremost in the minds of the designers was that this was not a flower festival, and several priorities had to be observed. Unlike a festival there would be no large overpowering pedestals which would obscure the views of any section of the congregation. No flowers would impede the positioning of the choir, the trumpeters and the soloists; the organist must have a good view of the choir; a clear passage must be ensured for the bride's procession through all doorways; and above all strict safety precautions must govern every detail of the designs. With all these things taken into consideration, with an overall colour scheme throughout, and with careful investigation into the positions of the cameras in every vantage point in the Abbey, the resulting designs included very precise details. Faultless mechanics were required; these were provided by a flower arranger's husband, a farmer by the name of Graeme Findlay. He designed, made and installed all the structures which played such a vital part in the success or indeed the possibility of the flower arrangements planned.

Once the team of arrangers had been chosen, two things were impressed upon them: (1) the need for secrecy as to the chosen colour scheme, and (2) the need for total accuracy in carrying out the designs given to them. There was no room for errors; there would be no opportunity to correct them. There were 45 members of NAFAS in the team of flower arrangers; they were chosen by ballot from each section of the Association, and all 20 areas of Great Britain were represented. They forgathered in Westminster Abbey three days before the wedding, bringing with them beautiful foliage typical of their environment. White heather came from Scotland, huge hosta leaves from Yorkshire, larger than life alchemilla from Cheshire and almost tropical foliage from Devon and Cornwall. The RHS Gardens at Wisley and the Saville Gardens at Windsor provided vast quantities of foliage, and the Royal Gardens at Windsor sent many beautiful carnations and chrysanthemums. Over 30 000 blooms arrived at the Abbey during the Sunday and Monday; many were gifts from growers in this country, the Channel Islands and abroad. English rose growers sent 4000 roses; superb orchids came from the orchid farm in Jersey; carnations were flown from Columbia; and the finest specimens of *Protea*, including the special 'blushing bride' proteas, were delivered directly to the Abbey from South Africa.

Unlike any other event held before, now whole vistas of flowers were caught by the cameras and relayed all over the world. They were enjoyed and commented on by people in every corner of the globe, and NAFAS' members watched with pride. In the days that followed the wedding, 54 000 people queued to file through the Abbey and to enjoy the flowers they had glimpsed on their TV screens. Many plucked rosebuds from the archway of flowers and from the choir stalls to take home as souvenirs – and daily we replaced them! They noticed the beautiful scent of the lilies, and they appreciated the charming tradition of the bride's bouquet, now lying on the tomb of the Unknown Warrior. This was a practice begun by Queen Elizabeth the Queen Mother after her marriage and carried on by every royal bride since, just as all royal brides' bouquets are presented by the Worshipful Company of Gardeners of London. Since 1947 this honour has been in the hands of Martin and David Longman of Longman's florists, both of whom have held the position of Master of the Company.

Once again flowers had told their story, and created happiness and pleasure for all those who viewed them. All races and all creeds, the old and the young, they came, they waited and their appreciation was immense. A TV reporter interviewed one elderly lady as she left the Abbey. 'How long did you have to queue?' he said. 'Three hours' she replied. 'Was it worth it?' 'I wouldn't have missed it for the world!'

Bibliography

Emberton, Sybil C. *Garden Foliage for Flower Arrangement.* Faber and Faber, 1968.

Emberton, Sybil C. *Shrub Gardening for Flower Arrangement.* Faber and Faber, 1965.

Newnes, Mary (ed.). *NAFAS Book of Flower Arranging.* Ebury Press, 1987.

Webb, Iris (ed.) *The Complete Guide to Flower and Foliage Arrangement.* Ebury Press, 1979.

Modern trends and new dimensions

MARIAN AARONSON

W HEN ASSESSING PRESENT TRENDS IN FLOWER arranging,it is necessary to look back over recent years to identify the factors that have fashioned the designs of today. In reviewing the past, it becomes evident that now and again there have been influences and changes of attitude that have altered or modified a style already established to suit new ideas. These developments have not evolved at a dramatic pace, or in definite movements, but through more gradual and subtle changes of direction.

Changing attitudes

For example, the mass arrangement of rather indeterminate shape with plant material assembled close together was gradually replaced by a more disciplined version based on a controlled pattern. This produced arrangements with a crisper silhouette and with more space between each unit. The more sophisticated aspect of the mass echoed the clean lines of modern architecture with its lack of ornamentation, and the simple forms of modern furniture and unfussy decor. Smart modern vases appeared, and designs became more restrained and linear.

There followed a phase when these sparser designs became over-stylized and rather stiff in appearance. Students in the classroom struggled with shapes based on the crescent, the Hogarth curve, and the L shape, which tended to produce prim, precise arrangements without a whisker out of place.

The reaction was a move towards a more graceful style guided by the natural line of the plants used. 'Free style', as it was christened, marked the beginning of more freedom in designing and a move away from repetitive methods. The pressure of working to rules was now relaxed. Crossing lines, for instance, were no longer taboo, and the principle was appreciated as a means of achieving depth or defining space. It became permissible for leaves to be furled or lightly trimmed, and thin flexible items to be looped or curved to make new forms and to create more original patterns. This greater freedom encouraged a more imaginative approach and designs that were less stereotyped.

Photo: Ken Lauder

A sparse arrangement with emphasis on line and space and each unit clearly defined. Arranged by Marian Aaronson
Scott Lauder Gallery

220

Photo: Ken Lauder

A subtly painted background adds atmosphere to a composition suggestive of a storm at sea. It picks up the colour and texture of the design without dominating it. Arranged by Marian Aaronson
Scott Lauder Gallery

As the appreciation for design itself continued to escalate, attitudes in using the plant material altered too. The value of its various qualities as elements and symbols for self-expression was now more fully realized. In line with this growing enthusiasm, interpretative themes at competitions became more and more challenging. The use of dyed and painted material became permissible, which increased the possibilities for interpretations through added colour. Impressionistic, expressionistic and futuristic effects were interpreted with fervour equal to the painter on canvas. Ingeniously coloured backgrounds to support the theme and to give added atmosphere became very popular. Used discriminately these greatly enhanced the composition, though alas they sometimes dominated the scene – as did too much painted material.

The influence of sculpture

The continuing search for new ideas extended interest to other contemporary art forms. Some of the concepts of modern sculpture inspired certain ways of assembling plant material. Exhibits lifted off the ground on metal or acrylic structures gave the illusion of con-

Photo: Ken Loveday

The expressive line of the cliffed fan palm, combined with that of the driftwood creates a vigorous rhythm suggesting the movements of a dancer. The vivid amaryllis flowers add extra sparkle. Arranged by Marian Aaronson
The Flower Arranger

tinuity into space, like a sculpture poised above its plinth or base. Space was used more positively within the design to create voids, and so enhance its depth and rhythm. Enclosed spaces were planned for the same 'eye-pull' as the pierced hole of sculpture. The mobile sculptures of Alexander Calder inspired floral constructions with actual movement, with the separate parts gently wafted by currents of air to give a rhythmic, ever-changing tempo. Likewise, the principles of the mobile were combined with those of the stabile to give actual and implied movement in a stamobile. Perpetual motion in floral design, however, was not developed to any memorable degree. Mobiles were included for variety in competitive shows for a while, but mechanical means of rotating the exhibits as organized at a few festivals did not seem to inspire much enthusiasm.

Achieving sculptural emphasis, however, certainly continued to influence the nature of many designs and to colour presentation. The more dramatic type of plant material became the most popular choice for achieving these effects, especially the dried and more durable items. Flowers, when used, tended to act just as contrast or as emphasis of the strength of the structure created. This led to more and more instances of arrangements without flowers. Major accolades awarded to such exhibits at the show bench strengthened the trend towards a division between conventional flower arrangement and sculpture with plant material.

Left *A flowerless 'sculpture' based on dried palm spathes and assembled so as to emphasize their form and structural interest. Arranged by Marian Aaronson*
Scott Lauder Gallery

Right *Nature's sculptural forms are combined here for rhythm, depth and areas of space. The ascending lines soaring upwards imply that 'objects never finish'. Arranged by Marian Aaronson*
Scott Lauder Gallery

Photos: Ken Lauder

Clearly the boundaries of *flower* arranging were becoming less sharply definable, and the presentation of plant material in ever more innovative ways considerably altered its image. Impressions of the changing concepts in other art forms opened up yet newer fields of vision with further breaks from tradition.

Towards abstraction

The shift of emphasis from the more naturalistic style to the more advanced areas of designing, with the ever-increasing exploitation of the material, led to abstraction. This concept involved a change of attitude in regarding the medium; its natural associations were now dispensed with in order to emphasize only its essential quality or qualities. Abstract is not so much a style as a means to an end. By simplifying, exaggerating or distorting, the subject is presented from a different point of view. Of all the progressive developments this probably caused the biggest controversy, for it raised the question of its compatibility with the nature of the medium. Those who favoured the more faithful representation of nature found the non-naturalistic manifestations and unfamiliar patterns hard to appreciate, and some felt the change of direction was unacceptable. Lack of understanding of the basic objectives resulted in rather poor presentations in the early stages. Good design and visual appeal were often sacrificed to sensa-

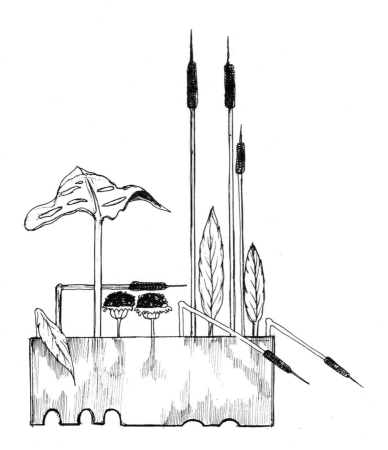

An abstract design

A presentation with simplicity and restraint emphasizing line, shape and texture. Arranged by Marian Aaronson
Scott Lauder Gallery

Photo: Ken Lauder

tional effects which had no real meaning, and the artistic freedom of concepts was abused. When greater insight was acquired, however, more acceptable versions gradually appeared.

The inclusion of abstract as part of the curriculum of students taking the City and Guilds examinations prompted further research into the principles involved, and their application relative to the medium of plant material. Greater general interest was also created by classes for non-naturalistic design at flower shows. This extra incentive through competitions has helped elevate the standard, and the more inspired presentations have established abstract technique as an acceptable part of the flower arranger's art.

Contemporary influences

Like every other artistic venture, flower arranging has been affected by major events and aspects of the times. Every so often fresh challenges and new opportunities are presented to encourage further developments. Perhaps the most significant single influence of recent times has been the ever-increasing contact between flower arrangers from different countries. With the ease of travel and communication today, it has been possible for a World Association to be formed. The strengthening of links through correspondence, publications and the exchange of teachers and demonstrators has been further promoted by several world symposiums. The resulting stimulus of the varying styles and trends delivered from different cultures and climatic conditions has proved most beneficial to flower arranging in all member countries. Clearly the enthusiastic exchange of ideas and concepts has broadened horizons, leading to greater awareness and appreciation of each other's styles.

Two competitive world shows have presented an even more comprehensive view of flower arranging around the world. At both events – the first in England, the second in Belgium – each member association staged an exhibition piece using the plant material typical of their country. The great variety of flora, and the very different ways it was presented, reflected individuality of outlook and resources in an unmistakable way, and not working to a set title gave each exhibitor complete freedom of expression.

The competitive sections, however, gave ample scope for the competitor to mirror the different facets of designing practised today, and an opportunity for the observer to identify the most significant aspects of contemporary trends. The premier awards, for instance, at both events reflected the continuing influence of sculpture on the designer using plant material, and the undiminishing popularity of dramatic dried items for establishing the structure of the design. The best-in-show award at the first competition was given to a stamobile; happily, on this occasion at least, there *was* enthusiasm! It was an immaculate design based on a large twisted vine to convey the illusion of movement; a couple of small orchids were the only fresh material included. The premier award at the second show contained a few more fresh flowers and leaves, but here too the structural strength of the design was sustained by its elegant sculptural framework of dried plant material. At this same event, the originality award could certainly have qualified as a piece of sculpture in a modern art gallery or, as the title suggested, a 'modern museum'. Here again the fresh plant, mainly bromeliads, added colour, but the drama of the design was captured mainly in the stunning way it conveyed the very essence of sculpture in its presentation of the dried units. These inspired art forms were all created by flower arrangers from South Africa, which again demonstrates the considerable influence of the available vegetation on style.

Sculptural emphasis, however, was featured also at both competitions in many designs of fresh plant material. Frequent use was made of large succulents, which last without water, and longer-lasting foliages. Leaves in several exhibits were manipulated into curves to create voids, and reshaped or overlapped in a series of planes to create dramatic new forms. Many of these compositions were presented on tall sophisticated structures, sometimes of natural material like bamboo stems, which enhanced their sculptural aspect. The Italian exhibit in the non-competitive section at Bath was a superb stabile of huge agave supported on a curved metal stand, with the bulk of the plant material held aloft several feet off the ground.

Photo: Rod Sloane

A composition for a 'modern museum' based on three painted scooped-out Calabashes. Arranged by Elsa-de-Jager
Garden News

Impression of a stabile

European trends

A fair proportion of the competitive exhibits at the Brussels show were by flower arrangers from Italy, France, Holland and Belgium. The Belgian Flower Arrangement Society had also staged an exhibition to feature distinctive aspects of the nine provinces of Belgium. Their bias towards fresh plant material and only natural accessories, in both modern and traditional presentations, was clearly illustrated. The Italian flower arrangers also generally favoured the use of fresh material. Their modern designs are now unmistakable, based most often on line-mass (see Chapter 4). They frequently use a considerable quantity of flowers and foliage grouped very close together to give virtually unbroken areas of colour and texture, but based almost invariably on a definite and dynamic linear pattern.

The compositions of vegetables and fruit at the second competition stimulated a new awareness of the designing possibilities with this kind of flora not as yet, in general, fully exploited. The European arrangers had assembled its great range of shapes, colours and textures into interesting structures, often with no other forms of plant material added.

The technique of designing in parallel lines has been a feature of

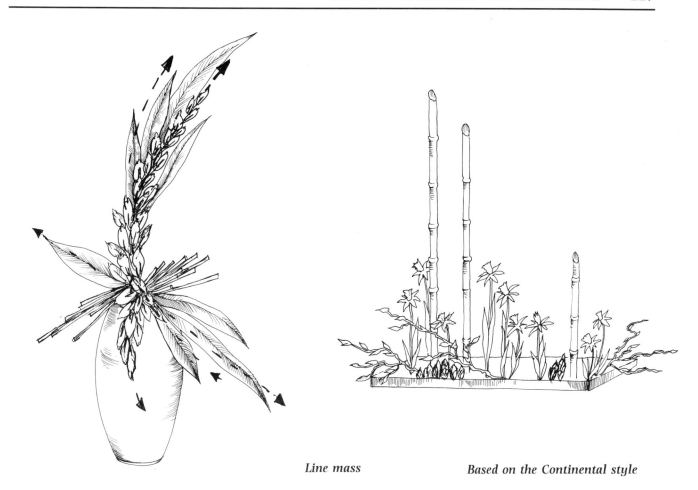

Line mass   *Based on the Continental style*

many European designs for quite some time, inspired perhaps by the spectacular florists' displays at the Ghent Floralies and other horticultural exhibitions on the continent. This is an interesting concept, and its influence has spread elsewhere. The units are arranged in a series of vertical lines, very much in the manner of their natural growth pattern. The upright stems are then sometimes contrasted by a number of horizontal or diagonal lines at the base, or flowers, often cut very short, are placed low in the container. Whilst not all the placements are entirely naturalistic, the overall impression evokes a scenic image. It is a technique that is particularly effective when staged in a long, low container, with the placements enhancing depth and distance as in a landscape design. In the more formal arrangement, too, this way of assembling the units makes a refreshing change from the more conventional practice of radiating the stems from the centre.

One of the most stimulating classes at the Brussels competition was that for the large 'tapestries' mounted and hung. The sense of depth and rhythm captured on a flat surface through colour and texture distribution, almost entirely with *fresh* plant material, was truly impressive. The overall effect of a picture gallery of living plants left no one in doubt of the resourcefulness of designers, even with a fragile, perishable medium. Indeed, perhaps it is the perpetual challenge of an ephemeral medium that inspires continuity of artistic endeavour in this particular art form.

Future trends

With the 1990s upon us, are there any true indications of what is likely to emerge as the trends of tomorrow? Will the continuing interest in the shape and structure of natural objects continue to promote involvement in sculptural composition? Or will the 'Continental style', as it is now called, establish an acceptable compromise between the more intricate presentation and the naturalistic arrangement?

Clearly, modern design no longer refers only to the sparse arrangement using a minimum of plant material, but can incorporate designs with a greater profusion of colour and texture, often with one type of flower or foliage bunched together for greater emphasis. During Euroflora '86 the Garden Club of Genoa organized a display of the modern designs of different countries, which illustrated the wide spectrum of styles now labelled 'modern'. The exhibits ranged from the very restrained and minimal to the quite voluptuous, from the almost naturalistic to the avant-garde, and from the simplistic to the complex. An overlapping of concepts and influences has produced a greater variety of moderns.

Abstracts, too, seem in general to be less stark and inhibited. A greater range of elements is often included for greater visual appeal, so that semi-abstracts, which are less restricting, have become the more popular choice and are more frequently practised. Interior designers have long favoured the less pretentious arrangements featuring flowers and foliage in an uncontrived way to suit the setting. This is a refreshing change from struggling with difficult mechanics, and such arrangements are pleasing and easy to live with. Those who have spent a long time acquiring more advanced designing skills, however, might consider this alone an insufficient challenge. Yet the simpler concept could inspire less complex compositions, using the plant material in a way that is more relaxed and natural but is based on the creative techniques of designing already mastered. This would combine past experience with a fresh approach; it would also make an interesting class in competition, providing some aspect of the intended setting of the composition was included.

In conclusion

It has not been possible in one brief section to comment in greater detail on the exhibits observed at other international events, whether demonstrations by highly gifted flower arrangers or other exhibitions overseas, and at the national competitions here in Great Britain, where over recent years many outstanding exhibits have been displayed.

Amongst the many factors that have contributed to this higher standard is more sophisticated and up-to-date staging, tailored to the newer trends in designing. The competitor is now far less restricted by always working in a niche. Free-standing backgrounds of very generous dimensions are often provided in some of the classes today, which has inspired designs more varied in format and dimensions. Sections with no height restrictions have also influenced presentation, with exhibits that soar higher and higher. For instance the abstract class at the 1987 NAFAS festival entitled 'Sequence' produced impressive examples unrestricted by dimensional limitations. Less restrictive wording in the schedules for classes, often just a title and the word 'exhibit', has helped to free the competitor from too many inhibitory requirements, and has therefore encouraged a more creative approach. These and many other factors have influenced the general pattern of progress, not only in competition or exhibitions but in other areas of flower arranging activities. The ever-increasing range of designs that keep emerging mirror the many new dimensions that have been added to the repertoire of the flower arranger in all parts of the world.

At the same time, it is reassuring to observe in world-wide trends a certain individuality still reflected in the styles of every country. The elegant, gently rhythmic traditional arrangement, so suited to the nature of the plant material of the British Isles, remains its most enduring style and is easily identifiable at international functions. In the same way, to name but a few, certain floral sculptures are associated with the Transvaal province of South Africa; exuberant, stunningly colourful masses of exotic material with Natal; and a distinctive way with leaves and striking methods of presentation with France. The retention of these differing cultural identities is a very desirable aspect of artistic progress. Designs might otherwise become standardized, with less originality of presentation to arouse curiosity and sustain interest.

Similarly, whilst general trends and new ideas can be incentives to creative development, ideally the concepts should be adapted to individual outlook and aspiration. For it is the personal emphasis, whatever the style, that gives artistic expression its infinite variety, with interpretations that are refreshingly different.

Bibliography

Aaronson, Marian. *Flowers in the Modern Manner*. Grower Books, 1981.

Brack, Edith. *Modern Flower Arranging*. Batsford, 1982.

Burger, Paola and Marsano, Loli. *Scultura Floreale*. Idea, 1986.

Clements, Julia. *The Art of Arranging a Flower*. Batsford, 1981.

Cowles, Fleur. *Flower Decoration*. Octopus, 1985.

Guild, Tricia. *Designing with Flowers*. Mitchell Beazley, 1986.

Healey, Deryck. *The New Art of Flower Design*. Collins, 1986.

Lambert, Rosemary. *The Twentieth Century*. Cambridge University Press, 1981.

Read, Herbert. *A Concise History of Modern Sculpture*. World, 1966.

Reister, Dorothy. *Design for Flower Arrangers*. Van Nostrand Reinhold, 1964.

Stockwell, Betty. *Floral Art – Modern and Abstract*. Warne, 1978.

Stratman, Lynn. *Modern Flower Arranging*. Robertson, 1979.

Index